T0151527

A Letter from Paris

Louisa Deasey is a Melbourne-based writer who has
published widely, including in *Overland*, *Vogue*, *The
Australian*, and *The Saturday Age*. Her first memoir, *Love
& Other U-Turns*, was nominated for the
Nita B. Kibble Award for women writers.

a true story of hidden art,
lost romance, and family reclaimed

a Letter *from* Paris

LOUISA DEASEY

SCRIBE
Melbourne • London

Scribe Publications
2 John Street, Clerkenwell, London, WC1N 2ES, United Kingdom
18–20 Edward St, Brunswick, Victoria 3056, Australia
3754 Pleasant Ave, Suite 100, Minneapolis, Minnesota 55409 USA

First published by Scribe 2018

Copyright © Louisa Deasey 2018

All rights reserved. Without limiting the rights under copyright reserved above, no part of this publication may be reproduced, stored in or introduced into a retrieval system, or transmitted, in any form or by any means (electronic, mechanical, photocopying, recording or otherwise) without the prior written permission of the publishers of this book.

The moral right of the author has been asserted.

Cover design by Scribe
Cover photos from Shutterstock.com: cards by Oleg Golovnev, leaves by Nonchanon, Paris by givaga, couple by George Marks/iStockphoto.com
Back cover image by Catarina Belova/Shutterstock.com

Typeset in Fairfield LH by J&M Typesetting P/L
Printed and bound in the UK by CPI Group (UK) Ltd, Croydon CR0 4YY

Scribe Publications is committed to the sustainable use of natural resources and the use of paper products made responsibly from those resources.

9781911617457 (UK edition)
9781925713312 (Australian edition)
9781947534612 (US edition)
9781925693034 (e-book)

A CiP record for this title is available from the National Library of Australia and the British Library.

scribepublications.co.uk
scribepublications.com.au
scribepublications.com

In loving memory of
Denison Deasey and Michelle Chomé.

Verba volant
Scripta manent

(Spoken words fly away
Only what is written remains)
Latin Proverb

Contents

Prologue

Melbourne, Australia

The first letter I ever received as a child came from Paris. It was magic to see the French postmark, Gisèle's address carefully printed on the back in her distinct script:

Apartment 10

24 Boulevarde de Grenelle

Paris, France, 75015.

Gisèle's love and thoughts reached out from her apartment overlooking the rooftops of Paris, France, to our weatherboard house in Melbourne, Australia. She was a connecting thread to my dad, too, even though he was no longer alive. Gisèle was my godmother, and had been dad's wife before he met mum.

The idea of a letter with words written from so far away seemed like science fiction: with a stamp, some paper, and a pen, I could receive a message across time and space from another country, all the way across the sea.

Paris was a world away from Melbourne, and all I could picture of France was held in the mysterious photos in our family album and the prints on the cards that came from Gisèle. The parks and gardens looked smaller and much prettier than the giant expanses of greens and browns that dotted our Australian landscape. My older sister, Ayala, with mum and dad, had even stayed with Gisèle in Paris before

I was born. I knew this from three photos taken on her balcony, laid out in Ayala's photo album, which also contained the only photos of mum and dad together.

Ayala, in a little blue pinafore, was playing with her flowers and a plastic windmill, Paris streets below.

As magpies carolled outside in the rambling cottage garden mum had planted after dad died, I pictured Gisèle in her apartment with that tiny balcony that reached out towards the Eiffel Tower. Her pots of pansies lit with sweet reds and yellows against a champagne sky.

Perhaps Gisèle was still working for French radio? I didn't know what she did, exactly, just that she'd once worked as a radio journalist. Her letters to us were always so much about us, anyway, about our special days, about how much she thought about us, wanted to see us again ...

My Australian family, she wrote, never referring to problems or anything bad, always on such beautiful stationery.

My-little-dot-on-the-map-of-Australia, on the back of a card for my birthday, packages and parcels wrapped in ribbon arriving all the way from a Parisian store.

For Christmas, she sent me a precious necklace, a ruby stone embedded in the pendant.

For my fifth birthday, a pearl on a gold chain.

I know it was strange, that we considered Gisèle family, but I didn't realise this until I was older. Gisèle had been dad's wife for many years before or when he met my mum (I never quite knew), and perhaps it was even stranger that she'd been appointed my godmother.

But mum encouraged our relationship, buying me stationery and stamps because I loved to write to her, because she understood the importance of a living connection to dad and the life he'd led before I was born.

I sensed that mum knew Gisèle held some of the secrets about dad. Perhaps even about me.

Prologue

✤

Dad died when I was six, and a precious *par avion* letter from Gisèle came on my seventh birthday a month later, timed to the day.

Seven little kisses for seven year old Louisa, she wrote on the back of an illustration of children holding birthday balloons in the Luxembourg Gardens. *Ask Ayala if she remembers Paris parks?* was in the postscript. Seven kisses marked X along the bottom of the card, to match my new age.

Gisèle calculated the lengthy overseas transits perfectly, and her carefully wrapped treasures arrived exactly on our birthdays, or a few days before Christmas to sit under the tree.

To see the little French stamps and her delicate handwriting on an envelope when I got home from school meant that something miraculous was waiting inside.

A link to dad, the wonder of air travel, words that had sped from a heart to page to letterbox across time.

When I learned that having dad's ex-wife as a penpal was a little 'unusual', I realised mum was quite avante-garde in her approach to life and love.

When I was a child, mum didn't have a car; instead, she'd take me and my siblings on Sunday trips to the library on our bikes, shopping on a shoestring at the local market co-op for fresh produce she'd then cook, insistent that we live in the inner city, where we'd be confident travelling around to school and events on our own.

We never had the TV blaring with sports on the weekend; mum preferred the national broadcasters, SBS or ABC.

I still remember my first trip to a suburban shopping centre in an actual car when I was twelve, because it was as exotic as an interstate trip.

✤

France wasn't just a place dad had once lived: there was a sense that I'd inherited some kind of French connection through the time he'd spent living there with Gisèle.

I took French lessons at school, we watched French films on SBS, and the living-room bookshelf held a thin, dusty book of cartoons called *Fractured French*. I used to pull it down sometimes, thinking of Gisèle, wondering when and how dad had lived in France, who and what sort of person he'd once been.

Through Gisèle's letters, I learned my first French words: *par avion, bonne anniversaire, joyeux Noël*, and *rue* for street.

I always planned to visit her in Paris one day, when I'd finished school and saved enough money. I didn't know how old Gisèle was, like I didn't really know or fully understand how old dad was when he died.

Just that they were both from a completely different time.

Ten years after dad died, Gisèle came to Australia. I was sixteen years old. She seemed full of life, impeccably chic — everything about her was so typically French. Something about her sense of self-containment and self-preservation stayed with me.

She carried herself with a formidable sense of dignity and enjoyment that wasn't at all self-conscious. I remember her taking mum and me out to dinner, and her smiling and saying things like *Marvellous* and *Aren't we lucky* every time the waiter delivered food to the table.

Mum said something depressing in the middle of the entrees, and Gisèle gently admonished her, insisting that we had better things to focus on at that moment in time. I remember it because I admired the grace with which she pulled it off. And her boldness made mum come to her senses and cheer up.

⚜

But a year or two later, Gisèle vanished. The *par avion* letters stopped. My cousin Mark said he thought she'd gone to stay with a friend in Brittany, but he wasn't sure where and had no address. She was retirement age, apparently, which I didn't understand.

She had always seemed so ageless. Sometimes, she even seemed younger than my mum.

When mum died, the same month as dad's last surviving sibling — aunt Alice — the last of any direct threads to him were gone. There were cousins who'd known him as an uncle, but no one who could tell me about who he was without the filter of such an age gap.

Gisèle was an unsolved mystery, aunt Alice died in her sleep, and then mum died, throwing out all the childhood letters and cards I'd ever made her before she chose to leave. It was like someone had burned down the family house, but by then there was no house and the only fire was in my heart.

My grief wasn't just for losing their physical forms, but for all the stories I'd never fully know about my family. Dad had crossed paths with me for six years only; the rest of my knowledge of him would have to be second-, third-, or fourth-hand.

I still had my brother and sister, but our ancestry was in the past — particularly, our dad's story.

Who was your dad?

Is a question I've never been able to answer.

Never thought I *could* answer, with any kind of certainty.

It was an unresolved wound, a painful longing, as mysterious as death and all the stories in one life someone takes with them when they go.

But a letter from Paris changed all that. A modern-day letter — an electronic message sent by a woman named Coralie.

5

Part One

Letters

Chapter One

Disparu

When dad died in 1984, on a hot Saturday night in February just before my seventh birthday, it was the only time I ever remember seeing mum cry. I'd slept in my new leotard the night before. Pale-blue polyester with stripes of gold, it was so prickly in the summer heat. Mum had bought it for the gymnastics classes I was about to start. So I wore it to bed — ready for a cartwheel on a high beam, not falling asleep on a sticky Australian summer's night.

How odd, the things we remember.

He had a blood clot, mum explained, after hanging up an early morning call from the hospital. *It travelled to his heart*, she said between tears.

It took me a while to comprehend that he wasn't coming back. That he'd gone somewhere I couldn't visit. That his death meant no more Friday-night drives past *Skipping Girl Vinegar* dancing in her red dress along the way to his big rambling house in Surrey Hills full of books, papers, the clack of his typewriter, that musty smell of dust and pipe tobacco, his cheeky grin.

And I'd never really know who he was.

I did get hints that dad was remarkable, but I also got hints that he was wild. There was the sense that he was inexplicable, someone I should perhaps be ashamed of. *The black sheep of the family.* I gathered he'd lived a life that was far from normal — or even acceptable — to the family and the time in which he was born. The only obituary I'd ever seen, printed in the Geelong Grammar quarterly *The Corian*, held a list of his 'unfinished' published work. I forgot all the rest.

Casual comments can create an entire story a child builds up around a parent — and the story's even stronger when you can't remember who made the comments or where or when.

He squandered three fortunes …

He wasted his talents …

What Geelong Grammar–educated man drives taxis … ?

The tone I absorbed was one of disapproval and shame.

The story was that he was impulsive, that he 'wasted' his money on writing and travel and never finished anything, that he should have been more stable, should have made more sense. He was 'difficult', possibly a bit of a lunatic. What hurt the most was the word 'amateur' — where had I read that? Was it from Geoffrey Dutton's memoir, *Out in the Open*, or Alister Kershaw's *Hey Days*? They were the only two books I'd ever found that mentioned dad. Or was it from the obituary in *The Corian*?

Denison conformed neither in his behaviour nor in his intellectual attitudes or aesthetic tastes, according to his obituary, written by prominent businessman Sir Robert Southey. A paragraph from writer and editor Stephen Murray-Smith was also included, claiming that dad was *caught up somewhere between the Celtic twilight, the South of France, and Ayer's Rock …* None of it had made any sense to me as a child.

The effort of packing up dad's house, and his papers, was enormous, and it took mum over a year. She always had an anxious, heavy face after he died, tight with remembering. The complication of his boxes and paperwork made her so sad. I learned not to say his name, sensing a guilt so complex I might make something explode by asking for details.

⚜

Two or three memories of dad stayed with me, like visions from a dream that quickly disintegrates when you open your eyes. I had to write them down to keep them safe.

The first was when dad turned up at my primary school, pulling up in his taxi outside the spot in the playground where I was playing with my friends. It seemed so miraculous that he'd found me, in all the giant playground and secret places I could have been hiding. I usually only saw him every second weekend, or birthdays, because by then he and mum had separated.

Dad, grinning with sparkly eyes, was holding something in his hand for me and strode from his taxi to the school fence to pass it over: a box of chocolate Smarties. It might as well have been a Willy Wonka bar with the golden ticket. Chocolate was a special treat — especially when given randomly, and in the middle of a school day.

'Make sure you share them, Louie.' He grinned, and waved goodbye.

Another time, he turned up unexpectedly with another gift — a soft toy bunny rabbit he must have seen in a shop and bought on a whim.

'Where is Lou?' he said theatrically, standing behind the flyscreen door at mum's house in North Carlton, pretending he didn't know it was me because I'd had my hair cut.

'It's me, dad!'

'Don't forget to give Lou her gift!'

And then — the broken bottle.

We made the trip to the shops near his house. He always had a glass of red wine with the Sunday roast, which we'd eat in his kitchen after church at 3.00 p.m. He called it 'Sunday dinner', and it was one of his favourite rituals.

He walked out of the shop with a bottle wrapped in paper, and realised he'd left something inside.

'Hold this for me, Louie?'

Inevitably, I dropped it. Red liquid and broken glass covered the footpath, and the smash made me so frightened that I ran down the street. Dad's long legs caught me within seconds.

The look of fear and sadness in his eyes was worse than any anger I'd expected over the broken bottle.

'Lou! Why are you running?'

'I smashed your wine, dad.'

'There's always more wine! But there's no more Lou!'

And then he died.

No more dad.

It was late on Saturday night when Coralie first contacted me. Despite a sudden summer storm, my inner-city apartment was stifling. I'd returned from a friend's house for dinner. An amazing cook, she'd made a small group of us seafood and salads, and we'd talked into the night as we waited for the storm to settle. Dinner at Carmen's was the highlight of an awful week.

In the space of seven days, I'd attended a funeral, been to the emergency ward, and had to call the police because my downstairs neighbour had gone off the rails.

I'd quit my job at the University a fortnight earlier after an impossible situation, and the prospect of starting from scratch depressed me. The job had been so ideal when I'd started, and ended so awfully, leaving a sad hollow in my stomach, a resistance to giving anything else my all.

I wanted to write, maybe freelance again — but I had to come down from the year-long stint at the University, the disappointment I felt at how that had all turned out. There was no space in my head to plan and dream — everything felt a bit scary. I wondered if there was something wrong with me, for not being able to 'hack' the situation at the University, if only to keep earning a regular income.

I felt caught between worlds, unsure of who I was or what I wanted, restless but tired. Anxious and disorientated. Disappointed in myself, somehow.

I sat trying to remember who I was, and what I wanted — if I could trust myself to want something again.

A Facebook 'message request' appeared on my phone as my neighbour's shouts of abuse reached up from her balcony below.

30 January 2016

Hello Louisa,
I hope you won't mind me contacting you in such an unsolicited way.

My name is Coralie. I live in Paris, France. My grandmother, Michelle Chomé, recently passed away and we found in her apartment a stack of letters written during the year 1949 to her parents in Paris. At the time she was an au pair in London.

In these letters she speaks of an Australian man called Denison Deasey. She met him on the train to London — he was there that same year with his sister. It seems he took her on some very special outings around London … she was very smitten with him.

Are you related to Denison Deasey? Again, I hope I am not disturbing you in any way …

Denison. His name was a shock and a surprise, like the stranger who typed it. I hadn't thought about dad on any conscious level for such a long time. His story was a scar that still tugged and pulled whenever it was exposed.

Seeing his first name and reading of him was an unexpected

visitation. It brought him back, it called him in. I realised just how much I missed him without knowing him, how much I still *wanted* to know.

I returned to that long-familiar longing, the knowing but not knowing, the unfinished story. Unsure what to hope for, unsure if I should.

I'd only reactivated my Facebook account that morning after a two-week break, to stop getting alerts from University pages. Even odder, I'd then changed my profile picture to an old picture I'd taken at the Louvre, an unexpected pang to return to France having surged over me as I sat up in bed after waking. I'd been trying to think of something that excited me, since I was feeling so lost.

I have to go to Paris again this year, I'd written in my diary.

But here was a message — from Paris. It seemed like a confirmation. I had to get back there. But how?

> Michelle met Denison on the train to London after the ferry from Dover. They went on some very lovely outings in London … they went to Westminster Abbey to see King George and Queen Elizabeth, they saw a John Gielgud play so she could learn better English … she describes him as handsome and charming … she adored him!
>
> My family was wondering if you have a photo?

I picked up a photo from my bookshelf, the one and only picture of dad and me, sitting in a park somewhere in Melbourne. He's holding me in his lap, looking away from the camera into the distance, his pin-striped shirt rolled up at the sleeves.

He must have been in his early sixties. It was 1981 and I was four. He had the look of worn fatigue and wistfulness, like he always did in in my memories. His grey hair was smoothly scooped to the side of his face.

The yellow undertone of illness. He probably had cancer when that photo was taken. I wonder if he knew it … ?

I never could imagine dad as a young man. All I'd known him to be was old, sick, the holder of history from an era I would never fully understand. I'd never asked mum — gathering, from their painful separation and then his death, that it hurt too much and that she felt guilty about leaving him when he'd been so close to the end. Of dad's six siblings — three brothers and three sisters, all older, though his brother Irwin had died as an infant — only two were still alive when I was born, and they were aged in their late sixties. Both were now dead. I'd never known my grandparents — they, too, were dead before I was born.

But here was Michelle — a woman in France, who until just yesterday had been alive.

And there were stories to tell.

Perhaps Michelle had spoken about my dad, for how else had this family been curious enough to contact me? Who was the 'family' Coralie meant in her message? Her message seemed to imply dad was someone special.

What frightened and excited me at the same time was that this stranger in a foreign country was able to tell me a beautiful story about my *own* dad.

From the moment I read Coralie's message, I knew I had to meet this family in France.

Coralie's face on her Facebook profile was pretty, sunny, light. Her face pressed up against her husband's, she was holding a little baby and smiling.

The Louvre, behind me in my own profile picture, *only changed that morning*, seemed almost like a cosmic joke. I thought of the night it was taken — the night, ten years earlier, when I'd walked for hours across Paris to try to find Gisèle.

Gisèle and dad had lived in France for a time and then in

Australia. At some point, Gisèle had returned to France, and dad had met mum. Like everything else about dad's life, I didn't know the timing. All I knew was that Gisèle had loved dad, and they'd been together 'a very long time', as mum had once said.

And because we were his children — Gisèle had loved us, too.

Was this dad reaching out from beyond, offering up a gift, a clue, a message? Imploring me to search one last time — if not for Gisèle, then at least for him?

I felt like a rare bird had landed on my windowsill.

A chance, an opportunity.

Something very fragile.

I started to reply before it flew away.

Chapter Two

Souvenir

Dear Coralie

Thank you so much for contacting me. Firstly, I'm very sorry for
your loss … Yes, Denison was my father, he died when I was six.
He was a lot older than my mum, so I don't blame you for confusing
me with being his granddaughter. Dad would have been 28 in 1949
when he met your grandmother Michelle. Most of his family was
gone by the time I was born, and I never really knew him … I would
love to read these letters …

We spent the night corresponding, from Melbourne to Paris.

I felt comfortable opening up to Coralie, for she opened up to me
— all that Michelle had written of dad, the context in which they'd
met, the family she'd come from, the way it all unfolded … To Coralie
and her family, dad was important, *significant*. Her family seemed as
intrigued about my dad as I was, which I found so startling, and so
strange.

I didn't sleep until five in the morning.

The flutter of excitement and anticipation with every new
message from Coralie was the kind of feeling I hadn't had for years.
It was the feeling that had pulled me into journalism — that sense of
excitement at a person's story that you just had to know. Of questions
seeking answers, of details that painted a portrait of someone — a life
— that you'd never have expected. Something beautiful. Something

secret, only able to be unfurled gently and carefully. A hidden thing that is only revealed with the right questions. Something that had to be seen through to the end.

Coralie referred to art, and writing, in a way that brought back to me all the respect with which the French treat these things, like a long-forgotten memory that in another country what I loved and valued wasn't considered strange. I felt myself emerging from a tight ball of fear of exposing myself that I hadn't realised had formed over the course of the last year.

With just a few emails to and from Coralie, I saw myself and my life differently. After she wrote that dad had worked as a freelance journalist in London and France when he met Michelle — which I'd never known — she *immediately* felt like family, because she was telling me about mine. It was so swift. I trusted her because she was so generous with information about my dad.

Information no one had ever shared with me before. Not even dad's elderly siblings, when they'd still been alive, had been so forthcoming. It wasn't their fault — I was too young, and how would they have brought it up? It was all just strange timing — my life beginning as theirs — and dad's — were ending.

We sent three very long emails each, with Coralie linking to a blog where I could find the first five of Michelle's letters, which Coralie's cousin had begun to transcribe. I gathered her whole family in Paris knew the story of dad. That this family — cousins, uncles, I wasn't yet sure of the size — had been holding these precious memories of my dad moved me deeply, and I wished I were in France.

Halfway across the world — the tyranny of distance pulled and tugged at me, and I yearned to jump on a plane the next day and land in Paris. But I also wanted to have something to give them back — some knowledge, some answers to *their* questions.

It was an earthquake, like everything else that had happened that week, but perhaps it was a good one? Paris pulled at me, again and again. I longed to be there, sitting in a room with Coralie and her family and learning about Michelle. I felt pained by the distance in time and space, and expense — wondering how I could make our meeting possible.

I was scared to spend my savings, particularly when I'd just left my job.

I wasn't even sure if I could believe this seemingly surreal story.

I threw myself into Michelle's letters.

Michelle had been only twenty to dad's twenty-eight when they'd met in the spring of 1949. It was Michelle's first trip abroad, and she'd met dad on the train to London. *The Australian from the train*, she called him.

He was her first holiday romance — a journalist, telling her about the beauty of Vienna, of searching for his Deasey ancestors in Dublin, mentioning places she'd never previously considered she could go, as she'd been brought up in quite a strict bourgeois family in Paris and it was bold of her to even be in London on her own.

Michelle had managed to extend her stay in London by finding work as an au pair with the help of nuns from her Parisian convent, a brave move for such a young woman, and I gathered her father didn't entirely approve. Michelle came from a respectable Catholic family, and her father was well known in France for inventing the ancestor of the breast pump. I gathered, from all the references in the letters to 'papa being worried', that her father also disapproved of the romance with dad.

But these letters about their dates were her *happiest souvenir*, as Coralie so beautifully put it in one of her emails, Michelle's year abroad in London one of the most significant times in her life. Coralie's younger sister, Clémentine, who also emailed me, wrote that she felt Michelle 'followed' dad's footsteps, travelling to Vienna herself and talking of pursuing a career as a journalist after the affair broke off.

Apparently, over the last few years, Coralie and Clémentine would find their grandmother Michelle reading and re-reading the letters, smiling secretly, humming the bars to an English song. She was frail and sick with complications to do with Alzheimer's, and got to the point where she couldn't recognise her daughters or her younger sister. But still, the memories of her times with my dad remained, and she talked of him often.

In her last days alive in hospital, Coralie wrote, remembering London and repeating the name *Denison* was one of the only things to make Michelle smile.

Coralie continued:

Michelle met your dad's family in London. She mentions his sister and her husband and their children. They spent quite a lot of time in Hampstead. They visited the city of London, went to Cambridge, your dad took her to his Club on Pall Mall, to the Theatre ... He had worked in journalism, loved writing and was a musician. He liked smoking Caporal cigarettes ... She described him as tall and handsome, blue eyes, brown hair. He had already been in London two years or so when they met.

They both went away for the summer — which is why there is a gap in the letters from July to October.

I could picture this man from her words, clear and concrete, no longer a blurry vague shadow. He sounded dashing, interesting ... *fun.*

And all I ever wanted to do when I was twenty-eight was travel and work as a freelance journalist.

The sense of longing and surprise at where this had come from was like a puzzle piece clicking into place.

Who was the sister Michelle had met — was it my aunt Alice? And what had dad been doing in London since ... 1947? All I knew of 'Pall Mall' in London was from the game of Monopoly. Everyone wanted to own a plastic piece on Pall Mall. How had dad once been a member of a 'Club' on its street?

With Coralie's emails, dad was becoming less the ragged, aged man who'd made bad choices and lost out in life, and more of a dashing figure, enjoying life as an expat in London after the war and wooing a Frenchwoman who never forgot him. I eagerly translated the first letters on my phone, cutting and pasting into Google Translate through the hot summer night.

May 1949

Yesterday afternoon, I received a phone call from the 'Australien du train'. He wanted to show me around London. We went to Westminster Abbey. Thanks to him, I was able to visit various chapels that aren't usually accessible to visitors. The organist was his friend, so he showed us many tombs of great kings and queens. We even saw the coronation throne … so very beautiful and gothic …

Afterwards, we went to Saint James Park, saw the 'home guard' without a horse, and caught a bus into the city of London.

Because of the bombing, many banks have been damaged and not yet rebuilt.

We ended the day in Hampstead at Denison's sister's house. A very nice little cottage: two children of eight and ten; the father is a naval officer who plays the piano very well. We spoke in English and sometimes French … I translated a letter for them … we sang songs together while we made dinner and washed up, in song.

They are a very nice family.

They invited me to spend the day with them in Cambridge tomorrow.

The 'sister' must have been aunt Alice, whose husband, Grant, had been in the navy. Had aunt Alice lived in Hampstead when her children — my cousins — were young? And who was dad's 'friend' who played the organ at Westminster Abbey?

This man — 'the Australian from the train' — seemed dapper, charming, well-to-do, and warm. No wonder she had remembered this time for so long.

He introduced her to his family. She met his sister, his niece and nephew ...

They washed the dishes 'in song'.

June 1949

Yesterday afternoon, I received a telephone call from Denison Deasey asking to take me to the theatre in the evening and offering me a chair on the terrace of his 'club', which is right on the course of the parade on Pall Mall that leads from Buckingham Palace to the ceremony.

Instead of leaving at six o'clock in the morning to get a bad place, I left the house at ten o'clock and was placed above the parade with Denison, his sister, and the children.

They took pictures ...

At eleven o'clock, the king appeared in a carriage, dressed in the uniform of a colonel, splendid and smiling. Before that, Queen Mary in a covered carriage, followed by the Duchess of Kent and her two children, the Duke and the Duchess of Gloucester, and other personalities, went to the place of the ceremony.

Princess Margaret and the Queen, both very elegant, in a black coach, smiled and greeted the cheering crowd ... the greatest ovation was for the King, with Princess Elizabeth on a black horse in blue uniform ... It was splendid!

The music, like all military music, was very 'engaging'. Before the end of the ceremony, we left our excellent squares to see the King's entrance to Buckingham Palace and greet the royal family who appeared on the balcony.

Even my Australians felt a little 'English'!

After the ceremony, we went for a quick lunch as I had to be back by two p.m.

The King and Queen of England ... Buckingham Palace ... 'my' Australians ...

They took pictures ... Where were these pictures ... ?

The letters went on ...

June 1949

Yesterday evening, I went to the theatre with Deasey. He took me to this play because he wanted me to listen to English spoken with the best accent by actor John Gielgud (who often recites poems on the radio).

He returned from Ireland content with his trip ... I forgot to tell you that he is a writer. He wanted to know all the old songs, legends, and traditions of Ireland. He found Deasey fishermen in a port near Dublin, he thinks they are relatives, because his ancestors were Irish.

He is also a musician. He currently studies music history as he wants to get into a music school in London. For the moment, I do not know any more, except that he loves the south of France, Le Lavandou, where he spent many months.

He only smokes 'Caporals' and is very sad because he is out of stock. He asks whether you can send me some packs of Caporal cigarettes and said he will reimburse me with English money. Is this possible ... ?

It moved me so much to read of dad studying music, talking to fishermen in Dublin in the hopes they were his ancestors ... I could picture it all. He had the same strong urge to find something in his ancestry that Coralie's emails had stirred in me.

June 1949

On Sunday, I agreed to go to Hampstead to Deasey's sister's house to spend the afternoon. We spent the day in the garden, took tea, played piano (Deasey, his brother-in-law, and niece), then

Deasey's sister, me, and the children, went to the edge of a pond in Hampstead Heath, to sail a small boat that their father the naval officer had built. In the evening, we prepared dinner singing in chorus and did the 'washing up' also all in chorus. So friendly!

I have the impression that Papa is a little worried about Deasey. I think this is wrong because he is like us. However, if for Papa's peace I should not see Deasey any more, trust me and I won't.

I will give you some more details for Maman, who likes to 'place' people:

Deasey is called Denison (tradition in the family), must be around twenty-eight years old, left Australia two years ago, worked as a journalist before travelling, and has a property close to Melbourne. One of his sisters was educated in Cambridge. He writes and makes music. Tall, blue eyes, brown hair. Loves Caporal cigarettes.

How lovely, for Michelle to be taken in by this Australian family in London, for the man she was smitten with to introduce her so quickly, when she had been so young and far from home.

I pictured dad with aunt Alice in Hampstead, and I felt I understood her better, too. Aunt Alice had worn handmade Liberty of London print dresses well into her eighties and nineties, drank a sherry before dinner, and asked me to play the piano whenever I visited — perhaps it reminded her of London, of those times with dad?

I wondered if any photos of those times existed. Although Alice and Grant had both died years ago, I wondered if somewhere, in our stack of dad's black-and-white photos, there might be some kind of memento of such a significant day?

And who was the sister that was educated in Cambridge? Was it aunt Kathleen, who was also dead before I was born? I didn't realise *Denison* had been a naming tradition in his family ... but my paternal grandfather had been a *Denis*. He, too, had died before I was born.

How close and nice dad's family sounded from those letters. Part of me longed to experience it like Michelle, but through her written words I felt in some way that I was.

The cigarette request made me smile. I thought of an Australian friend who once went on school exchange in Lyons when she was just sixteen — her host family had given her cigarette money every single day.

July 1949
My dear Papa, my dear Maman,
I want to reassure you: Deasey the Australian hasn't kidnapped me!
And I don't think he will do anything like that anytime soon, as he has left for Ireland to rent a cottage for the summer.

There was a gap in the letters, which Coralie explained was due to the English summer when Michelle travelled with her host family to Kent, and dad, apparently, went not to Ireland as planned, but to the South of France. They both returned in September.

October 1949
Yesterday morning, while I was out, Mrs Bryant received a phone call from Denison Deasey. He telephoned again in the evening to ask me if I had become English and if I could either go to lunch or dine with him soon.
    After refusing every day, I decided to go out to chat with him at the end of my course on Monday evening. I hope you trust me and that Dad is not going to have unnecessary worries, but if you really do not want me to see him again, tell me in your next letter.
    Deasey told me he had a great holiday in Austria and in the South of France. He fell in love with Vienna.

The next letter was dated what would have been dad's twenty-ninth birthday.

24 October 1949

I went out on Monday night with Denison Deasey. We dined in a restaurant in the centre of London and went to find his friends with whom we chatted, in English, from Austria, the South of France, and Brittany, where his sister spent the holidays.

We spoke of Australia, and I saw pictures of the Deasey family. His father is a 'clergyman' because in all the pictures he is in black with a collar like those of pastors. Very good evening, very friendly. As I was asking what English book I had to read to know good English, they read me some passages from the Bible.

All I knew of my grandpa, Reverend Denis Deasey, was that he'd been a vicar. Michelle had seen photos of him. Surely dad had been in love with Michelle, to share so much of his family with her … ?

I asked Coralie if Michelle had stopped seeing dad because of her father's disapproval — she seemed to agree. But she also said that Michelle had told her sister a lot more than what she wrote to her parents in the letters.

Michelle had thought — and spoken — about my dad for the rest of her life.

Coralie wrote again:

After returning to Paris in 1950, Michelle went on to marry my grandfather in 1953 and they had three children. My mother Laurence is the eldest. Their marriage wasn't a very happy one … She and my grandfather eventually got divorced in the 1980s when I was a little girl. Michelle never remarried and dedicated her life to her children, grandchildren and her passions for India, sustainability issues, yoga and alternative medicines.

I thought of mum. Just like Michelle, after dad died, she never remarried. She dedicated her life to us and was always very passionate about sustainability and environmental issues. An early advocate for alternative medicines and therapies such as yoga and tai chi, mum shared a lot in common with Michelle, it seemed.

How strange, the things that connected me to this family across the sea.

Coralie sent me two photos of Michelle, taken in 1950, and she looked so very chic and French, but with an air that was familiar. I knew, immediately, she was something special. She looked like Gisèle: strong, passionate, brave, and independent.

> As for why her parents seemed hesitant to know that their daughter was seeing your dad in London, I guess there was nothing personal … Her family were very French, very bourgeois, very Catholic. Not adventurous at all.
>
> Imagine: their daughter was in London, seeing an Australian who had fought in the war! They most certainly wanted her to date and marry within a very small French society circle.
>
> The reason we are so interested in that part of our grandmother's life is that clearly her time in London was her happiest souvenir. When she divorced my grandfather, she sort of retreated from any kind of love and fun life. I like to think that when she was younger she was enjoying London and fancied a handsome Australian man …

Dad had 'fought in the war'? I'd always thought he was the only brother of three not to have served. I thought he was too sick and had to get 'invalided' out of the Northern Territory before he actually did anything. At least, that's what I'd read in his obituary.

Coralie shared that her sister, Clémentine, was an actress and writer; her mother, Laurence, was a painter. Feeling we were having an intimate chat despite being so many miles apart, I responded that dad was the only one of his siblings to chase a creative path. Tears fell as I read her beautiful responses, and I promised to look for the Buckingham Palace photos of dad and Michelle.

I read and re-read Michelle and Coralie's words all night, picturing dad as a younger man, his sister living close by in Hampstead, his glamorous life in London — travelling across to Europe and having adventures, 'wasting' his fortune on life and love and discovery — so beautifully described in the letters.

I felt Michelle's excitement and gratitude at meeting this warm family seep through from her French words, and I wished I'd known them, too. But just as dad had introduced her to his family, it was as though this French family had re-introduced him to me.

I couldn't help but think of my own first travel overseas, crossing expanses of ocean and time in a journey so challenging and so exciting it stayed in my memory bank like an imprint that can never be removed. Those peak experiences of our lives, the first trip abroad, filled with wonder and romance and more than a little fear … No wonder Michelle had held onto those letters.

Her memento, her souvenir, of the time that had challenged and changed her.

I remembered Gisèle, thinking how similarly she and Michelle looked from the photos. Dark hair, bright smiles, strong faces, that chic air of pride and independence. Both remarkable women, who lived through remarkable times.

And I remembered my first trip to Paris.

Chapter Three

Voyageur

Paris, 2007.

The man at customs wanted to know where I would be staying. 'P-Pigalle' — I stuttered, hyper-alert after two months in New York, where the threat of terrorism is never felt more than at the airport. He paused, stared just a little too long, a slight flicker of amusement dancing across his blue eyes. I didn't know if he wanted more information or if it was just a pause. I'd never been to France before. Was he flirting … ? Or was this a test? Were they going to scan my eyes like they did at JFK?

'Here!' I handed him a card with the name and address of the hotel I booked online. His head pulled back to his chin, eyes twinkling in delight.

'Well I see you there later, then!' he laughed with a colleague, showing my card. They both smiled at me and I realised I was free to go.

I walked through the airport down the escalators to the Métro station, feeling relieved but a little embarrassed. New country, completely different rules to America …

Airport security man was still laughing and staring when I turned back to look.

The first thing that struck me was how different the crowds were in Paris. The Métro was packed and hot, just like the subway in New

York, but no one was encroaching into my personal space, no one was desperate to strike up a conversation or *perform* like in extroverted New York.

The *dang-ding-dong* of the train announcements, a musical scale in a minor key, sounded every few minutes, and the loudspeaker referred to us as 'voyagers', which made me feel like a passenger on a ship in the 1950s.

I exhaled deeply for the first time in months, feeling strangely at home on this packed train in a foreign country.

I could barely speak the language, but I felt at ease, familiar. Like I had a *place* there. Even the ground felt like I had walked it once upon a time in a past life.

The second I alighted from the Métro at Pigalle, the cheap flight from New Jersey to Charles de Gaulle — so cheap that none of the in-flight TVs worked, there were some dubious foodstuffs lodged into my seat, and I thought I saw a rat scamper across the aisle at one point — was forgotten.

I. Am. In. *Paris*.

I realised that I had always, *always* wanted to come to France. What took me so long? It had been a toss-up between travelling the world and pursuing a career as a freelance writer, and I'd chosen writing. It wasn't until I'd worked long and hard that I didn't have to be pinned to a particular location, that I could earn money from afar.

An unexpectedly large job rewriting a twenty-page website on the topic of *things to try before you die* had planted the *now or never* idea in my head, so I spent the whole fee on a return ticket to the USA. I was thirty, and I'd never really travelled internationally before. I'd spent the previous two years building up enough writing work to be able to live freelance in Australia, untied to any particular city or locale. Going further — living overseas — seemed the logical next step.

I picked New York because I loved Joan Didion and found the writing culture exciting, particularly the number of options and the sheer volume of print media. I had an idea that I'd find some literary companions — maybe even get a job as an intern at an eccentric literary agency or a busy magazine.

I was desperate to find people who talked about more than house prices, renovations, and football matches — all I seemed to hear about in Australia. Even among writers I felt like I was a frog stuck in a very small pond. The number of people employed in different writing fields in New York surely meant that by the law of averages, I would meet some like-minded souls and encounter more opportunities.

Since the airfare was so huge, and the flight so far, I'd decided to stay for three months. It was risky, but possible. I couldn't get a visa for any longer, or I would have made it a year.

Mum was worried, which was understandable, even when I lied and said I'd saved more money than I actually had. Mum's open-mindedness in some aspects was at odds with a more conventional anxiety about job security. She seemed endlessly disappointed by my inability to 'settle down' in one place or job for an extended period of time, and I didn't want her to try to talk me out of the trip. I told her I was going only after I'd purchased my non-refundable ticket.

But poverty in a foreign country was preferable to sitting in an office with the same group of people in the same room five days a week. I needed variety, I loved challenges, and if I wasn't learning anything new, whatever the job was, it felt pointless.

At that point in my life, I detested 'sameness' the way other people craved it for security. Many of my friends had settled into mortgages and started creating their own families, but I had a sense of urgency, a compulsion to jump without a parachute and try to live in a foreign country as a writer.

But heading to New York without a lot of money (or even a credit card) was a lot tougher than I expected. The Australian exchange rate was sixty cents to the US dollar, so my income from writing had shrunk from its already-meagre state, and accommodation cost twice what it did in Melbourne.

For two months I lived in a thirty-person Chelsea hostel where we had to be out by 10.00 a.m. each day and weren't allowed back before four. I lugged my laptop out in the snow to file my Australian newspaper columns at the New York Public Library, which was warm and had good wi-fi. I smoked cheap cigarettes on the steps while it opened — a habit I'd adopted since landing — patting the lions' concrete manes for luck in the cold but beautiful snow. I wandered through the library's free exhibitions, took breaks for dollar bagels and coffees from food trucks, watched buskers who rapped and moonwalked, and chatted to strangers everywhere because everyone was so interesting. There was just so much to do and *see*. The variety was overwhelming — in the best way.

The week before, an illustrator I'd befriended in Brooklyn had offered me a week's work supervising eccentric stamp collectors at an auction house on the Upper East Side. I made sure the men didn't steal the million-dollar stamps or touch them with their un-gloved hands (only tweezers allowed), and I was paid US$500 in cash. I used almost half of it to get that cheap flight to Paris.

What girl in their right mind flies to Europe with no money?

Despite all logic and reason, Paris felt like the best decision I'd made in my life.

Why, at thirty, had I chosen to live in a grimy hostel in New York, sharing a room with multiple snorers, when back in Melbourne I could have my own apartment and enough writing work to keep me happy and well fed — minus the giant rats and unfortunate exchange rate?

The real reason was that I needed to be in a place where more than one other person made a living in the same way as me. There was something lonely about always being the anomaly in my social circle. In Melbourne, I had only one other friend who earned her living as a freelance journalist, and I'd had to work quite hard to find her. My mentor, an astrologer who'd carved a writing niche with an unusual blog, lived in Sydney. Facebook and social media were barely a thing back then. Unless I physically flew to my writer friends interstate (which I did, out of sheer desperation for meaningful connection), most of my companionship came from email. Finding like-minded folk in Australia was hard, and I never wanted to be the kind of person who complains about something but never does anything about it.

Most of my friends at that time gazed on my freelance lifestyle as a kind of delusion, or a phase. Perhaps it was a mixture of envy, confusion, and pity. None of them really understood the ins and outs of my work, and I got bored explaining when I was still learning myself.

Mum didn't really understand it, either, and I think she'd been disappointed to learn it wasn't just a phase.

My sister offered the most support.

Ayala had miraculously been booked to go on a work trip to Philadelphia while I was in New York, so for two nights I slept in the twin bed of her four-star hotel room, and we went sightseeing together around her work. After that Chelsea hostel, the Sheraton Valley Forge might as well have been the Palace of Versailles. We explored the oddly contrasting sites of the biggest mall in America and Valley Forge National Park, which held hand-built huts from the Revolutionary War. She sent my clothes off for laundering on her hotel account and bought me huge American-sized portions of takeaway salad for lunch.

As we walked on the median strip of the freeway that led to the mall, just minutes away, Americans honked at us, confused we weren't in a car. I loved seeing my sister in the context of another country — walking despite the hotel begging us to catch the shuttle, laughing off the honks from the drivers.

Aside from the adventure of travel, the most content I ever felt was when I was in the zone of writing, tap dancing across the keyboard, creating stories — from the nugget of an idea or a curiosity, by interviewing people, by finding new things and weaving them into something else. It was really the only thing that lit me up, the only thing that made me feel alive. Every time I learned something, every time I met someone, every time I observed something wacky, mundane, good, or bad — I had to write it down. Everything else fell by the wayside in pursuit of that feeling: fulfilment and authenticity, like I was finally doing what I was meant to do. If I went more than a day without writing — even just in my journal — I felt physically ill.

To make actual *money* from it was the biggest high I could ever achieve, and I still got goosebumps when an editor sent me an un-pitched story commission. Occasionally, I'd be sent a reprint fee out of the blue, and that, too, felt like money for daring to be myself and follow my instinct.

New York hadn't disappointed me in its array of interesting new companions. The first person I sat next to at a cafe was a fellow freelancer who talked openly about writing for *Vanity Fair*. Everyone was always giving me their 'card' for possible future work or just correspondence. I went to a writer's meet-up I'd found on a forum, in a coffee shop near Bryant Park, and was one of ten who worked freelance. We went drinking at a bar in Soho and then had some kind of networking dinner at a penthouse on Fifth Avenue. The Americans were so eager, open, and enthusiastic about even the biggest pipe dreams — in New York, I had none of the naysayers and doubts-echoed-back-to-me that I'd always had in Melbourne when I dared to verbalise my crazy dreams.

The Writers Guild of America was striking for better wage conditions from the day I arrived, and I found it so incredibly inspiring to see such solidarity — hundreds of picketing writers in New York outside particular offices; just a handful of the 12,000 who were striking across the country. In Australia, I'd been a member of the arts union as a freelance writer, but twice they'd given me completely inaccurate information because Australia simply didn't have the size and scope to support such a 'niche'.

I realised what a cottage industry the writing profession was in

Australia, in the context of the world, when I got to America.

Perhaps if I'd waited until I could afford to eat and sleep better, I would have missed out on knowing the truth.

And now here I was in Paris, where things were even *more* fascinatingly different.

At airport customs, I'd listed *writer* on the disembarkation card, and the official had peered over his glasses at me with an approving smile.

'*Écrivain … ?*'

I nodded in reply.

'*Beaucoup d'inspiration*,' he'd said approvingly, before waving me on to the next round. It all felt so far from Melbourne, where whenever I mumbled out 'writer', people would look at me, slightly bored, adding (depending on how much they'd had to drink) something like 'but how much *money* do you earn from that?', which deeply offended me and made me not want to talk about it.

When I'd emailed mum about the trip to Paris, her reply had been happy and enthusiastic, which was rare.

You'll get to explore your French heritage, she wrote. I didn't quite understand what she meant. I wondered if it had to do with dad.

At Pigalle station, I began the steep climb up the Métro stairs with my suitcase, and an older man in a suit loudly tsked beside me, waving off my hands without touching me, silently taking over the responsibility of my heavy load. At the end of the climb, after an enthusiastic *merci beaucoup* from me, he nodded gruffly as if helping me was his Gallic duty, and I was slightly grotesque for thanking him so profusely. He went on his way.

Even the illegal market vendors spruiking rotten bananas near the sex shops by the Moulin Rouge looked glamorous. Dirt was *pretty*, in this city.

I.

Am.

In.

Paris.

I kept announcing it to myself, not quite believing it.

Unlike New York, which had been surprisingly full of rubbish bins, Paris was far, far prettier than the movies.

I'd never seen such a beautiful city in my life.

I pulled out my little map and made my way down Boulevard de Clichy, marvelling at the symmetry and detail of the buildings. The people in bistros and cafes all facing outdoors like on a movie set, the beautiful city in their outlook, scrawling on pages and looking thoughtful, or talking closely and passionately to friends. Something about the way the tables were placed meant that dining solo was an immersive experience. In Melbourne, I thought, eating alone was a bit more of a lonely affair.

The French language, which I adored but couldn't completely understand, made even the smallest overheard snatches sound like intense philosophy. Cobblestoned streets pulled me back into another era and the signs on windows played with my internal monologue, so that I started talking to myself in a sort of Franglais.

I feel like I'm dans une petite village.

Arriving at the Hotel Paris in Montmartre, I wasn't so surprised to find its interior was just like the exterior — *très petite*. I carried my suitcase up three flights of stairs, and squeezed and leapt around the door to get inside, because the bed filled the tiny room. But I didn't care.

A bed! A lamp! A French hotel room and a door I could close! I had never seen such a perfect little hotel room. I went to the window, which looked out to rows of symmetrical shutter windows directly across, and I saw an elderly man drinking a glass of wine at a table near his own window, poised in perfect elegance in his own private world, reading a book.

Merde, I was *beaucoup* tired. It was only around midday in New York, but by early evening in a Paris winter it was already dark. I hadn't slept much before my early morning flight, and this little bed in a room of my own with a door that closed was the most beautiful thing to happen to me in the past twenty-four hours.

But there was no way I was sleeping.

I dumped my bag, brushed my teeth, and whipped out my red scarf.

I looked at the map of Paris I'd bought at a bookstore in New York, and studied the walk from Montmartre to just near the Eiffel Tower.

I had come to find Gisèle.

By then it had been ten years since mum or any of us had heard from Gisèle. How could she just disappear? Trying to access the French phone book from Australia was pointless. Even in Paris, I knew I would need to physically go to her old address, because I couldn't conduct a phone call about much more than the basics in French.

Had I left this voyage too late?

24 Boulevarde de Grenelle.

I walked down the hotel stairs and stood outside for a moment, marvelling at the streets that were so beautiful, so different to streets of Melbourne, and yet so, so familiar. I felt this uncanny feeling, like I was *home*, and I had family living here. Being in such an ancient city had me feeling the past had half become the present. The ghosts of my ancestors seemed closer than ever. But mostly, it was dad who seemed close.

I had barely enough euros to last me two days, so eating at one of the many bistros I kept passing was out of the question. Instead, I spotted the red flashing lights of a cafe that was also a *tabac* and went inside. The place was filled with men of about fifty or sixty talking through stubs of cigarettes and drinking espresso and wine at the bar. Some wore berets.

They looked richer, to me, than any man I'd seen at a pub in

Australia. Something about their elegant sense of self-dignity defied their means.

'*Bonsoir,*' I murmured, conscious not to speak as loudly as I had in New York. '*Une café crème, s'il vous plait?*'

I drank my perfect little coffee with its perfect little sugar cube in that smoky little *tabac*, and paid my two euros to the man behind the counter.

I pulled out my map again and saw that I was close: Gisèle's apartment was just across the Seine. At the Louvre, I asked a couple to take a photo of me, the pyramids glimmering in the late winter light and my face lit up in hope with my red scarf whipping in the wind.

When I got to the Seine, I felt I'd fallen through a crack in the walls of time. The lights on the river, the reflections of the ancient buildings, the whirr of scooters going past, and a French accordion drifting from a bistro in the background — every few metres I had to stop and just stare, taking it all in, feeling like I'd been here before and yet it was also new and comforting. It was impossible to fathom ever being tired of looking and listening to everything in this city.

I felt so inspired by the beauty that I allowed myself to think crazy thoughts: Gisèle had moved across Paris, and the concierge would give me a forwarding address. Even if she was at the other end of the city, I would find her tonight, we could be eating dinner together by 9.00 p.m. *Aren't I lucky!* she'd say with her bright smile, kissing me on both cheeks and being strong and firm, a physical reminder of parts of dad that I'd never known.

Family.

I walked and walked, and finally made it to the apartment building I'd posted all those letters to, so long ago. The concierge was warm and smiling, but he didn't speak a word of English.

'Ah — *bonsoir … Je cherche Gisèle de Satoor de Rootas,*' I said, showing him her name on a piece of paper, flipping it for the French words for 'forwarding address' from the little yellow French–English dictionary on top of my tourist map.

But Gisèle was gone. He didn't know where. Taking over from the previous concierge who'd worked there for twenty years, this new man had only been working in her building for a month. He was indeed *désolée*, but there was nothing he could do.

He shrugged, looking very sorry for me.

I walked back in the freezing cold, disappointed and wondering what else to try. Time was running out and I had barely enough money to stay and search for two nights.

Once back at my hotel, I emailed mum and explained what happened.

She seemed sad that I'd got my hopes up, typing, *She's probably dead, Lou.*

But falling asleep in Paris that night, I had the clear feeling that I wasn't alone. I dreamed dad was in the laneway below, standing in an overcoat, smiling up at my window. He looked younger and happier than I'd ever known him to be.

Chapter Four

La peine

When I woke from patchy sleep after Coralie's first emails, the sun was heating my top-floor flat like a radiator even through the closed blinds. I needed sunscreen just to stay in bed; it would be another unbearably hot day.

I re-read the emails and Michelle's letters to convince myself the story wasn't a dream. Coralie had sent another during the night, respectfully emphasising how meaningful it was to connect with me when the time with dad in London had meant so much to her grandmother. Coralie's English, unlike my French, was almost perfect, which meant we could communicate easily about such a sensitive topic.

How could I form a relationship with a family on the other side of the world, seemingly overnight?

As well as gathering a picture of Michelle, I learned that Coralie was the eldest of three, with a younger sister and brother. Like my older sister, Coralie was married, with two children. She included her younger sister, Clémentine, in one of her emails, and Clémentine replied enthusiastically and affectionately, passionate about the romance of the story, excited about the whole thing. My urge to get to Paris was overwhelming but also painful — I couldn't afford it. But I just *had* to meet this family.

First, I had to tell my brother and sister, to get my head around this bizarre story, to somehow articulate it to someone not on a computer screen and make it more real.

I'll look through the family photos at my sister's today, I wrote, saying I'd search for the Buckingham Palace photo. I had a feeling a lot of dad's family photos had been burned in a house fire just before he died, but I wasn't quite sure. Alice and Grant, who'd been living in Hampstead, might have had the photos, but they were gone — and I didn't know where their albums had gone.

I wrote to Coralie:

Some of my dad's diaries are at the state library, because he was friends with the artists David and Arthur Boyd — who are quite well known in Australia. I think the Boyd connection is why the library has his diaries ... Perhaps there is a diary from 1949 ... perhaps he mentions Michelle? ... I'll have a look on Monday.

Coralie replied immediately, excited that dad was interested in Art with a capital 'A', impressed that his diaries were held in a library.

How amazing that Denison was interested in Art! she wrote, and, for the first time, I didn't feel the need to feel ashamed of dad's unconventionality.

Everything about Coralie's correspondence held interest, kindness, and a respect for what dad had been, these things I'd always kept secret, slightly hidden. While others had left me with a sense of shame whenever they referred to my dad, this family seemed to think that he was someone very special. And that I was, too, because he was my dad. She was so respectful in her words.

It was just so strange.

Despite it being relatively early on a Sunday morning, I knew Ayala would be up and about. Like Coralie and Clémentine, my older sister and I were a contrast of lifestyles. A different space entirely from my little solo apartment, Ayala's rambling Brunswick house was a flurry of Sunday-morning activity. With her husband and two teenagers, everyone was busy with preparations for various sports. I let myself in through the flyscreen door.

'Want a coffee, Lou?' Sean offered to make me espresso with their new machine, and I sat down at the kitchen table, moving my niece's homework and the Sunday papers to dump my bag.

Ayala knew more about dad than I did, by virtue of being seven years older than me, but even she was stunned by the emails from France.

Passing me milk for my coffee without looking up from my phone, she scanned through the French letters from the kitchen table. Finnian peered over while he laced up his boots for soccer, as if sensing something out of the ordinary.

Your grandpa ... I thought, considering for the first time the flow-on effect of dad's absence.

My brother, Declan, slowly came into the kitchen, tired and hot from a sleepless night in the studio out the back of their house. But his eyes flickered with interest, having overheard a snippet of the story as he'd entered the house.

A year or so earlier, Dec had used his own curiosity about dad to fuel an exhausting attempt at putting our stack of black-and-white photos into some sort of chronology. Until then, Ayala had been the sole bearer of all the family albums that had belonged to mum and dad, giant boxes of disparate photos and papers all in a jumble, the ones that escaped the fire.

I'd appreciated the extensive research work just to make sense of the tiniest parts of dad's photo documentation, but I could see, as Dec had worked through the boxes, which had never been properly sorted or annotated, that the job took its toll.

The living room of Dec's apartment became an archival records site, with sticky notes, plastic boxes, expensive plastic sleeves, and folders scattered everywhere as he discovered one thing or another was precious and needed to be properly stored. He barely did anything else when he was in the middle of the project. Tobacco and rollie papers appeared on his balcony, the addiction he'd fought to give up reappearing with the strain of poring over the past in all its half-explained details, which would inevitably have brought up grief, too.

Every time I called him, he seemed to be on another trip to the Public Records Office to try to track down some missing piece, and the photos he showed me were hard for me to even understand — I had no idea how old dad was when most of them were taken, so couldn't put anything into context.

After months of work, he'd only been able to guess at a vague time line. He'd sorted and annotated as best he could. From a military background and with more knowledge than Ayala or me of the context of World War II, Dec could put some of the history clues together and understand some of the photos of dad and his brothers and sisters from the 1940s.

But Dec hadn't contacted any strangers, and I knew that it was lucky Coralie had messaged me, because both Ayala and Dec were unlikely to respond to a random query from a stranger about dad — particularly on Facebook.

At the end of Dec's work, dad's personal photo album was still, largely, a mystery. I didn't know who the people or places were, or how old dad was in most of the photos. Who were the people around him? Where were they taken? My sister had a hand-drawn family tree she'd made as a teenager, but we all had to be in the right mood and the same frame of mind to want to even talk about the story.

It was so full of mixed emotions for all of us — mostly, intense grief.

Some of the photos were obviously childhood photos, but it was dad's twenties, thirties, and forties that were the biggest mystery — and had no documentation.

The years he spent abroad, the time when he'd met Michelle.

'Dec, when you did all that research, did you see any photos you think might be this woman?'

He joined us at the table, and I showed him Michelle's picture on my phone. Sean turned down the radio to hear more, offering me a second coffee.

'The letters mention it was taken outside a "club" overlooking Buckingham Palace, 1949 ...'

Dec stood up, disappeared into Ayala's study to get one of the huge boxes, lugged it onto the kitchen table, and pulled off the giant lid.

A post-it flapped from the front of the album:

DAD PICS. NO CHRONOLOGY. SUGGEST WE START OVER.

Two photos from the mid-1940s showed dad proudly shining a nice car — maybe a Mercedes. Just after the war had ended, we guessed. Possibly taken in Melbourne.

Another — this one torn in half, strangely — was of dad skiing in Vienna, Switzerland.

Was this the trip to Vienna he'd mentioned to Michelle?

Again, we had no idea of the year. I texted the photos to Coralie anyway, whizzing them from Melbourne to Paris on my iPhone so her family could see something when they'd already given me so much.

'So these letters were just in France ... all this time?' Ayala said, as baffled as me at the story, translating the French transcriptions from Coralie much easier than me.

'The sister Michelle describes was Alice,' Ayala confirmed. 'Alice and Grant lived in London after the war.'

I nodded, processing it all, missing aunt Alice, wishing I could ask her about it.

My cousin Julian, her son, was also my godfather.

I'd stayed with him when I worked in Sydney in my early twenties. As we sat down to dinner, he'd poured stories of dad out over a bottle of red. It struck me that he'd been the only relative to openly and fondly talk of dad without me having to ask or prod, feeling like Oliver Twist begging for scraps with my empty bowl.

Julian used to say dad was his favourite uncle, and when aunt Alice died he put together some of the things that were dad's and wrote little notes to explain certain parts of his life for us. *Denison set up the Oberon Press in 1947 and published a small number of books*, he wrote, inside a copy of a book called *Horned Capon* by Adrian Lawlor, apparently published by dad at age twenty-nine.

Julian's version of dad, like Michelle's, contrasted starkly with the sense of shame and failure that came from elsewhere. His fondness was one of the first trickles and hints that dad was fascinating and not someone to be ashamed of. It was a hard concept to reconcile with the view I'd absorbed back in Melbourne, where no one ever brought him up unless I explicitly and painfully asked. Julian, too, had since died.

Ayala continued translating the French letters out loud, wringing her hands anxiously. Her shoulders tensed.

'You could go to the State Library, Lou' she said, verbalising what I knew was inevitable. The only way I could try to find out more about Michelle.

Dec looked at the floor and left the room with a dramatic 'I'm out.'

My sister's work had been storing the heavy archive in one place for so many years. Dad's records and photos took up a huge part of her study, as well as the bookshelves in the living room. I knew how complicated it all made her feel.

Dec, too, had made a giant effort to try to sort the photos into some sort of order. Both of them had done what they did best — my sister worked as an archivist in global records management; her expertise was storing and preserving significant documents. Dec had spent months creating a system for the boxes. Perhaps my job was to investigate the material in the State Library?

I had tried to look at dad's library collection once, and this was maybe why Ayala wrung her hands, remembering the sobbing call I'd made from the steps ten years earlier.

I'd been twenty-seven at the time, researching a story on haunted buildings for a magazine, visiting the library's archives for some reference documents. I thought to type dad's name while I was there. I just wanted to know — *how many diaries were there?*

In my first year living as a freelance writer, I had wondered about his career. I wanted to know how and where he worked, how he wrote, what he did and where. I knew he'd been a writer, even if he had only 'finished' one book that I knew about — *Education Under Six*.

Aside from that one published book, there was a biography of an Australian explorer left half-finished when he died. Other than that, his career had largely been a mystery, filled with those echoing words *failure, dilettante, unfinished*, words I'd read or heard before I could even comprehend what they meant or question where they'd come from.

... there was something in Denison's nature which prevented him from finishing a work, had been written in one of his obituaries.

But asking to see the boxes was weird. I must have asked for the one box that was on the restricted list, with documents from mum and dad's separation.

Why were they even in the library? I'd never found out.

Aside from the Arthur Boyd connection, the only other reason I thought dad's stuff might be in the library was because of the material he'd compiled on explorer Peter Egerton-Warburton for the unfinished manuscript — I thought the library must have wanted the research material for reference.

But when I'd been at the library that day, the woman at information told me to wait, and a different man had to be summoned before she should even make the request. Nothing about the process was quick or easy.

I had to sign a lot of documents, almost like I was asking for something to be excavated from a tomb. I'd begged the librarians not to call my mum, because she was the person who needed to approve any readers for the restricted collection.

They didn't call her, but when I was wheeled over a trolley full of dozens of huge boxes, which only covered 1981, I had a feeling of panic at the size of the material. Why had I asked to see 1981? It was when mum and dad were going through the family court to separate. I'd felt so incompetent, so untrained to deal with such a story. It was more written material than I'd ever had to process — I had no idea where to start.

Was this how lawyers felt, having to prepare a case overnight from a story that required years of background research?

The trolley held reams of diaries, typed accounts of things, shopping lists — even a photo of me fell out of one of the folders, with dad's handwriting on the back. It took hours to even read through one folder of material. It was so complex, so *unsorted*. And that was only one year of his life. I felt like I had to make a decision about who was telling the truth about dad. It was awful.

The court documents from mum and dad's separation were harrowing to read, because he desperately wanted us to stay together as a family. God knows how they'd wound up at the library, because other halves of the missing documents were at my sister's house. I guess mum just handed it over in that messy, big year after he died — so much paperwork.

So many notebooks.

Oh, dad.

I'd never understood why they split up, or why they were even together in the first place. I could never ask mum, sensing pain and guilt so taut she might snap if I'd asked. Dad was twenty-seven years older than mum; all I knew was that they met at Monash University when she was studying and he worked in the History Department. Aside from us, mum seemed regretful about the relationship — or something. I never could understand it.

Why had she left him? What had they ever had in common? He seemed gripped by sadness, and there were endless letters begging mum to return with us, alongside matter-of-fact statements from mum citing missing clothes or late drop-offs as proof of his incompetence as a father.

Mum was an introvert who, despite her unusual leanings, craved routine and stability, not wanting travel or wild escapades, especially when you added three young children to the mix. She had always been such a practical parent: everything about the way she raised us was timed and planned and budgeted and sorted to the nth degree.

But one thing I never understood about mum was how she treated even the smallest details of life like she was battling for the Resistance — she always planned for, and expected, the absolute worst. She had impossibly high standards for everything — including herself.

Dad's style of living — impulsive and flamboyant and creative and extroverted and amused by the smallest details of daily life — seemed like the complete emotional opposite.

Perhaps you couldn't have chosen a less-suited pair.

Nothing became clear to me, except the sad and complex realisation that they were too different. They couldn't make it work. Mum had left dad when I was six months old.

I got the feeling dad hadn't even thought he could *have* children until mum fell pregnant with my sister. Perhaps that's why he was still married to Gisèle when Ayala was born?

I never did get to any place in my mind where I could see mum and dad in love.

There was no romance in what I read of their relationship. No joy, no fun. Just dad's longing for mum to come back with us — his children — as he faced death and sickness on his own, and mum's dogged determination that she could do better raising us solo, resolutely refusing to be vulnerable and return to live with dad.

I felt sorry for them both, and I felt annihilated by my grief. Opening those boxes of papers was pointless and futile.

My sister knew how awful that trip had left me feeling. How I'd wept and wailed about dad's sad final years separated from us and mum, the cancer which had been causing him pain for years undiagnosed until the final hour. I couldn't bear the feeling that he'd been in pain, alone, and feeling unloved when he died.

That's what the boxes stirred up in me — memories of dad's death, intense sadness at how his life ended, anger at mum for keeping us from him when he didn't have long left on the earth anyway.

But there were also precious pieces of my own connection with dad jumbled in there. On the backs of hymn booklets from Sunday church were scraps of dialogue from me and Dec on our fortnightly visits. *Louie insists on changing socks and putting lemonade in coco pops* ... Diary entries on a trip we'd taken to the country and funny words said, delight at our childhood personalities and how they formed, even though he surely would have been in a lot of physical pain.

Out fell a drawing of some crazy outfit I insisted on wearing, a description of Dec's Irish temperament coming out in a game with the neighbour, notes on Ayala's stubbornness ... alongside a plaintive prayer that mum would return to him and we could all be together as a family again.

Those prayers hurt my heart.

I'd learned nothing of the life he'd led before I was born. Dad had loved us, but he was dead. Why read that stuff again?

I hadn't returned to the library after that trip: it was just too huge and broken and emotionally difficult, even if the boxes I hadn't seen may have held some stories that didn't hurt.

Looking in those archival boxes was like putting your hands into a box of snakes and hoping you wouldn't get bitten finding a specific grain of sand.

Dad was dead, and now mum was, too. Mum's death had come in such a way that I'd had to accept she may not have seen the truth about life — or even dad — for most of it.

She'd been such a protective, practical mum when she'd been alive. But she'd also struggled with depression and had some strange versions of events that weren't based in reality.

I wondered, now, if the version she'd given us of dad had been accurate.

Sean broke my reverie, standing at the door jangling the keys, with the kids waiting outside in their soccer boots. Ayala looked at me before she followed them all to the car.

'Just request to see anything from 1949,' she warned me, as fearful of the snakes as me.

'Okay. I'll let you know if I find Michelle,' I said, waving them all off, staying at her kitchen table with the photos spread out before me, reluctant to leave.

I wondered how long it would take to sort through the 1949 material at the library, whether or not it was even dated. Would there even be any pages from 1949?

I turned over another of the photos on the table, a small black-and-white photo of a portrait painting of dad, some trees behind it, as though it had been painted outdoors. Pencilled on the back of the photo was 'portrait of dad by Sidney Nolan?'

The notion was crazy. Nolan had been one of Australia's most famous modernist artists, a member of the Heide circle, known for his depictions of bush life in Australia, most famously the Ned Kelly series.

Yet I wandered into the living room, where an Arthur Boyd portrait hung protectively over the room.

Dad.

I'd found the original painting in an online catalogue of the National Gallery of Australia just a year before. The portrait was of dad aged eighteen.

Mum had mentioned the painting just before she died. A writer had contacted her, saying Boyd had talked of the portrait, and wondered if mum had the painting. But mum assumed the painting had been destroyed, as the Ash Wednesday fires that swept through Macedon cindered most of dad's family keepsakes the year before he died.

But something had gripped me, and I'd scoured the internet one night in a frenzy, remembering a link a friend had once sent that I'd accidentally deleted, and randomly deciding to follow it up.

A cosmic collection of forces led to that discovery — from the gallery's digitisation and the descriptions in Darleen Bungey's book, to Boyd happening to have written dad's name and the date on the back of the actual painting, which was now housed in the National Gallery. Ten pages deep in a Google search, I found it.

Man Kneeling.

Denison Deasey. 1938.

After I'd forwarded the online link to Ayala and Dec in a blur of wonder, Ayala had ordered a print of the painting.

Three months later, it arrived.

And Ayala had it framed and hung in the living room.

A quick sketch done at night with a thick brush by an outdoor fire, Boyd had said when describing the painting in Bungey's book. In oils of green and brown, dad is kneeling over something, his features clearly shown.

The stories the painting told of dad and Boyd — their sensitive relationship, dad's look of intensity — made it precious to me. That it had been stored in a gallery all these years made it even more special. Where it couldn't burn or get lost … and where we could eventually find it.

I stared up at dad, still getting used to seeing him on a wall in my sister's house. Maybe we'd called him in by giving this painting such pride of place?

This painting had been a gift, and a clue to a bigger life than the one I had known of. Like Michelle's letters, it hinted at a life linked to art and artists, war, Europe, and a time in Australia when life was so conservative that people such as dad and the Boyds and their contemporaries had to struggle to find like-minded friends — when bohemia was a radical idea.

But the main reason I appreciated the painting was that it

lessened the feeling of shame. A little.

If dad had been loved by someone sensitive like Arthur Boyd, perhaps he wasn't the 'failure' I'd thought he was?

Arthur Boyd couldn't have known, as they both sat by that fire, that almost eight decades later we'd be reading his brushstrokes for secrets to an unknown father. What a miracle, that he'd donated that painting to the gallery. It was the clearest impression we had of dad as a teenager, but it had been so tucked away.

Perhaps the library would hold similar treasures?

I tried to be excited, but the memory of that awful visit in 2004 and how sad it had made me feel filled me with dread. What snakes could strike out, what pain might I find?

Stick to 1949, I repeated as I rode home, steeling myself like a boxer about to enter a ring full of ghosts.

Part Two

Art

Chapter Five

Serpents

On Monday morning, Melbourne was bustling. Late summer, in the first week of February, and everyone was returning from holidays, the new working year just begun and the sun high and bright. The city was full of promise and new beginnings.

But I was anxious and distracted, full of endings, the complete opposite. I couldn't bear the thought of bumping into anyone I knew. Everyone's happiness contrasted wildly with my feeling of foreboding and confusion; I was unsure where the year was headed or what I was doing with my life — or what painful surprises this trip to the library might yield.

I walked up the stone steps to the grand neoclassical entrance of State Library Victoria without looking sideways in case I lost my nerve. This was Australia's oldest public library — and one of the first free public libraries in the world. I'd always loved writing in the circular, domed reading room. Libraries have always been my church; the eternal nature of books and words, and the silence and peace of those rooms full of scratching pens and deep thought, had comforted me through so many life changes. But today it felt very different.

The doors were locked, so I went to a nearby cafe to fill the minutes until opening. At Mr Tulk, the cafe on the ground floor that doubles as a walkway from the street to the library, I ordered a coffee, recognising a friend from an old job and lowering my face so he wouldn't see me. I took my coffee to the hidden archway near the library's steps to read my emails, trying to calm my anxiety.

Coralie had messaged again in the night, bolstering me for the search. She seemed to care as much about the story of dad as she did about seeing a photo of Michelle and Buckingham Palace. She didn't seem to want or expect anything, other than to have found me and made our connection.

> You are on the other side of the world, these letters were written decades ago, and they tell us so much about people we love. To us it's our grandmother. We discover through these letters that she wasn't too different to us when she was 20 years old, living in London …
>
> To you and your family, it must be interesting to see what a charming man your dad was. Such a gentleman …

That Coralie understood such a sensitive situation, yet also seemed to believe dad was someone special, filled me with a new sense of pride that his papers were inside this historic building. When the crowd moved as the doors finally opened, I walked straight to the library's information section. Part of me was excited, like I was about to start a treasure hunt for Michelle. Romance, courtship, dashing days in London … fun and glamour and young love, all those things that had been missing from his relationship with mum. But the other part of me was apprehensive, the word *failure* whispering faintly from somewhere buried deep.

'I'd like to request to look at a particular collection, please … Or — a part of a collection, if that's possible … ?'

The librarian typed in dad's name, and pulled up the inventory.

'It's a large collection. It will take a while to load.'

She seemed surprised at my interest in her computer screen, the little mouse in a circle of thinking as we waited.

'How many pages is the inventory?' I asked her, when it had finally loaded.

'Um, let's see …' She clicked for what felt like minutes. 'Forty-four.'

Forty-four pages. Dear God. Thinking I could confine my search to 1949 was clearly stupid.

On screen, in each folder description, I saw that years were scattered non-chronologically, along with names, dates, and locations. Letters, books, and manuscripts had been dropped in boxes throughout the collection. Some of it wasn't even categorised: the folder would simply say, 'typed manuscripts … recollections'.

I groaned inwardly at the task ahead of me. Dad's material wasn't just a couple of clearly dated notebooks.

Or even — as Michelle's letters seemed to be — a small, precise sketch of a year in time. Neat and decipherable, wrapped in ribbon, sitting in a room in Paris. She'd even annotated which ones mentioned 'Denison', to make it easy for the family when they found them.

Dad's manuscript collection at the library was a chaotic, massive jumble of pages and papers, including letters, diaries, photos, and manuscripts covering the entire span of his sixty-four years on earth. I'd been too distracted when I looked at 1981, and I'd never seen the description of the inventory in detail. There were hundreds of manuscripts in there. Were they all unpublished?

Short stories. Book drafts. TV scripts. Radio plays. Memoirs. Poetry.

Letters from famous artists were mixed in with a Paris hotel receipt, a postcard from Gisèle with an outline for a radio script or a snapshot of dialogue from a pub in London in the post-war years.

Just looking at the inventory on screen brought back a memory I forgot I had.

In dad's house, he always had a big notebook by his side.

His bookshelves were full of spilled-out folders, with papers stacked high, under and over hardback books. Even the smell of the library took me back to him, that sense of academia, the fascination with higher concepts mixed with amusement at the mundane, scribbling away on any piece of paper he could find — the backs of envelopes if they were nearby and he found it too painful to get out of bed or his chair.

While I stared at the screen, searching for dates and times in folders that each needed a separate request slip, a memory of mum pushed through at the same time that I remembered dad.

'You've taken up the entire page!' she'd said grumpily over the phone, only slightly joking. After moving to Sydney from Melbourne, I was up to my fifth change of address and phone number.

Mum liked things to be neat and tidy. But by age twenty-two, I'd filled up the whole 'D' section in her old-fashioned address book, and she had to start putting me in 'E'.

Oh, mum. I remembered how well she organised everything. Tears threatened to surface. *No wonder.* How desperate she would have been to hand over the load when dad had died — the hugeness and the messiness of his life, her inability to quickly sort it into a methodical pile.

'Why do you need to see 1949?' the librarian asked suspiciously, puncturing my reverie. I felt unmasked.

She was young — my age, maybe. I decided to trust her. How else could I put it?

'Well, I received this email from Paris …'

My head spun just trying to articulate the story, hearing it come out of my mouth in a mixture of old and modern words forming a strange sentence: 'This woman's grandmother dated my dad in 1949 … in London … and that's … that's my dad's papers … so I want to find anything he may have written about her …'

She shrugged, uninterested, not bothering to reply.

'You can only request five boxes at a time. You need to sign each of these slips. If I get the order in now, they'll be waiting for you in the Heritage Reading Room by 11.00 a.m. And you'll have to put your things in a locker — you can't take any photos. Turn your phone off or put it on silent.'

'Okay.'

'And no pens allowed in the room.'

She clicked the screen shut and turned away.

My mind was on 1949, still trying to figure out what dad was doing in London, where he lived, and how he'd come to get there, trying to remember what I'd seen on the inventory on the screen. Had I imagined it, or did one of the folders say 'photographs' from the 1940s? Also — why did the folder seem to span Paris, as much as London? As well, I saw Vienna, Zurich, Dublin, Germany, Spain, and various other cities and countries on the description of diary entries and places visited in those late-1940s years.

I looked at my phone: it was ten fifteen. With forty-five more minutes to wait before dad's boxes arrived, I walked through the library. Past *Family History* and *Newspapers*, I detoured into *Arts*, finding an empty chair under a lamp to put down my bag. Quiet, cool, and less busy than the larger library rooms, I could forget the pace and noise of the city, the summer life outside.

I felt a strange mixture of intimacy and formality, as though I was about to meet a member of my family for the first time. In the background was sadness, too. The sense of futility that he was gone, and what was I doing, unearthing his life when I'd never have him back anyway?

I stood up to look through the shelves of books, flicking through Mirka Mora's *Wicked but Virtuous*, remembering an encounter with the French artist back when I'd been waitressing at Florentino's.

She had known dad. She'd told me so. But even then, I hadn't followed up. Something she'd said had frightened me, and I couldn't recall what it was. I made a note to look into my old diary, to remember.

Alongside Mirka Mora's autobiography was a book of letters from Sidney Nolan to Albert Tucker. Tucker, like Nolan, had been one of Australia's most famous modernist artists and a member of the Heide circle. Remembering the photo of the day before, when I saw there was an index I searched for dad's name.

There it was:

Deasey, Denison: 70, 71, 72, 73, 245.

I tore ahead to the first page, a letter from Albert Tucker to Sidney Nolan — dated June 1947.

… Deasey's in Dublin. Got TB on the boat ride over …

This information was more to comprehend than the fact that he'd lived in London in the post-war years. *Dad had tuberculosis when he was only twenty-six?* I hadn't known you could recover from that. And — how had he wound up in Dublin, particularly if he was so sick?

Nolan wrote back, asking Tucker to give his regards, referencing dad's earlier years and their friendship in Melbourne.

Dad *had* known Nolan — and Tucker. Perhaps that painting we had the photo of still existed somewhere? The notion seemed ludicrous — almost as ludicrous as the painting by Arthur Boyd, which had, in fact, proved real.

I tried to keep the three new pieces of information separate: Dad being close friends with Sidney Nolan, and Albert Tucker; that he once had TB …

But it hurt my head.

If the photo we had *was* a painting by Nolan, maybe *that* was the one mum had thought gone? Burned in the Ash Wednesday bushfires in Macedon, or sold when he'd hit hard times?

Maybe mum had even sold the painting when dad had died? I didn't know how she managed to scramble together enough money to buy the house we moved into the following year. All I knew was that mum always had that worried *money* face.

I guessed that to mean he'd left us nothing.

There was that sense of shame, again.

Dad had done something wrong, and I couldn't put my finger on it. It was tied into his open-handed attitude to art, or creativity.

It was a wound I carried inside, a sense of failure about pursuing life as a freelance writer, like it was inherently wrong that I could do nothing else.

It was all wrapped up in my impression that dad, the only other writer in my family, had been a failure, too. That his and my attitudes to art, creativity, relationships, life — were somehow too out-there. A bit cracked. A little broken.

Why couldn't I stick at boring things, stay in a good job for a good institution, and just think of the money like a 'normal' person? Why was I so obsessed with creative freedom?

Failure. Dilettante. Amateur … Wasted three fortunes … The words mixed and swam with the new information from the Nolan and Tucker book.

My head hurt.

Perhaps there *was* a Nolan portrait of dad out there in a gallery, still … ?

I snatched photos of the letters with my phone, texting them to Ayala and Dec. *I'm not in the manuscripts yet — just saw this in a book on the shelf*, I typed. *He did know Nolan … and Tucker.*

Then I went to look at the boxes.

At eleven o'clock, I walked to the Heritage Reading Room, past the Victorian portrait gallery and up the stairs. Swallowing deeply, I was aware I was about to reopen a wound. It felt fated and necessary, much like a family funeral, sombre and threatening and like I was about to come face-to-face with dad's face in a coffin like I had in 1984.

All the ideas I'd had about dad rested on what others had deigned to tell me. I'd caught snickers and snatches over the years — the repetition of certain words, those contrasting impressions of awe and shame, but mostly silence.

But private letters and personal diaries don't lie. This was the first time I would have the freedom to make up my own mind. Yet that terrified me, to reassess everything I'd unconsciously believed for over three decades. What if all his diaries did was confirm that he was, indeed, a failure?

That he did leave so much 'unfinished'?

This could be a disappointing task, and maybe I'd have nothing to give the French family.

I have to try to find Michelle, I said to myself, marching forward. *Romance*. The idea of the romance pushed me forward. I remembered Coralie's picture, and I thought of Paris.

'Yes?' a disapproving older woman looked down her glasses and opened the glass doors as I pressed the buzzer.

'Can I help you?' she said when I made it to the counter. The archive boxes marked *DEASEY* were in a shelf behind her. She wasn't smiling.

'Yes! I have an appointment. I've requested some boxes ...'

'Have you been here before?'

'Um ... no, I don't think so.' I looked around. The room didn't look familiar at all. I wondered if my failed attempt twelve years earlier had been somewhere else.

She didn't make any move towards dad's boxes.

'Are you aware this is a partially restricted collection?'

'Yes. Well, it's my dad's manuscripts. My mum was the contact, but she died —'

'It doesn't matter whose collection it is, these papers are library property. I'm going to need to see some identification.'

I kept my mouth closed while a visceral feeling of grief and anger filled my chest.

'You can't take any photos with your phone. You're aware of that?'

'Yes.'

I pulled out my library card, filling out two more forms and collecting a locker key, putting everything inside except my large spiral-bound diary and some pens.

'You can use one of these pencils to write.' The librarian pointed to a box of tiny blunt pencils. 'No pens.'

I grabbed one of the miniature pencils, putting away my biros, and she finally moved towards the boxes. The room was large, cold, and silent. Not being able to drink water in that room was a bit strange, but understandable, though it really threw me not being able to write anything down in pen. I hadn't written in pencil since I was a child.

'There's a lot of folders in this one box, so you can only have one box at a time.'

Fine, I felt like snapping, nodding instead. *Just give me my dad's papers.*

She placed one archive box down on the large table at the front of the room, where she could keep her beady eyes on my movements, and I moved the box directly in front of my notebook for some privacy. I wanted to be able to silently text my sister or see messages without her knowing.

But I didn't text Ayala that first day. For the next six hours, I was like a miner with a headlamp, chipping through a tunnel. I didn't bother writing anything down in my notebook with the stumpy little pencil, either.

I just read, and read, and read.

(from the diaries of Denison Deasey)
London 1949
Afternoon at the National Gallery among the Italian paintings. Returned by tube to Regent's Park, ascended into light and walked up the horrible Albany Road towards the butchers for my microscopic ration (two chops for the week, fit in my pocket.)

Heart heavy from the change from the gallery, I spy a small boy clutching a bottle of milk toddling towards me. I was astonished to see that he was approaching me and saying something;

'What is it, me lad?' I says.

With a confident, doleful note he says 'lead me across the road, please Mister ...'

Feeling vastly flattered at being mistaken for a confident crosser of London death-roads I drop a line for him to take a hold of and a small grubby fist clutches it. Gravely we traverse the road and part as do the oldest of mates, without a word.

What a thrill is the slightest touch of humanity!

Paris, 1948

As night fell on my second day in Paris, I left my room to walk, and chose the Boulevard Saint Michel, and was soon passing many bright cafes and looking at the smartly dressed 'artists' who inhabit them.

There, for example, was a man with a well-made tweed suit. But he had sinned by growing a beard — eccentric fellow. His eyes were interesting, though, something familiar about them. The bearded head was bent over a large plate of saucissons, and the artistic jaws chomped steadily.

I stood still for a moment, as I realized that I knew the face, that it was Bert Tucker, no doubt the only other person I might know in Paris, but whose address I had no idea.

I tapped him on the shoulder, and the sight of my face sent a saucisson or two down the wrong way. His mouth dropped open and stuck there for a few seconds. We exchanged mutual noisy Australian greetings. What a droll business, to stroll down a boulevard and find the exact man you had hoped to find, casually, munching a sausage and disguised by a beard. We both felt very joyful, on each other's account, because we were each in Paris. I congratulated Bert, and then he me, for being away from England and in the beautiful city.

For 1949, I would need to consult numerous boxes — and each box contained ten or twenty folders, overlapping with 1948, 1947, sometimes 1951 or later.

Each folder might hold a series of letters containing references to people I would have to hold a history degree to decipher, or it might hold a draft of a story for which I didn't know the context. And dad's handwriting — usually in pencil — was another hieroglyphic code entirely.

It would take me hours of reading just to understand dad's M's, the scrawl that meant 'art', the initials he used for his friends. That 'B.T' was Albert Tucker, 'Al' was Alister Kershaw, and 'A' was Arthur Boyd. But who was 'T'? Who was 'R.A'? Who was 'G'? Who was 'Nin'?

To read the entire span of 1949 seemed as though it would take months of research, for all the disparate references I struggled to understand. Famous literary names mingled with European places and snatches of dialogue so intriguing I wished I could devote the whole day to uncovering one identity, reading endless Wikipedia entries to make sense of it all.

1949 was so much more than Michelle and London — it was the South of France, a trip to Vienna where he looked for a flat and met a prince, references to poets and painters, and an endless battle to get English pounds or French or Swiss francs and food. A concert at Royal Albert Hall in London, a trip to Florence in Italy, psychoanalysis with a Jungian analyst in a place he called 'The Quiet Room' in London to deal with his 'problem' from the war.

Was it PTSD?

How do you look at one year of someone's life without looking at everything that led to that point?

The effects of World War II were everywhere in dad's writing. Tiny pats of butter after a long queue in London. An account of trying to replace his ration book after having to surrender the original to the boarding-house owner, and being denied. Endless lists of foods and their costs, and wondering if he'd survive the endless hunger when he was still clearly sick from TB.

References to the 'bleakness' of London, even after they'd won the war, because everyone was starving and many of the buildings were destroyed. But in stark contrast was the Art that fed him, the galleries and culture, the delight of being in England, finally, writing about how even the poorest Londoners knew so much more about history and music than even the most well-educated Australians.

And all this assumed knowledge of the war …

References to 'the time in the Territory', to the death they'd all narrowly escaped from the war years.

I realised, while reading, I didn't even know how or where or when dad had served. I knew the vague outline of his biography: born in 1920, studying at Melbourne University when World War II broke out, married briefly in Melbourne in 1946 … Where and how had he served?

And when did he go to London?

Trying to make anything chronological interrupted the flow of just letting myself be carried along by his writing. It was so honest, so filled with emotion, with so much feeling.

London, 1948

Back to the tube, back to my district. A half-hour walk brings me to the grocer and the butcher. The grocer looks at me suspiciously, 'no, we have no eggs …' I find the butcher. Closed. No word of explanation. Clutching a piece of butter the size of a matchbox, I totter home and cook a cup of coffee. Only the milkman doesn't come … I have to post my milk registration card to the dairy … Two chops for one week. Unrationed food (rice in tins) is on points.

Later return for eggs — get two. 'Persistent, aren't you?'

I felt like Gabin when the little man pushed his face in the soup. Persistent, yes one does become persistent in keeping alive even at the cost of tracking monotonously back to that cockney trollop's milk shop.

The London buses roar down the Marylebone Road …

Handwritten papers helped me get the sense that I was travelling with him in his first months abroad, and wild enthusiasm mixed with references to famous names I knew vaguely but had yet to absorb their significance.

There were descriptions of drinking at The George in Soho, where South African poet Roy Campbell introduced dad to his 'mate' Dylan Thomas, who was 'morose and only drank pints', then another random introduction on Oxford Street to Louis MacNeice, whose poetry dad had read and loved as a student in Melbourne.

Then we were on a train in Germany — dad had an unexplained broken leg, but there was a kind Russian who let him travel despite his expired documentation.

The writing was of a different time: when phones were telephones and cars were motorcars and anything involving swift travel or currency or communication cost a fortune.

And always — the references to the lack of food.

He recorded everything on paper because he had to — letters were the only way to convey a message, and diaries were his way of processing the enormous shift his life took after he caught what he referred to as a 'hell-ship' to London. The ship that gave him tuberculosis.

London, in the immediate aftermath of World War II, sounded a grim place to be, despite the glamour described in Michelle's letters. It seemed dad had done the hard yards in his two years there before he met Michelle, undergoing the requisite 'introductions' to become a member of the naval and military club on Pall Mall that had proved so seminal to her letters.

All the city buildings covered in holes, the general mood 'dark and sombre' (most probably because they were starving), how rarely Londoners smiled or engaged in cheery conversation on the street. Then an explanation of how he adored Roy Campbell so much because he was loud and blustery and animated, which contrasted so starkly with the usual English reserve.

There was a description of dad's first bedsit in Regent's Park, with wallpaper so ugly it made him hallucinate, and smells of cooking from downstairs while his stomach roared. The patron had confiscated his ration book in return for weak tea in the morning and one cooked egg each week. While dad struggled with hunger and tuberculosis — which still hadn't been diagnosed — a man gassed himself in the room next door to dad's, so the owner removed all the locks on the doors in case it happened again.

What a time to be in London ...

I learned he hadn't actually *wanted* to live in London, but it was hard for Australians to get out of England. Desperately in debt and fighting to recover from six years of war, the British wouldn't allow Australians — still considered part of the British Empire — to take themselves or their money across the Channel.

But he had somehow managed it. How, dad, how?

Suddenly I was on a random bus ride with him from France to the Pyrenees, where he wanted to see Andorra even though everyone said it was 'closed'. But he was refused entry back to France and instead smuggled in by a nice Spanish man who carried his trunk up the hills in the snow. Did he have TB then? The diary entry wasn't dated.

I pictured his six-foot form happily heaving up a snow-filled hill because the Spanish had been so friendly, mistaking him for a smuggler of contraband substances, so glad to be hosting such a celebrity that a random family had cooked him dinner.

Then we were back in London, as his diaries and letters dipped and flew around. There was another 'club' in Harley Street, and drinks with more poets — Dylan Thomas even came to a dinner in Holland Park.

From London, his Australian mate Al — poet Alister Kershaw, a friend he'd loaned the fare to England — sent him 'maddening' letters postmarked *Le Lavandou, France*. Al had moved in with the English writer Richard Aldington to a rented villa near the sea in the South of France. The food and the mood in France sounded so different to the post-war exhaustion in England.

Dad ached to get there and join them.

Finally, after producing the proof of his TB and a doctor's certificate saying the sun in the South of France would help him recover, he was granted thirty pounds of his own money to spend in France.

Then there were pints of 'warm beer' with Albert Tucker in Soho, where they hatched a plan for Tucker to get to Paris, too, to see some original Picasso paintings. Tucker gave dad a couple of small Foujita paintings he'd acquired when he worked as a war photographer in Japan, in return for a loan. He told dad to sell the paintings in Paris when he needed French francs, because the art dealers near the Seine would know their value. Foujita had once lived and painted in Montparnasse.

However, dad wound up in Dublin instead of Paris somehow — and I still had trouble making out the dates or the reason — but he seemed desperate to look for 'that spark in the eye' that was his Irish ancestry, and Tucker offered to wire *him* a hundred francs instead.

Don't miss Paris in the Spring, Dease. And, if it helps, a curse on all your blights! Tucker wrote, affectionately.

Months later (or was it a year?) when dad finally made it to Paris, after a stint in the South of France with Al and Richard Aldington (was this the year he'd met Michelle?), he'd walked and walked the city at night, which is where he'd stumbled upon Tucker in a laneway in Saint Germain, bent over a plate of sausage.

I chuckled and smiled, reading dad, searching for more. A hundred pounds given to another writer, sums of money flying about, so many risks and so much money just to travel and expand and see the world. Even simply exchanging money required so many signatures and international verifications. The time and cost involved in getting foreign currency in the 1940s was outrageous.

But the throwing about of art and money between those who didn't have much helped me see dad's figure come closer to light.

Words, a life, thousands of pages. *Dad left us all this.*

I turned and turned the pages in the folders in the boxes. Here was a slip from a 1949 service at Westminster Abbey, inside a diary entry about Spain.

After a villainous journey in a Spanish bus crowded with priests, peasants and poultry, I reached the frontier ...

Then a whimsical idea to move to Vienna and search for a flat reminded me of when I went flat-hunting in New York, sifting through CraigsList, one listing offering free rent in exchange for a tenant who fed their pigeon in the nude.

Vienna, 1949
The Prince discoursing on the installation of bathroom fittings for a paying guest was rather strange.

Then back we galloped to those first days in London — he'd arrived it seemed, on 1 August 1947. He was so excited to be out of Australia, he called the date his new Birthday.

Rambling diary entries on art, music, love, and life. How music was more spiritual to him than the church, how love was the only reason for life. The pleasure of being in Europe, where knowledge of history and aesthetics and music and art weren't considered luxuries for an elite few.

The diaries and letters took me across the world.

Vienna, 1949
Asked a policeman the way. Said he was going there too. I limped along but he didn't mind dawdling, he said. The weather led to policeman's uniforms in summer. I said Australian ones wore shirts open at the neck. He said 'yes and shorts?' I said 'no', he thought then said 'no of course not, that wouldn't be right would it with some policemen with big fat knees and others with thin ones' ... what an aesthetic view. Ha.

The local madman raised his hat to me.

There were memories of Melbourne, too, with names I recognised from the Angry Penguins movement and the Heide circle, such as Alister Kershaw and the infamous Max Harris and the painter and writer Adrian Lawlor, whose book about bohemia dad had bought a printing press just to publish, back in Melbourne before he left for London.

I got to know dad in his pages. The friends he loved were interesting, not repressed or conservative or stuffy. He loved people who were honest; he kept going on about honesty and lack of pretension.

I remembered another reference I'd read or heard somewhere, that dad had associated with 'unsavoury types' in Melbourne. Was it the artists who were considered 'unsavoury' back then? Why was it so 'wild' to hang out with artists? Why was modern art — or just thinking vaguely outside the square — once considered so morally reprehensible?

This was the closest I'd ever felt to dad. To touch his notebooks and the address book he would have kept close to his heart in his inside suit pocket felt almost religious, like I was reaching into his tomb and waking him up again. The words were alive, his life was alive, and the feelings transferred to me in a way that filled me with grief and return at the same time.

Michelle, Michelle, must look for Michelle, I'd vaguely assert, but then another encounter on a London street, or a monk bowing to him in Italy, or a description of the power trips of London shopkeepers would distract me.

I didn't expect dad's life to be so interesting, to be honest. I didn't expect him to speak to me so deeply. His travels and thoughts, reflected in his diaries, mirrored my own. Even the way he recorded snatches of dialogue, feelings leftover from a dream … my own diaries are echoes of dad.

Dad's diaries filled parts of me I had no idea were empty, so that within minutes of opening the first box I was in quiet tears, oblivious to the librarian who just minutes ago had pressed 'enter' on this strange and ghost-filled journey.

On that first day, in that first hour, every page I read led to more questions.

There was London, where he had to queue three times in one day, trying to get an egg. Then he was in Paris, being cooked nightly omelettes at the Hotel Floridor, treated to a litre of wine.

The Hotel Floridor sounded like a Wes Anderson film — the hotelier always drunk, the Nigerians on the top floor who blocked the lift so their radio would work, the widowed *Maîtresse* with the sick little dog who lived in the room beside him, had a lot of 'uncles' who came to stay, and offered dad shots from her whisky bottle. Dad really liked her, because *she knew how to enjoy life*. I loved his open and non-judgemental nature.

Every entry in France went into extensive detail of the food, acknowledging the luxury that it was, post-war. No wonder he adored France — and of course, he would have immediately recognised Michelle as being French. He fell in love with the place because it rescued him from starvation. France didn't just mean staying alive; it was where he could heal and recover.

They had *eggs*.

I forgot where I was, what I had to do, who I was. I read so many of his thoughts at certain points, I felt as though dad was *within* me and that it was me walking those streets, marvelling at beauty, searching for eggs, awe-filled and intensely moved by a first trip to the hallowed halls of the British Museum in London, almost like a pilgrimage to a cathedral, then that first train trip to Paris, and his recognition that the French knew how to enjoy life. His eerie feeling, in France, that he'd finally come 'home'.

⚜

Why the hell can one only feel truly alive when writing, or trying to write? he'd pencilled in the margin of one diary, after writer Richard Aldington had requested he research some letters at a library in London.

Aldington. Why did this figure seem so important to dad? I made a mental note to look him up when I got home.

I read my way through the diary to September 1949, and found that's when dad's own mother, Maude, died — it was unclear how, just that she'd been sick and confined to bed with crippling arthritis for decades. *My grandmother.* Dad's emotions, coursing across the page, ranted and raved at how much she suffered, in ways I'd written when I lost my own mother.

At the time, he was back in London; *just before he'd called Michelle*, I remembered from her letters.

When Maude died, he'd been staying at his sister Alice's cottage in Hampstead. The sad news was delivered late at night via telegraph boy. Dad described sleeping on a camp bed in their spare room after staying up by the open fire with Alice and Grant, drinking sherry.

Just as I'd slept on a camp bed at my brother's, and stayed up drinking and talking with Ayala after we got the news about losing our *mum.*

No sooner had I visualised this eerie parallelism than there were descriptions of the funeral service he and Alice held at a little Church of England in Kensington, walking the streets to give the news to his mother's elderly brother Charlie, who was also visiting London at the time. *All these family members I never knew, described in post-war London.*

Then, in his diary, was the description of how eerie it was to receive a letter from his mother two days after he'd learned that she'd died. The ghostly sense of reading her, holding her written etchings in his hands, when she'd already left the earth.

As it was for me, sitting here with dad.

Between scrawled notes for his mother's eulogy and references to his chosen Bible verses were lines from a poem by A.E.

I had found that exact book of poetry, transcribed lines from that very same poem, in my own diary. It had always made me think of dad.

I'd pull myself back to try to find Michelle, remembering they were in contact in October 1949, but learning about dad, and my grandmother, and all of this intense family history, had changed my focus.

I forced myself to search for Michelle's name, even though I wanted to know about everything else. All I found was a scrawled entry from June 1949:

… lunch with Michelle, dinner with Michelle.

No further detail, no descriptions of Michelle or how he felt about her, just a personal admonishment to focus on working and try not to let the hunger in London dull his senses.

I felt awful that I had nothing to send Coralie about Michelle. She'd found me just two nights ago, and her beautiful emails had guided me to the library. If it wasn't for Coralie, and Michelle's beautiful letters, I wouldn't have found my dad.

After thirty-two years, he was back in my life. The decisions that he'd made — things I'd heard whispers of, hints of, never quite known — I was hearing in his own voice, in his own words.

I tried to be methodical. I pulled out a blue folder marked 'diary — January 1948' and found myself in Zurich, Switzerland, where he was apparently confined to a sanatorium with TB. But I had to go back, even from Switzerland, to find out why he'd come from Dublin, so then I had to open a diary from 1947 and look at his passport, just to check one of the hundreds of date stamps. From there, I'd pull out all the notebooks, searching for one with a corresponding date, eventually finding one that jumped from 1947 to 1951.

Desperate to learn more about his Irish grandfather, who'd

emigrated from the Constabulary and never spoken of Ireland again, dad had made his way to Dublin (*me! In Dublin!* he jotted gleefully), but he only managed one or two conversations with friendly Irishmen in a pub in O'Connell Street before the rain and cold sliced through his infected lungs and he was unable to walk.

Dublin, 1947
Doctors say I have signs of a TB condition. What this means exactly I don't know. They say that if I 'go slowly for some months, build up resistance and avoid cold' I may clear it up for good. Or not? Maybe just waste a few precious months of wild living … ?

Medical bills. Dates. Times. The results of an X-ray: double pneumonia, left-lung tuberculosis. More medical bills. The struggle to get currency on the black market (*fifty pounds just to get a hundred*), approval notes from bank managers, calls back to Australia (*a shilling a minute*), no luck getting Swiss francs.

It must have been 1947 or 1948, because there was an undated letter to his mother, telling her not to worry about his health, unaware it was she who would die soon and not him.

All my love, Denison.

His life zig-zagged wildly — letters from Arthur Boyd were stuffed into a folder alongside a card for one of David Boyd's first pottery shows in London — and there seemed to be no space between the TB and his recovery when he was suddenly back in London, drinking beers with Roy Campbell or heading to the military club on Pall Mall.

Ah. He was a member because he *had* served in the military, it seemed. Little pieces of his history, and Michelle's references, started to fit into a larger story.

There was a long diary entry on the sanatorium: stark white with perfectly numb nurses; how he wished he was in the ward with all the other patients (*inmates*, he called them), not stuck in silence with no one interesting to talk to. Being bored seemed worse to him than being sick. Through it all, the determination not to waste time. The hatred of confinement.

More references to money — to the power games between the haves and have-nots in London, and this sense that he despised money not for what it was, but how it made some people *not tell the truth*.

It was mysterious and extreme, his attitude to money, and seemed intricately tied to this sense I got of his wildness and impulsiveness, to the reason I was supposed to feel ashamed of him.

Reading on, I found this diary entry from Paris, 1951:

It was a fine day and I stayed out late into the evening, visiting various offices and businesses in my work as a translator and freelance journalist. When I returned up the narrow flight of stairs to the Hotel Floridor, there were people everywhere, and as I brushed past them to get my key off the hook one of them grabbed me and showed me a Press card. Two others started to talk to me about my plans and where was I from?

What was all this? I sighted the hotelier, my mate Louis, who had known me three years. He gave me a big wink and raised a glass of wine in salute.

I had never seen wine in the office before, and now there were bottles everywhere.

The man from the big American daily was at my elbow, asking questions. Who was I, where had I been, where was I going? He wanted to know. I brushed through to Louis, followed by the mob, and demanded what the hell was going on.

'It is all right, Denis, the whole Press has been in and out tonight. They think you are some missing Englishman, and they are all buying drinks.'

A correspondent I knew slightly caught me by the sleeve and started making more sense, and backed it up with a glass of good champagne. 'Have you heard of a chap called Maclean?' he asked me. 'You look a bit like him, and half of Europe is on the hunt for him.'

We adjourned to my room, looking out over the square with a few of the journalists and a bottle, and sorted the matter out while Louis fought off the rear guard or sent them out for more wine.

I began to understand. I had been meaning to visit a friend of mine in Berlin, calling into Pan-Am office in the Opera district to ask about ticket prices. I had not concluded the deal. Oddly enough, my friend was in American intelligence, but not in counter-espionage. George (Bailey) was in interrogation of Russian defectors with the U.S. Army unit. Someone from Pan-Am must have reported a British type, over six feet high, dark, seeking a way out to Berlin.

Who was Maclean and why was he so important? The Times correspondent filled me in while he asked me a few questions and we sipped his Veuve Cliquot.

Fortunately, I was known to our Embassy — there were other Australians like Roly Pullen, the Herald correspondent in Paris, who knew me, and Louis (if he ever sobered up) could vouch for me. About midnight, we all parted the best of friends and went to bed.

Next morning, wondering if the whole thing was a dream, I read the morning paper and caught up on the Foreign Office scandal. I was at the little basin shaving, with my back to the door, when it burst open, a rugged-looking dark Frenchman in a blue suit, probably a southerner, took me in a jiffy, simultaneously staring at everything in the room at once. He kept one hand in his pocket and said three words: 'D.S.T. Monsieur, Passeport?'

D.S.T. I had heard of this sinister department — the French equivalent of the Special Branch. A very undercover organization for operations against foreign spies on French territory. I produced my passport very quickly. He examined it and spent another minute or two examining me and a photo he held in his hand. I told him, with some malice, that the International Press had left the trail cold the night before. With a typical French monosyllable, he turned on his heel and left.

Shortly after this, Alister Kershaw dropped in for a chat and warned me to be careful. 'You'd better be on the watch. These D.S.T. people don't act like French police — and you know how different they are from British police forces. We had better see Jacques [Delarue].'

Jacques was a very civilized, well-read police inspector. He used to drop into the Hotel for chats about poetry and life at odd times. Small, dark, very French.

Jacques came round to see us and we told the story again. He was sitting on the bed, smoking a Gauloise. Alister occupied the only chair. There was yet another knock on the door. I opened it to a small sandy-haired man in a raincoat who cupped his hand with a card in it and rapped out 'D.S.T.! Passeport!'

This time I didn't hurry to show my passport. 'Look here,' I said, made bolder by the presence of Jacques. 'Why don't you ask your colleague about it, he was here this morning?'

Sandy-haired went red with anger. 'Colleague? What colleague, what did he look like? Which way did he go? No-one was assigned to this job but me.'

Jacques interrupted drily from the bed. 'Permit me to point out, Monsieur, that you are rather late in arriving. The whole Paris Press was here last night.'

Sandy-hair was not amused. Furiously he demanded more details about the short dark visitor of the morning and went off to interrogate Louis about this new spy mystery and raced off to chase, not Maclean, but the pseudo-D.S.T.

Tucked into the diary was a newspaper clipping:

May 1951
AUSTRALIAN NOT MISSING DIPLOMAT
Sunday Telegraph Service
PARIS, Sat. — Scores of police and British Embassy officials

combed Paris last night for Mr Dinison [sic] Deasey, of Melbourne.

Deasey, 30, is a son of the late Canon Deasey, of Melbourne.

When he went to the office of International Airways to book a passage to Berlin, the clerk thought he was Donald Maclean, one of the missing British Foreign Office men.

The clerk told Deasey to wait, then rang the British Embassy from a backroom telephone.

Tired of waiting, Deasey left the office before Embassy officials arrived.

Police joined the officials in an all-night search of Paris hotels and ordered a watch on all aerodromes and railway stations.

Deasey was dressing at 7.30 this morning when police knocked on his hotel room door.

IN UNDERPANTS

The police questioned him as he stood in his shirt and underpants.

They refused to believe that Deasey was not Maclean until British Embassy officials arrived.

The officials, who knew Maclean well, said that Deasey bore a remarkable likeness to the missing diplomat.

But their questions soon revealed that he was not Maclean.

Maclean and Guy Burgess, another Foreign Office official, disappeared on May 27 while on a visit to France.

Dad, mistaken for a spy! Was Michelle back in Paris at that time, too? 1951, yes, she would have been. Did she see the newspaper clipping? I would have to find out if she had lived near the Hotel Floridor.

The voice in his diaries — the sense of snap decisions, intense observation, love of adventure, and instinctive, impulsive boldness — was so familiar.

Mum had been brave, but she'd never been so plucky and adventurous.

This was my dad. One half of my DNA.
Me.

Just as he'd chanced upon Tucker in Saint Germain, he bumped into his ex-wife's mother, perhaps the only other Australian he might have known in France, staring at the Nike statue at the Louvre. The next day, he'd taken her to Versailles, where gossip and small talk of Melbourne life reminded him why he'd left.

In Europe, Melbourne feels like an alien-land … I realized they are looking forward to going back there soon. Why?

Dad's handwriting was difficult to understand, but if I stayed with it, almost like listening to the particular sound intonations of another language, I could sense the rhythm. If I squinted and read out loud, I got used to his shorthand for certain words. I had to keep my head down or I'd lose the thread.

He came into my brain, his writing 'voice' replaced my own, because I read so many of his thoughts. But all the questions I had, only he could answer, so I kept reading, catching up on decades of lost conversations.

He was *here*, again. Alive through the printed word. *If only in my head.*

But still, it felt so real.

Each piece of material — every new letter, every new page — revealed more information than the last. It reminded me of that first night I spent in Paris, wanting to walk down every street but being distracted by every new vision and encounter, every precious thing. I felt possessed by more gifts than I could hold.

Michelle, Michelle, must look for Michelle. But then dad was in the South of France, which seemed another world entirely, living in a villa with Richard Aldington, being visited by his literary heroes such as Henry Williamson.

Here, I see the war was worth it, he wrote. Then, just as soon, he was back in London. From 1948 to 1949, he travelled from London to France so many times, endlessly catching the train.

The character I met on those pages had managed to squeeze multiple lives into what others would struggle to put into one. I started to see him more clearly, understanding how even in his older years he would have still been the man in these pages. I could finally see how mum must have found him intriguing, despite the massive age difference, despite how the relationship ended.

The strangest events were brushed off like they were nothing — was it a sign of the times? He didn't mind being mistaken for a Cold War spy when he could have been shot by the secret police — because Louis Marandou, the hotelier at the Floridor, where he'd been confronted, opened a bottle of champagne in *Monsieur Denison's* honour! He'd even found a way to make tuberculosis work for his life plans, using the medical papers to ensure he got out of London and back to France.

I read so much that first day. I read until my vision blurred and my stomach roared and I was so thirsty I couldn't even voice a 'thank you' to the librarian at the desk when I signed the requisite forms to be let out through the glass doors.

I stumbled down the library stairs to the hot night outside — Melbourne, Australia, summer 2016. But underneath my skin, I was in 1940s France, still travelling with dad. I thought of how much he adored France, how happy he was there, regardless of the health problems that seemed to plague him.

It's impossible to sustain melancholy in Paris, he'd written.

That seemed significant, somehow.

That a family in France had reintroduced him to me.

I'd gone to the library to search for Michelle, but instead found dad. Her beautiful letters had helped me brave the snakes.

But now I couldn't close the boxes.

Chapter Six

Chance perdue

There had been chances to learn of dad's story, breadcrumbs that had come before Coralie's message and Michelle's letters, hints that his life was interesting, references to famous names. But something had always frightened me off diving deeply. The knowledge that he'd suffered, perhaps. Or the sense that his story was too big for me to ever understand.

Mirka Mora, a Frenchwoman who narrowly escaped Auschwitz and relocated to Melbourne in the 1950s, had been one breadcrumb. She'd also been an artist and a member of the Heide circle, closely entwined with Nolan and Tucker, and John and Sunday Reed, and that whole bohemian time in Melbourne.

But Mirka had also said something that had warned me off, all those years ago. Much like the first trip to the library when all I found was sadness, something she said had hinted at the pain I knew had filled the end of dad's life.

I spent a decade whipping across the floors of Mediterranean restaurants in the city, first as a university student, and for a few years afterwards. As I tried to figure out how to make writing work as a career, I'd occasionally look up and realise I'd spent more of my time delivering plates of food and drinks to strangers than sitting at my desk and actually typing. But I always kept a diary.

What I loved about working in each of those restaurants, was that it felt a bit like I was travelling. Even if there was a crazy Italian chef who fired all the staff and then hired them back in weeping apology ten minutes later, I found that more interesting than sitting in an office, and I loved witnessing the differences of culture in European restaurants. I seemed to gravitate towards the more intense and busy places, mostly because I loathed being bored, even if my arms did feel like they were going to fall off from the weight of carrying plates for a sixteen-hour shift.

It was hard work, but the simplicity of serving such a basic human need and having interesting interactions kept me waitressing even after I did start to work as a freelance journalist.

At Florentino's, one of Melbourne's oldest Italian restaurants, at the top of Bourke Street, Mirka Mora had a ritual where she'd come in every Monday for oysters at midday. A well-known character in Melbourne, she and her husband had once started Balzac, the first French restaurant to open in Melbourne, in the early 1950s. Her being a French-Australian artist, and born in the same era as dad, made me wonder if they'd met.

Something about Mirka, by virtue of her French-ness, also made me think of Gisèle. She felt *familiar* to me. Melbourne was small in the late 1950s, and dad had returned to Melbourne with Gisèle sometime around then. There couldn't have been a large French-Australian population. Perhaps they'd met?

So Mirka would appear every Monday, bright-red lipstick, wide eyes, and warm greetings, dressed for what seemed such a beautifully *French* ritual, ordering a dozen oysters for lunch and a glass of champagne.

She had this playfully young sense about her, despite her age. She captured the sense of style I imagined of older women across France — an innate self-possession, confidence in her own particular type of femininity. A sense of the necessity of luxury, yet a beauty that had nothing to do with material means.

I also loved that she couldn't care less about outside opinion. Her irreverence to authority and conservatism made me comfortable.

Her face would change when I set down the plate of oysters on her table, and she always squealed something funny in delight, like 'Look at their little faces!' or 'My friends have arrived!'

Glancing at the butcher's paper we always placed on top of the tablecloths, I'd see she'd been drawing wide-eyed doll faces. She always left a trail of art wherever she went. Whenever I cleared the table after her, I'd keep her drawings, and the manager once pinned one above the phone.

After working up the courage for weeks, I stood by the chef plating up the oysters to ensure no one else got to the bell before me. The manager was upstairs, and I knew I had a few moments alone.

I placed her 'little friends' down and cleared my throat, tumbling the words out before I had the chance to get scared.

'I'm sorry if this is an odd question, but I — I just wondered if you knew my dad?'

'Who was your daddy?' she said to me in her French accent, unfazed because she was like that, changing *dad* to *daddy* in a way that made me feel she understood. I was twenty-seven. She was about eighty, and her tone was kind, if a little confused. She studied my face, looking up from her seat, and I felt guilty for pestering her.

'His name was Denison Deasey,' I replied, feeling foolish.

Time passed as I could see her scanning her memories — all the people she'd known, the lives she'd lived.

'No ...' She looked like she was trying to remember something. 'I'm sorry, I didn't know that man ...'

My shoulders fell, the drama was all for nothing.

'Oh, okay, sorry, sorry, enjoy your oysters. *Bon appétit!*' I said, embarrassed. I walked to the back of the restaurant to hide my red face and give her some space, but then I heard her chair scrape back, so I turned around.

'HIS EYES! YOU HAVE YOUR DADDY'S EYES!' she shouted across the restaurant floor.

I sped back to her before the manager could hear, and she took my hand in both of hers, warm and beautiful. Like we were *family*.

'I remember your daddy. I remember your daddy! Yes. Yes. I remember him. I remember him … *Deasey*. I don't remember *Denison*, but I remember *Deasey* you see. You confused me. I remember *Deasey* …'

Tears welled in my eyes, and she studied me again.

'He is still here,' she said — like a fairy godmother — pointing at my face and then my chest. 'You have your daddy *in* you,' she said, looking me deep in the eyes, which by then were openly spilling tears.

Then, just as unexpectedly, she started telling me a story and her face changed to twinkling amusement.

'We were at a party at our restaurant,' she said. *Balzac*, it must have been. 'Some "notable" men, you know the sorts, important or something, anyway they arrived and they were stuffy. Too stuffy. Everyone was acting so stuffy …'

She made me giggle. I loved that she didn't like stuffiness.

'Anyway, I decided to throw some cheese, and nobody liked that of course … but your daddy stood up, clapped, and said, "Bravo!", which made them all join in …'

Sibling subversives, I thought. No wonder she felt like family.

'Yes, yes, I remember him,' she said, pointing as she spoke with her beautiful red-lipped smile. 'I can tell you more if you come to my house in Richmond,' she said, writing her address on a napkin and forcing it into my hand. She was still staring into my eyes, as though dad was there.

'Your daddy … he suffered a lot,' she added before she left, looking sad.

What did she mean? I had to sit out the back in the laneway to recover, and I kept coming back to those words, unsure if I could handle the answer. Why did she say that?

I worked split shifts in that restaurant for a year. By the time I had some space to even think about travelling to her house in Richmond, I wondered if she'd forgotten our encounter.

I never did go and visit her, feeling intrusive and foolish because I didn't have a phone number and I didn't want to turn up unannounced. I saw her on the streets of St Kilda a few years later, and tried to say hello, but she didn't remember me.

For she was elderly by then, like everyone connected to dad.

Perhaps the truth was, I didn't want to know more details of his suffering. When I'd first tried to look at the boxes in the library, a year or two after meeting Mirka, all that had met me was his pain.

I only wanted to know he'd laughed and encouraged her to throw cheese.

Chapter Seven

Manuscrits

Aunt Alice had still been alive all those years ago when I'd met Mirka. Seven years older than dad, minus a day, I thought they'd been close. The diaries in the library confirmed she was his favourite sibling, listing secret calling codes and nicknames they'd use in London and France. Perhaps that's why he'd introduced her to Michelle.

She was his most adored sister, his dear *Azzy*. But even his adored *Azzy* had pestered him about his spending. He'd shouted her lunch in London and she'd told him off for 'wasting' his inheritance, I found in one of the diaries.

Of dad's three sisters, Alice was the only one still alive when I was born, but I'd always thought of her more like a grandmother, because she was in her seventies in my earliest memories of her. Impeccable, scarily observant, and extremely independent, even in her eighties she'd wear her handmade Liberty of London dresses with polished nails, opening up the piano in the front room or a book of art on the living-room table and asking me about school. After her husband, Grant, died, she lived alone in that house in Point Lonsdale by the sea until she died in her nineties, even driving her car well into her eighties.

Until she retired, Alice had been a headmistress in Geelong, and I loved her but she intimidated me, which is perhaps why I didn't ask her more about dad. Also, what could I have asked? I didn't know much about world history, had no idea what all the reference points would have been.

Alice once took me out to lunch on one of those visits to her house in Point Lonsdale, and I remember serving myself some salad without waiting for permission, or something similarly casual. She flashed her eyes at me without a word and I felt so ashamed. The event makes complete sense, now that I know she'd lived through the the Great Depression, World War II, and rationing, but when it happened I remember feeling I'd broken some great moral code.

That sense of austerity, of clear right and wrong, seemed to hint at what dad must have experienced in his family — particularly when they were so connected to the Church of England. If my casual serving of salad was bad, what must they have thought of his spending so much money on travel and art, on living large?

When I finished my arts degree and applied for a postgraduate writing course, I only told my sister. I doubted I'd make it in, because the course was so competitive.

Sure enough, as I pulled in the newspaper from the front doorstep on the Saturday when results were publicised, my name was nowhere to be found. My sister consoled me, knowing how badly I'd wanted it, taking me out for gelati on Lygon Street for a distraction.

By the time I got home, I'd decided to get a job on a cruise ship that was to go to Europe. The thought of travel was the only thing that lifted my spirits, and a week later the cruise liner was already checking my references. I visualised a fully stamped passport replacing that paper degree — maybe travel would give me something worth writing about?

But a week later, aunt Alice called early on Saturday morning.

'Lou,' she said in her formidable, slightly breathless voice. She never spoke about them, but I knew from her host of ancient ailments it would have taken an effort for her to get to her phone. 'I'm looking at your name in the paper, next to Professional Writing and Editing,

Royal Melbourne Institute of Technology.'

I'd mixed up the newspaper's announcement dates. Pre-internet alerts and digital updates, if she hadn't read the newspaper front-to-back at her dining table over her morning toast every day, perhaps I would have got on that ship.

As steely-eyed and intimidating as Alice was, she could surprise me with her perceptions. I'd always felt a sense of shame and *how dare I?* about pursuing writing, but Alice didn't treat it that way. I learned one day, she'd warned mum not to expect me to 'settle down' into any kind of 'normal' career.

She called again the day I had my first article published, which gave the occasion some gravitas, clipping the newspaper and keeping the story to show visitors.

In the last trip I made to Point Lonsdale, not long before she died, aged ninety-five — when Barack Obama was inaugurated as president of the United States and I could tell she was confused as to what era she lived in — she pulled out a magazine to show me dad's first published creative piece in the literary journal *Overland*. It's one of the only memories I have of anyone being proud of his writing — and actually showing it to me.

I didn't tell Alice, because she had twilight eyes and I sensed she was losing her grip on the earth, but *Overland* was the first magazine that had paid me for a poem, a few years earlier.

Michelle had *met* Alice in 1949, according to the letters, an event I still found beautiful to think about. Coralie's French grandmother had met my aunt Alice! Dad had taken Michelle to Alice's cottage in Hampstead for a picnic with the children, and afterwards they'd washed the dishes together.

In song.

At home, re-reading my own old diaries, searching for the discussion with Mirka Mora, it struck me how romantic it must have been, for dad to introduce Michelle to his sister and family. If I was far from home and had just started dating someone, I'd be touched if they took me for picnics with their siblings and their children in Hampstead Heath. And there was so much literary history in that area of London; I wondered what literary connections he'd made other than Dylan Thomas and Roy Campbell and those names dotted across his diaries I'd swam through in a blurry frenzy.

I emailed Coralie and Clémentine, pasting a small photo of the page of the diary that mentioned Michelle. I'd snuck it quickly and silently, wedged behind one of the boxes, wanting to emerge from that cave of a library room with some sort of visual proof of dad — some part of him to take with me.

It felt too small, not anything like the reams of letters they'd already transcribed and sent me. But it was still Michelle's name, all the way across the ocean from France to Australia, uncovered from a box, and written in dad's personal, cursive script. A little record of that time with Michelle, proof that our families had once been connected — and maybe still were.

It was *something*.

I'm sorry that this is all I could find of Michelle, I wrote to Coralie. *I saw that there's a folder full of black-and-white photos, but I have to request them in a different room, on a different day. I'll go back.*

For the rest of the week I was at the library by opening time, reading until the warning bell went for closing, feeling foolish that I'd waited so long to know the story of my dad.

The photos — which I did eventually get access to — were black-and-white shots from London, France, and Vienna in the 1940s and 1950s, just after the war. No Michelle. No Buckingham Palace.

But still — they were so precious, so new and intriguing.

There were weathered black-and-white photos of soldiers and a camp in the outback, a man I knew to be dad's friend Alister Kershaw, and I also recognised Arthur and David Boyd. There was a black-and-white photo of the writer Richard Aldington, and a small strip of photos of a gathering outside a bistro in Paris, and numerous travel shots from what appeared to be the 1940s and 1950s with men and women I couldn't name or place.

They were beautiful photos, and showed dad travelling in post-war Europe, laughing, smiling, wearing well-made suits, shirts, and coats. I'd never seen him looking so dashing, if a little thin. There was even a photo of him at school with friends, as a teenager. But my favourite of those secret photos in the library folder was one where he was striding down Oxford Street, London, with Alister Kershaw.

He looked happy, well-to-do, approachable, and handsome, just the kind of man you'd like to meet on a train.

But no photos of Michelle.

I started to have dreams of dad, as his words seeped further and further into my heart and I could envision him as the person he was, not the sick man who'd died before my childhood brain had the chance to comprehend him.

The first dream came after the second day at the library: we were emailing each other despite his being on 'the other side'. He asked about Ayala and her kids, and I told him she'd had a girl and a boy — he had grandchildren. He sent me a poem as life advice to give to them, and I can only describe that dream as a visitation.

He was alive, back in my life, even if it was all on a level that I couldn't quite express or yet understand.

When I woke, I realised he was asking me to keep reading his diaries.

It was as clear to me as if he'd come back from the dead and asked me to complete a task. It was so real — *he* was so real. Even though I'd found him in the library, it was Coralie's message that had started the journey. I couldn't express to her how grateful I was. I still desperately wanted to visit her, and the rest of her family, and I sent her another emotional email of thanks and apologies for not finding more about Michelle.

Clémentine, as emotional in her emails as me, told me not to be stupid and that it was all so important, regardless of whether I found Michelle in his diary. I felt comforted by that.

Each morning that week, as my neighbour woke and started shouting abuse upstairs, I'd check my emails to see if anything had arrived from Paris. I found myself hoping a message had flown its way over in the night, searching for Coralie and Clémentine's names in my inbox. I should have been looking for a job, or a new place to live, but I was obsessed with this story of dad and the French family. Everything else came second. Soon, their uncle Edouard emailed me, too, telling me that he was so thrilled Coralie had found me, that his precious *Maman* had spoken of dad since 1984, that he thought the whole story was like a movie script, and that he wanted me to come to France.

On the third day, after the visit from dad in my dream, an email came from Clémentine. It held a link to a short video that was password-protected. I tentatively clicked open, a little afraid of what it might hold.

The video was of Michelle talking about my dad, just days before she died. A tiny, frail Frenchwoman propped up in her hospital bed, obviously nearing the end of her life. Edith Piaf's 'La Vie en rose' played softly in the background. It looked as though the family had decorated her cubicle with a beautiful patterned sheet to make it more comforting.

Laurence — Michelle's eldest daughter; Clémentine and Coralie's mother — swayed to the music to make Michelle smile. She wore a white top and reminded me of my mum; they had a similar way of moving, looked a similar age. It was uncanny. I remembered she was a painter, just like mum had been.

As Laurence swayed, Michelle clicked her fingers and called

her in closer, speaking quietly in French. All I could make out was *Denison*.

'Denison … *Où est Denison?*'

Laurence replied, in English: 'He is in Australia … I think …' She smiled.

I wailed and wailed, watching that video over and again. Clémentine had recorded it just a week earlier, not long before Coralie's first message.

An actual living, breathing connection to my dad.

In Michelle's twilight time, she even thought dad was still alive.

That all of this had been happening in Paris only a week or so ago made my head spin. Though I'd lost Gisèle and that connection to dad's life in France, Michelle had been there all along. She seemed a sacred treasure. I grieved for her after watching that video, like I'd lost a member of my own family.

When I'd gathered myself together, I sent Clém an email to thank her. I wondered if she'd needed permission to share such an intimate video.

I rode back to the library and continued the search through his letters.

To Dec and Ayala, Clém and Coralie quickly became *the French Sisters*, and when Edouard, Michelle's eldest son, expressed his passion for the story, they all became *the French Family*.

My sister used her research skills to find newspaper clippings of the Gielgud play dad had taken Michelle to see and the Royal visit they'd witnessed at Buckingham Palace, wishing we had more to send *the French family*.

After talking about the library papers one night, Ayala and I agreed to ask *the French Sisters* if they could search for a record of what happened to Gisèle. Coralie had explained in one of her messages that their uncle worked as a special investigator tracking down people owed large fortunes. As he was based in Paris, we thought he might be able to find her death certificate, at the very least so we could have some closure.

I messaged Gisèle's full name, and her last known address on Boulevarde de Grenelle.

While Coralie and Clémentine and the rest of their family travelled from Paris to Brittany for Michelle's funeral, I established myself in the library, negotiating boxes in a subterranean world of papers and stories from another time.

Edouard emailed me the video of Michelle's life they had played at the funeral. I was so deeply moved by all of it that even though Michelle had just passed away, I felt my family had expanded.

In the library, I requested the maximum number of boxes I was allowed each day, and read in that cold room like I was cramming for an exam. I found an entire typed and bound memoir written when dad had returned to Australia in 1955, one I'd never known existed; I scanned it quickly to search for Michelle, but found instead Gisèle, 'my French wife' as dad referred to her.

I photographed thirty or forty photos, precious photos I could add to our record of dad's twenties. He looked so happy in France, his face radiated delight all the way across time. *He'd made it, at last.*

But I didn't find anything else about Michelle.

I snatched photos of dozens of typed diary entries from Saint Clair, in France, because the writing was so beautiful and filled with poetic descriptions. Dad's cursive script appeared on French hotel stationery that oozed luxury, where, in Melbourne, paper had been rationed so strictly that dad's purchase of the printing press — and paper — to publish Adrian Lawlor's book was apparently considered obscene.

The days in the South of France were dad's happiest days, I realised, reading the joy in his words at finally making it across the

Channel and meeting Richard Aldington. *The Writer*, he called him grandly, feeling an affinity with Aldington almost like a father–son relationship. Aldington had also been affected by the war, exiling himself from England to France to get away from the 'wreckage and the waste'.

Aldington, Richard Aldington. The name felt important, inextricably intertwined with dad's. Why? I searched for letters to dad from Aldington, but they seemed to be in a different library — hundreds were kept in the National Library, in Canberra. My research expanded every time I looked up a new piece of information.

I found an Aldington letter in a book held in the State Library describing dad treating him to a meal in Paris that was so decadent I wondered if most of his wasted 'fortune' went on French food.

I filled the entire memory of my phone within the first week.

I found a note about the time he bumped into a distant ancestor on the street in Ireland:

Galway, 1949

I met Jack Deacy in the street in Galway this morning and we went into the pub. Jack bought drinks. A hornpipe was playing outside. 'Well, when ye come back to Galway, I've a house out about a mile and there'll always be a room for ye. Now remember you're first preferred. Come back for the races, now.'

I copied letters from Albert Tucker, and David and Arthur Boyd, and a postcard sent by Barry Humphries, and by necessity I swung my research to the mid-to-late 1950s. I understood why the library must have wanted this material: it covered such an interesting time in Australian history, and dad recorded so many quotes and anecdotes drawn from artists and friends who later became famous. There was correspondence from writers and bohemian figures such as Manning Clark, Tim and Betty Burstall, Stephen Murray-Smith, so many names I'd seen on spines of books or related to Melbourne or literary history.

Dad had even written a film script with my cousin Julian, who'd been a TV director. *The little boy Michelle had met.* I'd had no idea dad pitched a film script — I started to understand why Julian adored him so.

In the boxes from the 1950s, a letter from dad to his brother Randal appeared, and he talked about Gisèle. I wondered if dad had met Gisèle at the same time he met Michelle, as it might explain the lack of correspondence about Michelle.

Dated 1953, the letter gave me some clues.

We met in London, years ago, and recently reunited in Paris. She's small, dark, and very French. Soon we'll be married.

It would mean a lot if you could send her a note.

Dad and Gisèle, too, had met in London through 'friends'.
Who? How? Was 'years ago' 1949? Or 1950?
More diary entries about Gisèle's father: his name was Gerard.

A gentle and softly-spoken man, much like a zen master, he held the same scars on his legs from infections from the war …

Gerard — that was my brother's middle name. A French name and I'd always wondered why …

There was more about World War II, about Gerard. He survived four years as a prisoner of war with the Japanese in a camp in Java, where he'd climb under the fence to tear up weeds he'd give to the other prisoners so they could have some food. For four years Gisèle heard nothing. Unable to stand not knowing, she joined the army, intending to go and find him, but the war ended before she could be sent overseas.

Gerard was expatriated out of Java and returned to Paris by the Australian Red Cross at the end of the war. Tiny and thin, wearing clothes also donated by the Australian Red Cross, with permanent marks on the back of his head from the canes used by the Japanese in the camps, he woke screaming from nightmares for the rest of his days.

When dad lived with Gisèle in Paris, he felt so peaceful in Gerard's presence. In turn, dad drew Gerard out of his shell. Rather than finding dad's nationality a bit frightening, as Michelle's parents had (Australia was so far, he might take their daughter away, I assumed was the fear), Gerard and Gisèle may have been drawn to dad *because* he was Australian. For the Australians had returned Gerard to France. To life.

Dad wrote so intimately of those nights spent talking with Gerard, and how much he admired him. How close he felt with Gisèle, how warm he found her companionship. He nicknamed her 'Rat' and she called him 'Mate'. The two were married at a registry office in Kent, England, in July 1954, even though they'd been sharing a flat near the Eiffel Tower, in the world-famous 7th arrondissement, for at least a year by then. David and Hermia Boyd were their marriage witnesses. Were the Boyds their mutual friends?

Perhaps Dad, Gisèle, and Michelle had all lived in the same arrondissement? Perhaps they'd passed each other on Paris streets, circling each other like cats in the dark, completely unaware of me sitting here in the future, picturing the past.

The librarian who'd been so strict the first day seemed relieved when I returned for the third day in a row, because she didn't have to repeat the rules. I'd been asking for dad's inventory on her screen at the end of each day when I requested the next day's boxes, but on Thursday she slipped over to my table.

'Don't tell anyone I did this, because we're not supposed to print things out,' she whispered conspiratorially as she slid the forty-something pages of the descriptive list across the bench, clipped together like the book that it was.

Oh, that token gesture helped so much. I could record which folders I'd actually seen, which boxes I'd requested where and when, what held what. I even began correcting the descriptive list in the margins of the library inventory, when I discovered the boxes and folders actually contained different things to what was listed.

I tore through the diaries from 1947 to 1949, trying to figure out how and when dad caught the boat from Melbourne to London, where he stayed, how he'd got to Dublin.

I'd never really registered how close to the war those days in London had been, how the circumstances of the time would have affected everything he wanted and tried to do. The bombed-out buildings, the hunger, the debt, the rationing. The six long years of the Blitz, which would take over a decade for England to completely recover from — nine years after the war had ended, food rationing was finally lifted.

Crippled with debt, used to the sirens and having to cover their windows for blackouts, the English in the immediate post-war period sounded anything but jubilant the war was over. They were hungry, depressed, and *exhausted*.

Dad's first meal at a bistro in France, by contrast, was almost a holy experience. *Meat, wine, bread, butter, mussels … this seems like life again.* A detail from this meal in Marseille struck him: *The French sit facing the sun.*

Despite the diagnosis of TB, and difficulty being allowed currency that wasn't English pounds, dad had seemed determined to cover as wide an amount of European terrain as possible. His passport was filled from 1947 to 1949 with stamps *across* stamps — Spain, Switzerland, France, Italy, Germany, Ireland … I had trouble making out the dates.

The feeling of *shame* again, hitting that part of the solar plexus I associate with survival. *He squandered three fortunes …* The painful words came back. What were those fortunes? All I knew was that his father, my grandpa, was a Church of England vicar, who would have raised six children on a parishioner's salary. I made a note to ask my cousins where the 'fortune' would have come from …

The cost of exchanging Australian dollars for pounds, the medical bills, the open-handed way he gave to his friends … Dad was extravagant, it was certainly true. But it was as though he thought he didn't have much time left, and I understood that feeling of urgency, even though I wasn't sure where it came from.

There was 'squandering' to encourage David Boyd by paying for his music lessons in Melbourne, more 'squandering' on one of Arthur Boyd's earliest paintings of Rosebud, more encouragement. Music, art, beauty, travel. Random loans to artists. A hundred-pound fare for the boat from Melbourne to England given to poet mate Alister Kershaw, then another hundred pounds loaned to mate Albert Tucker. The cost of the printing press. Printing a poem into a book for Al, then printing Adrian Lawlor's book …

In London, he even saw *Swan Lake* two nights in a row because it filled some spiritual need — falling in love with the lead, Anna Cheselka, and waxing lyrically in his diary about how love and art and beauty could fill a hunger that mundane concerns could not. He was a mad romantic. Art, music, and love moved him spiritually much more than the church, and he felt this differentiated him from his family. His father had been a clergyman — was that why dad was considered the 'black sheep'? In Paris, he'd describe himself 'galloping' every time he heard music coming from inside a church. Music moved him more than anything.

The war was over and he was always starving hungry, it seemed, but he wanted to live as well as possible, with as much friendship and culture and poetry and romance as possible. He was always shouting people meals in London. But he was never full, always describing a 'dull ache' in his stomach.

Until he got to France.

⚜

I shifted in and out of journalistic objectivity, remembering to look for clues about dates, names, times, then falling into this strange, obsessive, trance-like state, caught up in the marvel that he was actually talking to me, through these diaries. Once home from every library trip, I'd pull a diary of my own down from the cupboard, locating eerily parallel lines written by my own hand, at similar ages.

A short story about a trip to the country echoed lines from my first book. The similarities in our writing style had me wondering about what we inherit without even knowing: a focus on snatches of dialogue, the idea of freedom and spirituality, and love versus traditional religion. A deep distrust of hierarchies and pretension. All the parts of me that had never made sense were here in dad's pages.

It was intimate and intense, this relationship I'd formed with dad's words, and I didn't know what it meant or how it could be a good thing — I had nothing to compare it to, no one to ask about it. If I said it out loud, I would sound like I'd been possessed by a ghost. I kept it all quiet, only expressing my feelings in emails to the French sisters, in my diary, and to my siblings.

I couldn't focus on anything else, I found dad's writing so entertaining. Even the most banal diary descriptions were interesting. How had this been tucked away from me for so long? Why hadn't anyone told me?

I had to consciously remind myself he'd written these diaries for no one but himself.

1949

The Russian boys get on at Ennsbrucke. One of them smiles and says 'Guten Abend.' We are suitably astonished. He looks at the passes, holds mine for a long time. Then he says, 'This is too late. It has expired.' I gasp. The others all turn around. I stand up and start talking bad German with him.

He is quite right, the damned thing had run out. Fat monocole has moved back a table to be out of the way, but he suddenly says: 'He has broken his ankle, can't you see? That's why he is late, he's been in hospital.' I suddenly play the foot argument, showing the plaster monstrosity. But the boy half grins and says 'I must see my officer', disappearing. I am shattered. A sallow, hooked-nose man who has been talking bad French with another, both wearing violent American feature ties says, looking at me, 'Now we will be late in Vienna …'

I walk back to my compartment to look for hospital documents to confuse and stupefy the Russkis. After ten minutes the train moves, slowly, but it moves. I put my head out the window and laugh for glee.

Damn the passport, we're off. But the porter comes along with my passport. The nice Russian boy had just taken it outside the carriage, hung rough for a minute, then given it to the porter. Nice boy. The second nice Russian!

We're off again. The fat monocole returns. 'Er war sehr nette, jener Russe, sehr nette. Ja, er war sehr net, nicht wahr?' Grey hair agrees with him.

The Arlberg Express, held up by one figure on a grey card for twenty minutes, roars off to beat the clock.

Despite whatever mysterious ailment he seemed to have on those train rides, he galloped from place to place at a giant speed, hungry to devour the culture and interact with everyone, so grateful to be out of Australia, to feel like he was 'living' again, even though his medical records painted a different picture.

Then somehow we'd gone from London to Paris again, and he was living in an upstairs room at the Hotel Floridor in 1951. There was no hot water, the lift was broken, the hotelier couldn't speak a word of English, but he was happier there than anywhere he'd lived in his life, parking his bags in an upstairs room overlooking a square for over a year. It was close to the nearby international train station, and he could zip off to Brussels or Berlin or Bern whenever the mood took him.

I could understand his excitement at being out of Australia, particularly after what sounded like a harrowing six-week voyage on a 'hell-ship' with 'no windows' in a cabin with five other men and no trips out on deck, but the rate at which he travelled was overwhelming even to me. He seemed determined not to miss out on something. Like perhaps he had, before.

Thinking I was picking up another page from 1949, I opened up a ten-page memoir about his army service in Australia during World War II. It was typed up as if for publication, but one line threw me:

... and the next detail will be of interest to my children ...

Simply titled, *1942*.

I surrendered to what had become clear that first day in the library. I couldn't understand 1949 until I understood everything that came before.

Particularly, dad's experience of the Second World War.

Chapter Eight
Le régiment

What would we do if the Japanese came? I had a Tommy Gun, but we were under strictest orders not to shoot a single round. Meanwhile in the heat, without news of the war, sound nor sight of a plane or a civilian, eaten by insects and forgetting the taste of fresh food, we sank.

The entire ten-page essay, and another tucked just behind it, were both penned decades after the war had ended. Perhaps they were drafts of a story for publication? The manuscripts recounted, in detail, dad's experiences during 1941 and 1942. His handwritten letters and diaries from 1939 to 1943 filled in the gaps.

I learned he'd joined one of Australia's first Commando units, and was sent to guard the Northern Territory from Japanese invasion.

I'd never really looked into dad's war service — never known how much World War II had affected my family, my grandparents on both sides, even dad's eldest sister, Louise, who'd lived through both the First and Second World Wars. His obituary said he'd been 'invalided' while still in Australia. I had never understood how or if dad had 'served', not really understanding what the Australian contribution had been, or if you could still say you'd 'served' if you'd never been posted overseas.

But it all connected to his feelings about France.

How that feeling of being trapped in Australia by the confines of his family had marked him so deeply, he'd been determined to see as much of the world as he could when it was over, though this meant breaking the conditions of the 'inheritance' from his maternal aunt's husband, Randal Alcock. (I learned through my cousins that Alcock was a prominent businessman who'd never had any children of his own; he'd left dad and his five surviving siblings a small inheritance when they 'came of age'. The inheritance came with conditions, though, and dad seemed to get in trouble a lot for exceeding the stipulated amount they were allowed to spend on travel.)

I'd looked up dad's war records online once, in a midnight Google search that went for hours but only gave me more questions than answers. I had zoomed in on scanned PDFs and tried to translate war-speak and army code, but the signs and handwritten references in his records were too hard to understand. I hadn't understood *Independent Company* referred to the first Commandoes. All I could clarify was that dad was 'taken on strength' on 12 December 1941, went AWOL a lot after 1943, and wasn't discharged until 1945.

But he never left Australia.

This memoir read almost like a translation of the 'official' story of that first Commando regiment in Australia.

In September 1939, when Australia's prime minister announced the country's involvement in World War II, dad's history studies at Melbourne University paled in significance with what was unfolding on the wireless. On 3 September 1939, he wrote:

> Tonight while dad was at Church, Chamberlain spoke suddenly to declare war. After, we did little but listen to news bulletins. When will the bombs fall on London? He sounded frightened, poor old man. Frightened at the things he was letting loose … the distinction Chamberlain made, between German people, and Nazi war-lords … I don't yet realize what it will mean to me. If Hitler gets Poland, he threatens us.

And later that year:

Poland taken. Paris has fallen. Des marches out in uniform.

Dad had been hospitalised with sinus infections numerous times as a teenager, and the family still called him 'bubs' at age nineteen. As he saw his older brothers leave — Desmond to somewhere in the Middle East, Randal in the Artillery, even his sister Kathleen to help form the Australian Women's Army Service — the frustrated, always-missing-out feeling that came from being the sickly 'baby' of the family grew so intense that by the time the Japanese had joined the Germans in threatening the Pacific, he skipped his history lecture at Melbourne University to catch the tram to Town Hall and enlist.

Melbourne was small back then. Someone had given 'word' that a sergeant major was taking volunteers for 'especially dangerous and immediate service'. It was the first special-forces group Australia had ever formed, on directions from the British, intended to support the Australian Imperial Force in the Middle East.

Dad was apparently rejected in that March 1941 attempt for sounding too 'la-di-da', so he learned to soften his English-intonated speech for the next interview. That first Independent Company — the one he missed out on being selected for — was the first to be killed in action.

But by December 1941 he'd made it through. Hours after volunteering (this time, in suburban Caulfield) he was on a train to the tiny country town of Foster to be trained in guerrilla warfare at the Australian mainland's rugged southernmost point, Wilsons Promontory. His father, through some kind of connection, managed to identify the train, and climbed the fence at Spencer Street station to see him off, appearing at dad's window, determined to say goodbye. This visual of my grandpa was immense.

I could finally picture someone further up the family line than dad — and I loved who I saw.

'What are you doing?' dad had apparently said, worried the officials would discover his dad had uncovered classified information, because no one was supposed to know where the group was being sent to train. Not 'I love you' or 'Goodbye'. Dad berated himself for years afterwards.

On the Victorian coastline of Wilsons Promontory, with no family to constrain him with their concerns and criticisms, no one calling him 'bubs' or saying he was too sick to attempt the gruelling routine or admonishing his impulsive streak, he trained with his fellow crackpots who'd signed up for 'dangerous and immediate service', burying limpet mines and explosives, conducting mock raids and hand-to-hand combat, taking target practice, and learning secret tactics only entrusted to the chosen few.

No grog, plenty of grub, dad wrote. They ran up to the peak of Mount Oberon every morning, and if you didn't make it up to the top by a specific time you were sent back to be a 'regular' soldier. Oberon was the difference between 'regular' and 'dangerous and immediate service'. Unlike the soldiers stationed in outback Katherine or elsewhere, waiting for movement, the Commandoes would be deployed — and soon. *We were sure of it.* Dad made it up and back from Oberon in the specified time, every morning. Determined to get away.

Something twigged, and I realised why he'd named his printing press *Oberon Press*.

Soon, he'd be deployed overseas. *Overseas*, a distant notion taken from the wireless or the newspapers or history lectures. Alamein. Africa. Europe. *Abroad*. In a time without internet or long-distance air travel or television, the notion of 'abroad' must have been about as exciting as outer space.

As they prepared in that training camp, dad considered what he knew about the fight against fascism and the Germans, how he'd be making his own contribution first-hand, a part of something global he'd only read of or heard in snatches on the radio.

Finally, I'd have the chance to learn of my bravery, he wrote. *I could make the choice.*

How refreshing it would have been to meet men from all over the place, not just the Church of England types from his boarding school, not just people who'd known his family, with all their loaded expectations of what was proper and 'right' behaviour, the weight of religious conservatism, that connection with his father being a vicar that made him feel endlessly monitored back in Melbourne.

He wrote of how interesting the other guys in his company were. Though most of them came from the 'lower classes', he felt safer with these 'good blokes' than those he'd schooled with at Geelong Grammar (the Australian version of Eton). Why was that? He seemed to imply it was because they were honest.

Here he was finally with some rebels and misfits. Men rewarded for taking risks. A little cracked. A little crazy.

Brothers in the adventure.

When the Japanese bombed Darwin in February 1942, his company was ordered to Katherine, to protect the Top End of Australia from further invasion by 'harassing' and 'disorganising' the Japanese.

We'll finally be in the fight, he wrote. *Connected to the rest of the world.* It was hard for me picture life in Australia without the ability to cross oceans through communication, at whim. As I pored over dad's diaries, Trump's fight for the US presidency was being televised globally and discussed all across the internet.

From the moment dad stepped on the train north, his letters to family members — also held in the library — had such a sense of impending adventure. Signing up for active service was the most exciting thing he'd done in his life so far.

No more grey skies and cold Melbourne winters. Here it was: fast travel and warm skies and palm trees, strangers bringing sliced pineapple as gifts to the men at the stations like the whole thing was a spectacle and the soldiers were the stars.

He didn't mind having no idea what came next. Perhaps it was the perfect outlet for a nature like his. The Commandoes, unlike the regular soldiers, were chosen specifically *for* that particular irreverence to authority and structure. Their ability to make snap decisions without needing to be expressly directed how to act and when was why they were chosen for this 'dangerous and immediate' service.

Halfway to their destination were 'Wet' canteens at Alice Springs and even an outdoor cinema. *What a luxurious business this War thing is*, dad wrote.

In one letter to his mum, he warned his sister Louise to stop asking about where he'd be going. *I don't want another word of it. Stay right off it, — please.* He seemed scared she might take something away.

It took over a week on the train to make it to the Top End. Katherine was arid, full of crocodiles and wild pigs and a blazing sun. But there was so much hope in dad's early letters home that there's no way he could have known he'd see nothing but the dust of that desolate landscape for the next six months.

Somewhere next to a swamp in the Northern Territory, dad spent six months of 1942.

No radio, no information, nothing but the Daly River rising and falling, and the leeches and the mosquitoes and the same ten faces of men soon suffering from dengue, malaria, and severe malnutrition. Armed with a tommy gun and enough ammunition to last a few minutes, if that, they had no food except a few cans of corned beef and dried rice, and no water to cook it in.

Worse, they had no barely any cover from the Australian sun except a tent and a small net for the ten of them.

They'd been taught how to fight in hand-to-hand combat, but no one, particularly the British, who came from a cold climate, knew what special-forces soldiers would need to survive the searing temperatures in the landscape of northern Australia.

There is a war, somewhere, and we'll be in it soon, dad kept telling himself.

Sleepless in the Territory heat while mosquitoes hammered them relentlessly with what dad deliriously described as 'bayonets', their wounds soon getting infected, his group took it in turns to pile three apiece underneath their one square of netting from March to September 1942.

He was twenty-one.

Perhaps the War had ended … ? How would we know? he wrote. The idea of Europe, and the German occupation, was an abstract and illusory thing with no radio and no British officers keeping them in the loop.

The mozzies were so bad one man shot himself on Hermit Hill. Similar things happened on the Roper … Others just wandered off into the featureless Northern Territory landscape …

He couldn't even fathom the meaning of the word 'fascism' at one point, hallucinating and delirious and unsure of who or where he was. It had meant so much in Melbourne: it was the reason he'd enlisted. Yet 'fascism' seemed unreal when he was surrounded only by the Australian outback and the faces of the same men caving in on themselves around him.

They were actually dumped there, I realised. Dumped by a swamp and left to 'disarm the Japanese if they come'.

His commanding officer went MIA, after two of the men in his group had also wandered off. Eventually, another officer turned up in their miserable camp, like something out of a hallucination. He oddly demanded dad's group pull their boots on for 'March Out' (parade in formation).

What was this 'March Out', and why on earth did it matter in the outback? One of the men, in pain beyond bearing, unable to get his boots over his swollen feet, and by then covered in infected sores, threw his boots with a yell into the scrub and was put on a charge sheet.

Good show, really, wrote dad, scornful, like the rest of the group, of the bizarre order.

The soldier with strikes on his record for throwing his boots into the bushes wandered off, too, eventually.

While another man shot himself ('accidental death', the official line), choosing to end the mosquito hell and the confusion and the anticlimax of staring at the same starving faces next to a swamp full of leeches, dad battled his torrid inner world with the determination that *there is a War, and I'll be in it, soon.*

In September, half a year after they'd been dumped near the swamp, a truck appeared, taking the remaining soldiers to the Adelaide River. There they saw fresh, flowing water for the first time, a shaded eating area, food brought in by truck, and, most importantly, a wireless radio.

But they still didn't know what they were supposed to be doing. After a few weeks, another truck appeared, taking dad's group to a camp in Katherine filled with thousands of other soldiers.

> But why had they trained us as commandoes to fester out here in the scrub? No answer. We were to move to a prepared camp with amenities, regular mail and so on, just like human soldiers.

These soldiers were well fed and had plenty of water. They even had ammunition.

Instructed to join the 'regular' soldiers to dig trenches for hundreds of toilets, dad was digging with his mate Matt, who was then accidentally shot in the back by one of the 'regular' soldiers carelessly taking target practice.

It seemed particularly insane that the regular soldiers were allowed unlimited ammunition. The Independent Company were given 200 rounds each and the instruction not to use a single bullet in practice. *Just disarm the Japanese ...* That's what the hand-to-hand combat training had been for.

While getting his ulcers lanced in what seemed a glamorous camp, because it was shaded and had a medical tent, dad heard the Sergeant Major call.

Finally. *My luck had turned — I'd get to be in the action.* He allowed himself to think, *Alamein, definitely.* He was sure they were needed in Egypt.

It was different news, but still exciting. The second part of the Independent Company — the men they'd trained with in Wilsons Promontory — had made it to Timor-Leste by boat. Behind enemy lines, they were 'disrupting' the Japanese, just as they'd been trained. But 20,000 Japanese were apparently looking for them. Overtaken by the enemy and cut off, they hadn't surrendered. Could Dad's company join them?

Dulled by a variety of ailments including malaria and malnutrition, dad allowed the information to sink in. Soon after, a telegram appeared, delivered to the Sergeant Major.

Private Deasey is to be returned south on compassionate grounds as his father is dead and his mother a cripple.

He took himself outside and sat under a tree to absorb the news. *Father ... dead ... mother a cripple.*

The harshness of the word 'cripple' in reference to his mum made him reel — he'd never considered her inability to stand or walk like that. She was just his *mum*. It's all he'd ever known her to be, bedridden by arthritis. Not a 'cripple'.

And now his father, Denis, was dead.

Denis had died of a heart attack on the train from Geelong to Fawkner, remaining upright still wearing his hat, so that no one knew he'd stopped breathing until the train got to the end of the line and he was still in his seat.

Denis's death was yet another casualty in a war in which dad hadn't even stood in battle or left the country.

After the telegram, dad was ordered onto a cattle truck packed with *sickos and psychos and ex-inmates of the boob*. He stood for days on end, making it back to Melbourne almost two weeks later. He wrote that the truck stopped in Adelaide on the way, and 'Ninette' met him at the station. Hers was the first friendly face he'd seen in so long. He told her, and himself, that he'd be back in the fight after a brief return to Melbourne. (Was this Ninette Dutton?)

Yet in Melbourne, he was confined to desk duties while still technically on 'active duty'. He never did make it back out. Put in the army communications department, he was given reporting duties on the army magazine, *Salt*. Health and science were his beats, and he soon moved across to the civilian broadsheet the *Herald*. (Its successor, the *Herald Sun*, was the first place I worked as a journalist.)

I wondered who wrote that telegram, talked about it to Ayala and Dec, and read everything I could to try to find out. Eventually it became clear: his eldest sister, Louise, had written to the government. She didn't want their mum to lose all her sons. She probably didn't want to lose all her brothers, either.

Des and Randal were both too heavily embedded in their postings to be let out — Des now in the Middle East, Randal preparing to go to Borneo. Their sister Kathleen was by then leading the women's army in Mildura. Irwin had died as a child. Louise likely hadn't wanted their mother to go through any more anguish. Telegrams had already arrived announcing that Des had been 'wounded in action', with no further details.

Besides, dad was the 'bubs' of the family — he shouldn't have enlisted to begin with, according to his role in the family opera. Let alone in the Commandoes, the least likely to survive.

The sickly one, the black sheep, he said they always called him.

He should have been at home with his mother.

He wrote of those years after returning from the Northern Territory to Melbourne with a deep sense of loss. The house was cold and grief-stricken; his mother's nightly shrieks of pain pierced his sleep and dreams.

I realised, when I cross-referenced the memoirs with the obituary I'd once read — that I'd had the wrong information about dad's service my whole life. He *hadn't* been invalided out, and it *hadn't* been in 1944, as was written in his obituary. What other stories had I taken as truth?

Melbourne in the war years became a place of austerity, pain, and other people's wishes, a place where dad was forced into a role he had no interest in playing. *Where he felt confined.*

He was angry his sister had taken his choice from him — he'd never know if he'd be up to battle, if he could have played a role in history.

His company did see action, the action he'd wondered about and prepared himself for by that revolting swamp for six months. The 2/4 Company made it to Timor the week dad's train arrived back in Melbourne. They carried out ambushes, blew up bridges and roads, secured observation posts in the mountains, and relayed information on the movements of Japanese ships and aircraft.

They deployed.

But dad went back to *that cold house which reeked of death.* Angry, confused, starting to go off kilter in the confinement of life back in Melbourne, he gained dozens of AWOL strikes on his military record whenever he was told to turn up for March Out. Perhaps it reminded him of the boot episode near the swamp.

His friend Bill, a calm and measured friend from school, died in his first deployment with the RAAF during that time, too.

The war memoirs conveyed a feeling of powerlessness and randomness — that who lost out to war, and who survived, could never be predicted. And that all dad wanted was the freedom to choose what to do and when.

Dad also hungered for honesty, to the point where he'd throw money (his 'inheritance') at people who he considered 'authentic' and 'stimulating', those who marched to the beat of their own drum and didn't care what others thought. The war years were when he started kicking around with artists and non-conformists who had nothing to do with his Geelong Grammar crowd. He met Alister Kershaw in 1940, introducing him to author Geoff Dutton.

I saw dad was looking for the truth. He didn't want the 'social' position the family conditions — and their connection to the school — imposed. It can't have been easy being the son of a vicar (who was also on the school board) in such small circles. Sometimes, he'd search for a homeless man, just to shout him a beer and have an 'authentic' conversation. In one diary after the war, he wrote of driving all the way to Gippsland to have a drink with some 'real' people in a country pub.

The artists that he started knocking about with in Melbourne — irreverent, a little wacky, completely unpretentious — refreshed him. They weren't bowing to some invisible hierarchy. They were a little cracked and crazy, like him.

What use is money, if you can't use it to further the things you value and love?

There seemed such disparity between what the world saw of dad, and what he confided into his diaries. He was so lonely in those post-war years in Melbourne, even during his brief and impulsive-sounding first marriage. I didn't understand why he married a woman who also came from quite a well-known Melbourne family, but he did love her, until the 'petty concerns' got too much and he realised she was happy to live in Melbourne for the rest of her life while all he wanted was to get out of it.

He was desperate to travel.

Alister Kershaw, by then his close partner in crime, cheered dad with his extreme nature and similar tendencies to rail against social expectations. He hated conformity as much as dad, and when they both met Irish artist Adrian Lawlor at a bar, they hatched a plan to publish his first book. Dad funded it all, as well as Kershaw's first book of poetry — but I understood, now, that the money was all tied into that feeling of constriction and *conditions*. Spending it on some form of creative expression, on things he valued, gave him a sense of freedom. Like he was building a bigger world in the conservative Melbourne of the 1940s.

There was a receipt in the boxes dated July 1947, signed by Albert Tucker, confirming that dad had given him one hundred pounds to get out of Australia, *away from this accursed country*. I knew dad had thrown another hundred pounds to Kershaw, too, paying his fare to catch the boat to England.

But this confounded me the most. Why did he support everyone else on their creative journeys — but not himself?

With his good mates gone, but still technically married, he did eventually buy himself a ticket to England, cementing his role as the 'black sheep'.

So he'd gone overseas on that awful boat where he caught TB — I guess five weeks on a boat to somewhere was better than six months waiting in the outback, only to have a letter from your family bring you back home.

He left behind land on the Yarra River, a car, and a wife he'd been married to for less than a year. He felt enormous guilt for the 'shame' he'd brought to his mum.

But he had to get away.

By Friday night of that first week in the library, I was battle weary. Ayala and Dec invited me over for dinner, and I was desperate to share and unload. I cycled straight from the library, wanting real live family, not pages in notebooks, ghosts and stories. And I knew this was just as important to them as it was to me.

My brother padded in with his walking stick, and joined us with eyes aflame in interest.

'What'd you find today, Lou?' he said as Ayala joined us. I spread the latest printouts on the dinner table in front of them like spoils from the battlefield. Dec examined all the photos I'd taken of the library photo collection, and explained which ones must have been taken in the Northern Territory during dad's Commando posting. My sister showed us a photo she'd downloaded from the Australian War Memorial after I'd sent her copies of the war memoir.

The man in the photo looked at first like a complete stranger.

The date, place, and company corresponded, but this man was shirtless, skeletal, and in a camp that could only be described as squalid. In another photo, Dec pointed out that a dead pig was strung up on a tree just behind the man. There was no cover to the man's bed, which appeared to be a bit of plastic lying on the ground. And this man had a moustache.

'That's his tommy gun,' said Dec, pointing at a blurry piece of black in another photo of a man we would have had trouble recognising without the memoir. *The tommy gun he wasn't allowed to use.*

Dec flicked through the rest of the army photos, zooming in on particular details of the camps and the train, explaining the details as only someone who's served in the same kind of unit would know.

No wonder dad loved Gisèle's father Gerard — they'd both had that shared war experience, although Gerard's was more horrifying. Each would have filled missing pieces of history for the other.

'I never knew why I had the name Gerard,' said Dec.

Food arrived, and we all kept talking and sharing. It was a campfire dinner, a room full of family, and even though everyone we were talking about was dead, I felt them join us, perhaps relieved that we knew their stories, and how they joined to ours.

Dec's first deployment, in the modern-day offshoot of the Commandoes, the Special Air Service — was to Timor.

The place dad never got to go.

Through no influence of his own, he even ended up in the exact same regimental letter and number configuration: 2/4 Bravo Company.

When Dec broke his back parachuting in the unit, we found he'd signed a form that said his family weren't to be informed if he were in danger — as if he'd inherited that fear of interference, that someone would block him from making his own choices.

In Paris, the French sisters met to try to sort out the chronology and send me more information.

> We have just returned from Michelle's funeral … her younger sister remembered well the story of your dad … even that his mother — your grandmother — died when they were seeing each other.
>
> Michelle was totally smitten, but their parents apparently asked her to stop seeing Denison.

Coralie sent me a photo of Clém sitting with one of Michelle's letters about dad. While Ayala and Dec and I had been talking about dad and the war over dinner in Melbourne, they'd been examining dozens of Michelle's letters about dad in Coralie's apartment in Paris.

> Tonight Clém brought over more letters from Michelle's apartment. She nearly had a heart attack when she read this letter from 1950.
>
> '… I regret losing Denison … he was so interesting, and played the piano well, he could speak about the war against Japan in the Pacific islands, and he took me to the theatre. In short, he was the perfect man.'

Chapter Nine

Crise d'identité

As I worked my way through dad's gargantuan collection of diaries and letters, life trundled on, oblivious to my seismic shifts.

Somehow in that first week of documents and library opening hours, I'd interviewed for and landed a six-month contract job. Employed in a high-security government department, I was to write half a dozen or so tweets and update their website with compliance certificates for speed cameras, as well as perform the odd editing or rewriting task. It was extremely boring, but the team I worked in was lovely, mostly because they left me alone to process everything that was shifting and sliding underneath my skin.

To think of how much hustling I would have had to do to earn the same wage from freelancing exhausted me. And while I was looking into dad's life, I just didn't have room in my head for any other stories. I needed to save for Paris — but I couldn't justify going to France until I'd made my way through all of dad's boxes.

My new job was on the top floor of a city building, located beyond various security checkpoints, on account of the number of death threats sent to the department's director. As the weeks passed, I was always having trouble selecting the right printer, and sometimes printed documents I'd found the night before — a story dad had written, or a library collection listing, or a reference — only to find, with horror, I'd sent them to a printer at the Magistrates' Court instead.

Finding dad's papers was a privilege and a gift, but it was also draining. It was a little like I'd signed up for a PhD, but I had no direct supervisor, no one telling me when the research might finish, just dad subtly guiding me from another plane.

Even though the times of his life were fascinating, I'd developed this constant hollow ache of loss in the background. I lost my sense of humour and became sensitive to anything anyone said when I tried to explain what I was doing with all my spare time.

At the same time, I learned that the library had actually *paid* for dad's material — mum hadn't donated the collection, as I'd always assumed. The money they'd paid, documented in a series of letters, had allowed her to buy our house when he died. It wasn't that it had been kept a secret, more that mum had always implied to me that dad's writing hadn't amounted to anything. Or maybe that's what I assumed?

Mum had often mentioned dad's connection with the Boyds, but his life in London and France, before she'd met him in Melbourne, was a mystery. Maybe no one knew about that time. Or the ones who did were already gone — like Gisèle. Coralie emailed from France, one of those days, with the sad news that Gisèle was nowhere to be found, even though she and her uncle had both searched French records. Gisèle's surname wasn't French, but rather Dutch-Indonesian, it seemed, and perhaps she hadn't been born in France, which might have been why they couldn't find a death certificate.

There were dead ends everywhere I looked. I left messages for Mirka Mora with her son's gallery, and eventually tracked down another son. But Mirka was old and frail, and, I later found out, had completely lost her memory.

Somewhere in that time, my sister mentioned some cassette tapes of dad's from the 1970s that she doubted would still work. I rode over to her place and collected the box: there were seven tapes in full. I stayed up late in the night working my way through the ones that didn't play, until I found one that was from a dinner party in Highgate, London.

It was dated 1974.

Dad's voice … he was here again.

Recorded at Arthur Boyd's Highgate house (where dad, mum, Ayala, and Dec were then living), it was dad hosting a dinner party with what I assumed were two Londoners, 'Bob' and 'Val' (I later discovered it was Robert Southey, who wrote the large *Corian* obituary, and his first wife, Valerie). Dad sounded in his element, talking about the education books he was writing, the Boyds, France … He was animated, excited, serving up some mussel dish for dinner and chattering to Ayala. Mum barely spoke. I worked my way through another three tapes — a radio interview dad gave when the education book was published, a speech at a cousin's twenty-first birthday …

By the final tape, I was a wreck.

It was from a summer Sunday afternoon — 1980. I must have been three; dad was sixty. He was trying to organise a trip to the swimming pool with me, Ayala, and Dec, playfully urging me to sing, intent on recording my voice.

Lou, Lou, skip to my Lou …

Sing a song of sixpence, Lou …

From what I knew of all his illnesses and ailments, I couldn't believe how energetic he sounded. Friendly, lively.

I was shattered from tears when I got up for work the next morning. The man on that tape was a *good* dad. Affectionate, fun, loving. Interested in history and books and songs, and sharing it all with me. But I'd left him to gather dust in boxes all these years.

It took months for me to put parts of the letters in any kind of timeline. I'd use my lunch break to return calls to historians, art dealers, galleries, librarians, journalists, cousins. I kept repeating the story to strangers who might offer clues, my throat tugging and pulling while the words formed themselves on repeat: *I never knew my dad.*

It was the constant reopening of a wound, to say it out loud.

Guilt and grief and loneliness and obsession all got mixed up with an exhausting sense of futility. My workdays became a strangely opposing contrast. During days in the office in the city, I'd stretch out my tasks, trying to work as slowly as possible just to fill in the hours. But before nine and after five and in any break in-between, I was juggling phone calls and emails and library collections and request forms for collections overseas, chasing leads for people who may or may not have still been alive, who may have been linked to dad.

After numerous lunch-hour trips to the State Library reading room, late-night Wednesdays in the same room, and most weekends spent in library archives, I stopped cycling to work, so that I'd have more time to read my emails on the tram.

My life became one-dimensional — work, home, library, research. So far I'd found sixteen library collections around the world with material about dad and numerous new books with references to him.

One place and one name kept appearing and reappearing. In dad's diaries, his letters, the books in which dad was mentioned: Richard Aldington, the English poet and author who lived in Saint Clair, in France.

Saint Clair, Le Lavandou. As Melbourne skies went dark with the coming winter, I tried to picture the South of France but came up blank.

Aldington's letters to dad were interstate — a seven-hour drive away, in Canberra — and I couldn't fathom when I'd have time to get up there and read the collection.

I'd never been so antisocial. But my sense of self was melting, and some of my friendships moved on ground that felt like water.

All the painful reasons I'd never looked into the boxes before fought with my obsession at the task. Resistance began to show up in careless remarks from friends, reflecting my own thoughts and doubts. When the conversation inevitably wound to this story I was still trying to articulate that was taking all my time, I'd be met with statements like 'It's not good to live in the past' or 'Why didn't anyone tell you this before?' and I found myself wondering, too.

I became reclusive and quiet, reluctant to share the story with anyone new.

Even to explain why the library had his diaries made me uncomfortable. The library had *paid* mum for those papers. Thousands of dollars. I had to keep repeating the knowledge to myself to believe it. It didn't just shift my view of dad, it shifted my view of myself.

Dad's writing is how she'd bought our house. The belief that he'd left us with nothing was wrong. And my understanding of mum and dad's relationship was also shifting. He'd known Gisèle for twenty years when he met mum, and he hadn't thought it was possible to have children. Gisèle had been back in Paris because her mum had been ill. Dad had travelled to Paris in 1968 to stay with her for Christmas, returning to Melbourne in late-February 1969. Mum and dad were in the middle of a 'casual' affair when mum unexpectedly fell pregnant. Neither mum nor dad had wanted anything more than a brief liaison. Mum had known dad less than a couple of months and, of course, he had still been married.

I wasn't just learning of dad, I was learning of mum — and why she'd never spoken about his life. She'd barely *known* him. The mum I'd heard in the background of those cassette tapes in London and Australia was the mum I'd grown up with: serious, anxious, tired. When she'd been alive, I'd just thought that was her personality. And it wasn't until now, years later, that I could reflect on the contrast with dad's enthusiasm and gregariousness, and why my parents had always seemed such a strange match. No wonder mum had never talked happily — or even openly — about living in London and Europe with dad. The depression in her voice on the cassette recording was audible.

All I ever remembered her saying about the years she spent in Europe with dad was that it was freezing cold.

It became harder and harder to talk with friends, even close ones, because unravelling the truth about my parental stories was excruciatingly deep and painful. Some friends understood with minimal explanation; others fell by the wayside.

When one said he'd rather watch a game of cricket than read his dad's diaries, I was so hurt I couldn't talk to him again.

You *know* your dad, I thought. What he did, where he went, the major dot points of his life.

Whether you liked him or not, at least you *know*.

I felt grief, as if dad had died all over again, but this time I had to process it as an adult.

I'd never really talked about dad's life in detail with my sister before. I was reluctant to prod her for memories of her childhood, aware that it brought up all her grief, too.

'Well of course who could forget the story of me losing dad's war medals,' she said one day when I sat at her table searching through her childhood photos for clues to something else.

'Ay, I didn't even know he *had* war medals. When and how did you lose them?'

We broke into laughter at the insanity of it all. Ayala, locked in tension and guilt at this family story she assumed we all knew. Me, surprised and delighted to hear about dad proudly taking her on the Anzac Day march when she was ten — and on her dress pinning his medals, which then fell off, somewhere on Nicholson Street near the Carlton Gardens.

After what I'd read about how much he suffered in 1942, I was glad to hear that he even celebrated Anzac Day with his fellow comrades, and, later, his daughter.

Bugger the medals!

I must have looked confident in my search, because I was at it every day, but every day I questioned what I was doing. I particularly hated making people uncomfortable — which I knew I did — asking questions about dad. Some of the surviving people who'd known him didn't give me answers when I asked, and that hurt the most.

Maybe what I was doing was destructive — pulling his life out of those boxes and forcing other people to look at it, trying to unravel the mess? Why couldn't I just accept the story that I'd always been told, that he was a failure, that his writing didn't matter?

Because I'd uncovered enough from his papers already to know that wasn't entirely true. And he was me, and I came *from* him. I didn't like the feeling of anger it all stirred up in me — anger that I hadn't been told the truth, or hadn't questioned it, or something. Anger that all I'd had was that obituary, which focused on his failures. Anger that no one had told me the rest.

On a Saturday afternoon at my sister's house, while I was sorting through another box, a friend dropped around to return a book. I had cards strewn out in front of me as I looked, fruitlessly, for records of Gisèle's mother's address in Brittany in a futile attempt to send another clue to the French sisters to continue the search.

The friend came to the back room and looked at dad's portrait by Arthur Boyd.

'That's a beautiful Boyd painting,' she said.

'Yes, it's dad!' I said, proudly. That treasure of a painting had become a talisman to ward off thoughts of giving up on dad's story.

But she shook her head and left.

Sitting in my apartment with a wad of the tissues I had to keep on hand since I'd opened the boxes, I emailed Clémentine.

> I just don't know if I'm doing the right thing. Maybe it's not right if it makes me — and others — feel so terrible … ?

Immediately, from Paris, she replied.

Louisa

Sometimes people can't hear about the past, they don't know how to deal with it … or it disturbs them. But don't let their behaviour damage your research. What you're going through is so important. It's your dad, your roots … It's a gift to have that opportunity, a gift for you *and* for your dad. Don't doubt it, ok?

Follow your intuition, Denison is guiding you Louisa … You're finding so many beautiful and meaningful things.

I know the importance of it. What you're discovering is huge.

One other thing: Michelle was very intelligent and she saw something special in your dad.

Lots of love …

I trudged along at work, tired and sensitive, clinging to my emails from Clém and what I'd already uncovered of dad's life to remind me that there was beauty in among the pain.

Our office was sent on an all-day training seminar, organised to help foster better verbal communication with members of the Indigenous community. The training involved learning to use the right types of language to connect with their history and be culturally sensitive to their historical situation.

The woman who took our day's training bravely told us her family story, which, like that of many Indigenous Australians, was a harrowing tale. A member of the Stolen Generations, she was a living, breathing reminder of our government's fairly recent decision to take Indigenous children from their families and force them to assimilate in a white family, far from their kin. This woman hadn't even known who her blood father was until after he'd died.

When we finished work that day, I walked straight to the State Library to make the most of their last two hours open. Her story had given me perspective on this huge privilege of sitting at the library — even if it could be painful.

I found a book I suspected might have something of dad in it in the larger reading room. It was written by Alister Kershaw. Since I'd learned they both 'escaped' Australia within months of each other, I suspected there might be more about dad in Kershaw's memoirs of living in France.

The book, *The Pleasure of Their Company*, held tales of Melbourne bohemia and Paris life at the Hotel Floridor. Dad was there, written of in most chapters, relevant to the entire book, transforming the Hotel Floridor into 'Little Australia' at one point when Kershaw and Geoff Dutton moved in. And there were fascinating stories about his life in Saint Clair, including a tale of a man who arrived, pretending to be a Count, and swindled the entire seaside village.

This was the *seventh* new book I'd found that referenced dad since first receiving Coralie's message about Michelle. It was clear there were more.

Something about the photo on the cover of the book was familiar, and when I double-checked at home, where I now held the massive pile of dad's unchronicled black-and-white photos, I realised it was from a strip of photos dad had taken in Paris outside a bistro in the 1950s. I'd always wondered who the people were. According to the book, they were the tribe from the Floridor, including the hotelier Louis Marandou, sitting outside over a drink.

One of dad's photos, one that had sat blankly at the bottom of a pile, until now an inexplicable mystery — was on the cover.

Maybe that was enough. Maybe it was enough to know how and where he'd served in World War II, about the Hotel Floridor, that dad had loved France. Maybe one day I'd get to visit the Hotel Floridor and meet the French sisters. Maybe ... I still couldn't bring myself to book a ticket to Paris.

The money was too much, I'd have to use my credit card, *he squandered three fortunes* … I feared I was too much like dad. It all felt too risky.

The supposed Nolan painting had proven to be another dead end. The experts I'd contacted had all said Nolan didn't go through a portrait phase.

Maybe it was time to stop searching, to focus on the here and now. Get back to my old self, whoever that was, pay attention to Melbourne in 2016. Get out of the boxes.

But I just couldn't let dad's story go.

On Sunday, I crept out of my apartment to try to cure my blues. I had to leave home despite the incessant rain, because my downstairs neighbour had been screaming and bashing the roof for over an hour. I'd called the police and didn't want to be there when they turned up. I should have looked for a new place to live, but I felt frozen. I'd worked so hard to save that money — it was supposed to be for France, not moving house.

My life felt like it was imploding from its very foundations. Everything I'd felt to be so secure until just a few months ago was suddenly not at all. That apartment, in one of the loveliest areas in inner-city Parkville, had been my home for the last three years. Thanks to one scary neighbor, it now felt like a squalid slum.

I drove to Northcote and wandered into a second-hand bookshop. A friendly and eccentric older man greeted me at the doorway to the shop, which held paperbacks stacked floor to ceiling in two rooms. I tiptoed around the bookshop, trying not to bump the towers of books. I peeled out a few nonfiction titles from one shelf, opening one on the science of memory, which filled me with story ideas I wanted to scrawl down. I suddenly missed freelance writing and felt relieved my contract in the city was coming to an end.

I put down the book and moved to the back of the shop, flicking through some poetry and a stack of Australian memoirs. *Ninette*

Dutton. Nin. I recognised the name from dad's diaries. Geoffrey Dutton had been dad's other close friend in Melbourne. Like Alister Kershaw, he'd pursued a literary life.

Ninette picked me up from the train, dad had written.

Geoff, Ninette's husband, had enlisted with the RAAF in 1942, had been dad's friend since Geelong Grammar.

I paid the sweet man at the counter for Ninette's memoir, then dodged pellets of rain to get to the car. Once home, I opened the book on my kitchen table.

There, in the collection of photos in the middle of the book, was dad.

Denison Deasey, Saint Clair, 1949.

The tuberculosis, the South of France … I calculated the date — it must have been taken the month before he met Michelle.

I'd never seen that photo before in my life.

I googled Ninette, who had died many years earlier, it seemed, but her diaries were also in the National Library, in Canberra. I stayed up until midnight reading the book from cover to cover, learning more and more about dad, and that time in Saint Clair. *A fisherman's boat to an island, an idyllic retreat with a poet in the South of France …* The affection with which she wrote of dad filled something in me, so that I felt just as I had with Michelle's letters, as though she was a long-lost aunt sitting me down and telling me about my dad.

The photos in the middle of the book explained more of what was in our family collection, particularly the photos of the Duttons in London. I was sure Geoff and Ninette had met Michelle, had been the friends they'd met at the club in 1949. And the photos taken in Saint Clair gave me names and dates.

An artist herself, Ninette had found inspiration in the South of France for one of her first series of lithographs, and in her memoir she described Richard Aldington, and dad, and life in Saint Clair. One chapter chronicled a boat trip with dad to the island of Port Cros. I looked at my collection of photos, of which about ten were taken on that exact day.

I could finally annotate their year and locations.

There were so many of Saint Clair.

Ninette had loved dad, as friends who've been through wars and known each other since their twenties and lived in foreign countries together do. She described him as *one of the most beguiling ne-er do wells I have ever known*, writing that he deeply loved music, and reading, and driving far and wide. The new books about dad were growing in a stack beside my bed.

I fell asleep feeling that perhaps not all my godmothers had died.

As eager as I was to tidy things up and move on, I also understood there were still more secrets to my dad, hiding in boxes and bookshops.

Chapter Ten

Chasser la joie

As I numbly returned to work in the winter dark, June became July. I found a pen the shape of the Eiffel Tower and placed it on my desk, wondering how I could write my way across the sea. My contract was ending and I didn't want to seek another one. I was battling stronger urges to get to Paris, go back to freelance writing, move house to get away from my awful neighbour, perhaps drive to Canberra and read the Aldington letters.

But money, money …

In my last week at the government job, I sent out five pitches for stories and freelance writing work, getting three commissions quickly. It felt like a sign, like maybe I could trust myself to take some creative risks again.

I'd been thinking more and more about when I had made writing work, and how. When all my inner voices had told me that I'd come from 'failure' and there was no future in it, and how I'd fought to reverse that belief.

Because I couldn't *not* write. It was the only thing that made me feel relevant to the world as the best version of myself — carving stories out of ideas, figuring things out on the page.

I remembered how I used to feel about dad as a writer, knowing he'd had one book published but thinking he'd left hundreds of other ideas unfinished and incomplete. Someone had written of dad that he was 'amateur', and so I'd always fought to be the complete opposite

— to change that family story.

Yet by now I'd read many of dad's short stories and essays — and they were really good. I found his writing lively and intelligent. He'd had so many essays and articles published. Once I started recording his list of published work — and knowing from experience just how difficult it can be to get published — I wondered how I could have ever believed the 'amateur' comment.

Perhaps *dad* was the one who had felt a failure? In one two-year block when he was working full-time as a teacher back in Melbourne, building a house in the country with Gisèle, and fruitlessly pitching stories about life in France to Australian publications, the word 'failure' recurred in his diaries again and again.

Coralie and Clém continued to keep up our correspondence, reporting career highs over in France from their creative pursuits. Coralie published her first book, *Créer, jouer, rêver: toute une année créative en famille* (*Create, Play, Dream: a whole creative year with your family*), which contained hundreds of DIY games to play with children under six, while Clém auditioned in New York and secured a lead role in Ron Howard's epic series *Mars*, a huge coup that soon saw her flying to Morocco to shoot the series. I scanned their Instagram accounts daily for visual news, cheered by their successes.

It made me question what I was waiting for, because once upon a time it had always been me with news of wild creative pursuits and crazy new dreams. I felt I'd lost something, or forgotten an old part of myself, caught up in fear and restriction and the sadness of missing dad and dealing with my neighbour. Perhaps it was time to do what I always told friends to do when they were confused. To chase joy, follow the feeling that brings the most peace, however illogical it might seem to the ego or the bank balance.

Screw misery and martyrdom. What was money for, if not for freedom and happiness?

❧

My neighbour's shouts reached a higher decibel, and I found myself shallow-breathing, tiptoeing to see if her reflection in the window would show me what was going to happen next. As she jumped up and down screaming and swearing, I pulled the blinds shut and searched online for new apartment listings.

I remembered my friend Deanne from the lovely apartment I'd once rented where we shared a cat named Catty. Then two years after my mum died, Deanne and her partner had asked me to mind their big house in the country. They furnished a spare room just for me and gave me a reason to flee what had become a traumatic city full of reminders of sad events. For six weeks I fed their chickens and cats in quiet and peace, and walked on crunchy country paths until the kinks in my psyche began to unravel. The quiet of the country — how their house shaped like a boat had healed me.

In that house, I'd written so much until finally I had formed some kind of clear narrative around the destruction. It was winter when I stayed, and the trees grew silently in the dark beside my window, the fog always lifting, no matter how cold the morning.

The thought of their friendship made me smile, and I impulsively messaged Deanne:

I have to get out of here, my neighbour is really scaring me. I think she might be on ice …

Deanne replied at once:

Lou — grab your cat and come stay with us in the country. But also — your old apartment is available … It went up on Domain this morning …

I typed out my application on the spot. It was after one in the morning. My neighbour was, by then, bashing the roof with what sounded like a large hammer. I pressed send and went to bed, shallow-breathing until the sun came up.

❧

Nine years, four interstate moves, numerous deaths, and a lot of life in between, and the only thing that gave me peace of mind was to think of returning to that sunny apartment with the communal garden. The place I'd made good, loyal friends, drafted my first book, and manifested freelance writing work with a lightness and ease I now found extraordinary.

In the morning, while Melbourne skies poured with rain, the real-estate agent called to say I could move back in straightaway.

I started packing.

When I ran out of boxes only three-quarters of the way into packing, I saw how much paperwork I'd accumulated in the last six months of research. Piles full of printouts of dad's letters from the library, books I'd found that mentioned him, my own notes, a printed draft of a memoir dad had written about his childhood, and then my own diaries — A4 spiral-bound notebooks I'd been keeping every day since I was sixteen.

Just moving them from house to house was annoying — how had dad managed to keep his records preserved so well when he moved overseas? *They would have come by ship.* More money, more expense. How expensive reading, writing, and living in a world of letters would have been in his time.

Once I had the internet connected in my new (old) place, I would be able to write, send photos, even Skype without a second thought. But dad would have had to lug his typewriter, manually copy and bind drafts, and physically mail his writing to publishers and magazines, waiting months for replies. He'd have to send telegrams and pay by the character if a message was urgent. It was a luxury. One of his letters referred to how 'squanderous' he was, because he didn't write over both sides of a sheet of paper.

But he *didn't* waste money. The joy and peace he found in the printed word was not a waste. Anyway, if he'd written on both sides, I'd never have been able to read it. His letters were now *my* luxury, too.

✦

I moved house in one day, letting my cat roam the empty apartment before the truck arrived with all our things. I looked outside to see the succulents mum had lovingly planted on one of her visits, nine long years earlier.

I started to unpack my things in the new space, feeling mum's presence as real and loving and thriving as the garden outside. I felt her like relief, like she might be coming up the garden path sometime soon. And even if she didn't, she was still there in the living garden she'd planted.

It was profound, returning to that apartment, like I'd returned to a family home. I thought of all the times, since mum's death, that I'd wished there was a house to return to, somewhere to gain a palpable sense of her presence.

Moving back to that place felt like she'd returned, not me. I could even see her tiny form, bent over and rustling about in the dirt like it was one of her canvases and only she could see the finer points of how to make it bloom. The relief and happiness I felt at choosing something just because the thought made me smile confirmed that I needed to go to France.

Chasing joy isn't extravagant, Lou. You only get one life.

Without a screaming neighbour, I could finally hear myself think.

A familiar shuffle hobbled up the garden path, and I recognised Mick, the elderly man who'd lived upstairs ten years earlier. My God — Mick was still alive? An eighty-something man with a giant hearing aid who'd been on dialysis for his liver, he'd seemed like every day might have been his last *back then*. But he'd even managed to outlive his ancient Siamese cat.

'Mick!' I waved from the kitchen, surprising myself with how happy I was to see him again. He waved back and stooped down to pat my cat with a smile before shuffling off to his waiting taxi.

I sat on the front step in the winter sunshine, staring at mum's plants, marvelling at their blooming health and the ability to keep growing. They seemed somehow connected to Mick: a reminder that life is just as strong as death. Sometimes — stronger.

On Monday, I saw him stubbornly walking up and down three flights of stairs to drag his bins in and out of the street, reeking of beer as he passed me with a pink, smiling face after his dialysis appointment.

'Whatever you do, don't bring his bins in,' whispered a visiting Ayala. 'The weekly exercise might be keeping him alive.'

How strange it was, those who had staying power on this earth.

Chapter Eleven

Saint Clair, Le Lavandou

When I'd first opened dad's boxes for 1949, certain wafer-thin pages had script so evocative I couldn't let them go. *Saint Clair is a dream of the South,* he wrote. *There is a simple inn nearby, unrationed food, books, records and wine.*

Saint Clair, Le Lavandou. Even the name sounded like a song.

Typed on monogrammed stationery from Les Sables D'Or, the local inn, the letters and memoirs chronicled life in a small village in the South of France after the war. The waters of the Mediterranean were within a stone's throw of Richard Aldington's rented villa.

There was endless laughter. An innkeeper named 'Berky', who knew how to make twenty types of hors d'oeuvre and charged dad a pittance for his lodgings. Sunshine and fresh fish. Talk of Poetry. Nights of music and romantic interludes with visiting Americans. Wine in bountiful supply. Visits from his literary idols — Roy Campbell, Henry Williamson, and others.

But mostly, a feeling of kinship and homecoming. Because *the French know how to live*, he kept writing.

Catha goes to bed. Dusk falling. Richard goes for a bottle of champagne. Returning with the long bottle in his gargantuan hand, Richard begins to talk about superstitions and poetry.

⚜

While dad had still been stuck in London, Alister Kershaw had managed to sell a radio talk to the BBC, thanks to Roy Campbell, which got him the fare across the Channel. From Paris, Al had written to Richard Aldington, praising his poetry from a chair at the famed Art Deco brasserie La Coupole in Montparnasse.

At La Coupole in the 1940s, anyone who appeared to be a poet, such as Al, would be given access to hot and cold water, soap to wash, even pencils and paper. Such was the French respect for anyone considered an *artiste* or living *la vie de Bohème*. Al found that in Paris there wasn't a constant sense that you didn't measure up as a human if you weren't materially well-to-do.

Aldington's response to Al's letter was to invite him to visit Saint Clair. He was renting the Villa Aucassin, apparently a huge mansion, the only one of its kind in Saint Clair, built for the regal Harmsworth family of newspaper founders by a famous French architect in the 1920s. Aldington had moved there earlier that year with Netta, his second wife, and Catha, their young daughter.

Twenty-eight years older than dad, Aldington had moved in London literary circles that included W.B. Yeats, T.S. Eliot, Ezra Pound, and D.H. Lawrence, and was once married to the American poet Hilda Doolittle. He'd served as a Captain on the Western Front in World War I, travelled Europe, and spent World War II in the USA, before relocating to France. Dad revered Aldington, regarding his bestselling *Death of a Hero* to be one of the greatest anti-war novels dad had ever read. Like dad, Aldington had been damaged by his experience of war, and probably suffered from a form of post-traumatic stress disorder.

Al soon invited dad to join them.

There's food here, Dease. Fresh fish, even a piano. You can eat well, and talk books. Come to Saint Clair.

The English told dad to stay put, whispering that the French had even less food, that they'd 'failed to prepare for the war' or something odd. But eventually, after finally securing the necessary medical certificates and a sum of his own money, dad set out on a plane to Marseille.

> Winter has ended for me, the long winter of Australia and England, all I have ever seen, where people sit in gardens hidden behind houses, avoiding the street, or drink in closed institutions with their backs to the street.
>
> Escape to the South is, at last, escape from that conformity feeling. There is an unpolluted sea crammed with succulent red mullet and shellfish, abundant sun, grapes and contempt for red tape.

He first stepped foot in France in April 1948, feeling, immediately, *a peculiar sense of homecoming, despite never seeing France before in my life*. He was twenty-seven years old.

I can pinpoint a monumental shift in dad's view of life at the moment he entered France.

Although that initial trip to Saint Clair in 1948 only lasted nine weeks, he returned later that year, and every year until 1951, when Aldington moved to Montpellier. But the importance of dad's relationship with Aldington, and how that all tied in with his feelings about France, was cemented from that initial trip. It was here he decided to become a writer.

Aldington was dad's dearest mentor, his inspiration and ally, but most of all his confidante and friend. Dad didn't give out trust or respect very easily, especially, it seemed, to the English. But with Aldington there was a mutual understanding of life and literature rooted in their experiences of war and social pretensions.

Aldington had sought out a place, in France, where he could make the writing life work. Like a protective father, he seemed determined that dad do the same — advising, admonishing, even commissioning dad's first research work, which would prove integral to the notoriety of Aldington's book *Lawrence of Arabia*. Aldington was no dilettante, which is also, perhaps, why dad respected him so much. He wrote from 6.00 a.m. to noon every day, military in his approach to the typewriter. Often, he'd return for another round of writing in the evening, but only after a long, long lunch.

> Lunch at the villa was a sort of quest, a gateway to finding out what was left undestroyed in our worlds … the talk was often about war, the wreckage of it, the waste …

In one of dad's diaries from 1950, I found him sitting in the British Museum in London, compiling research for the book on T.E. Lawrence. Scrawled in the corner: *Writing, here, I am truly happy. Here I am at peace.*

Aldington helped dad find what truly fulfilled him.

Back at the library after I moved house, a photocopy of part of an article fell out of one box from the 1950s, and I searched and searched to find the full story online.

Entitled 'Lunch at the Villa', it was a published version of dad's typed diary entries from Saint Clair. The 3000-word essay chronicled the meeting with Aldington, the time at the Villa, and what made Saint Clair and France so special to poets and artists after the war. Published in the highly influential Australian weekly magazine *The Bulletin* in 1981, the article, written over thirty years after that initial trip, made it seem as though he was still walking around the Villa.

Caught up in the South of France … Stephen Murray-Smith's line in the obituary started to make sense.

'Lunch at the Villa' was the most beautiful published work of dad's that I'd read. If that one piece was all he'd ever published, I would have been proud.

I wrote about France, I taught French, he wrote in the piece, detailing how hard it was to let France go after he returned to Australia with Gisèle, reflecting on how Al had made the right decision by never leaving France.

I searched and searched through the diary entries for the origins of what became that story. I even contacted Aldington's biographer and literary estate, to see if there were more letters that might shed some light on that time. In the *Corian* obituary, Geoff Dutton wrote that *Aldington once remarked that Denison wrote the best letters he'd ever received*.

Did these letters still exist, somewhere?

I searched online, finding numerous collections overseas and contacting librarians in America and England, yet they only revealed letters that *referenced* dad. But 150 or so letters from Richard Aldington to dad were held in the National Library of Australia. There was also a 'notebook' full of dad's written research for *Lawrence of Arabia*.

I knew I had to get to Canberra to see those letters, and I went through the requisite rigmarole to make the bookings. Inexplicably, I felt like I was about to travel to France. Canberra wasn't Paris, but to think of touching and reading so many letters written in Saint Clair and around France had me feeling I was already there. I drove to Canberra with the radio howling, feeling I was moving towards something again.

London, 1949
In my worst hours I think of any street in Paris, or of the Point at Saint Clair; and when I remember they are still there, I am content.

It wasn't just Aldington's letters and dad's notebook that were in the National Library. There were a number of other writer's collections I suspected might have relevant information. I'd become obsessed with reading Ninette and Geoff Dutton's extensive collections since finding Ninette's memoir and wondering if she had any record of his appearance at the train station in Adelaide during the war. I also suspected some of dad's letters to Geoff in those first London years would shed more light on his character, particularly the letters from 1949. Perhaps Michelle was in Canberra?

Altogether, there were seven collections in Canberra that contained letters to, from, or about dad, and hundreds of letters from Saint Clair. I set myself the ludicrous goal of tearing through them all in two days.

In all my library research, the letters from Saint Clair were always a treat — dad's happiness in France seemed like a key to a hidden part of myself.

I felt pulled by an invisible cord up the road to that library full of letters.

Finally, I had a vague chronology.

Dad left Australia for London in 1947, returning in December 1954 with Gisèle. Gisèle had returned to France sometime in early 1968, and dad had joined her for Christmas, returning to Australia in February to work at Monash University in the History Department. Mum was in her final year of studies. My sister was born in March 1970.

In September 1970, dad returned to France with a writing grant to research French education for his book *Education Under Six*, as well as another book on education he was researching for the International Bureau of Education in Geneva, called *Initiatives in Education*. He took mum and Ayala, who was only six months old. Gisèle cleared out her apartment and went to live with her mother to let the three of them stay in her tiny little flat! In September 1973, my brother Declan was born in Oxford, England, when they'd all been living downstairs in Arthur Boyd's Highgate house. In a congratulatory letter from Gisèle, she playfully implored dad to finalise their divorce because Gerard had joked that he was Dec's grandfather.

Dad had been working on *Education Under Six* in London in between trips back to France. In 1976, they all returned to Australia.

I was born the next year.

Why was his heart so trapped in France? Why was that country so bound up with his true identity?

Perhaps Aldington would help me understand.

One of the seven books I'd discovered since Coralie's first message from Paris that referenced dad was a book of Aldington's letters. Dedicated to the memory of former members of 'The New Canterbury Literary Society', dad's name was listed above Lawrence Durrell.

Inside the National Library of Australia, set up at one of the shiny formica benches on the top floor, I pulled out the folio of Aldington's letters to dad. Unlike the scrambled documents in Melbourne, these were arranged chronologically, held in plastic sheets, and arranged in a book. The first letter was dated January 1949, and the last, some 300 pages later, 1959.

What flowed through in those letters was too much to take in.

You wanted answers, here are your answers, dad whispered, or perhaps it was Aldington, as I sat entranced by this world of France, after the war.

First, and most disconcertingly, I saw a reference to my sister's name, *Ayala*.

Aldington was writing to dad about Alister Kershaw's new baby in 1956. Her name was Martine, but Aldington, inexplicably, insisted on calling her *Ayala*. I quickly texted a photo to my sister. Just as reading dad's name in a Facebook message had been such a shock and a surprise, seeing my sister's name in a letter dated 1956 was unsettling.

Later, chewing over the day's discoveries in my hotel room, my sister and I talked about how and why dad must have chosen the name. *As though he'd repeated the name in homage to his literary hero.*

Perhaps he'd forgotten where he even first heard it …

From Ayala's name, I moved across to an unpublished letter from D.H. Lawrence to his wife, Frieda, written in 1927. The contents were fairly banal: something about a bottle of beer and cordial greetings, but still — it was a letter from D.H. Lawrence. Dad had come to own the original, it seemed, in the course of his research work for Aldington.

Chapter Twelve

L'écrivain

The 300 or so letters from Aldington to dad chronicled the highs and lows of the writing life in 1940s and 1950s France and England.

Aldington was intimate, affectionate, detailed and forthcoming. He was endlessly cheering dad on, congratulating him on any moves forward, confiding literary facts and details that implied a relationship built on mutual trust and deep companionship. The years they spent in Saint Clair were so beautiful that when dad returned to Australia, almost every letter from Aldington contained a reference to something in Saint Clair.

Aldington hadn't just loved dad's company as a friend and companion. He'd seen dad's potential as a writer and a creative. And that's what transformed dad's perception of *himself*.

As I read the letters, I realised that just as dad had unintentionally found a mentor on that first trip to Saint Clair, I had found the same kind of guidance when I first lived in Sydney.

In my twenties and working at a women's magazine, I wrote an email to a writer whose website I loved. Though her website was technically about astrology, her wild tangents were grounded in a background as a journalist, and she had the ability to pull facts and figures from history and psychology to twist funny tales that somehow related to pop culture and the news. Reading her sometimes made me laugh out loud.

Mystic Medusa wasn't just an astrologer, she was a poet, an

educator, and an entertainer. Her irreverent writing style had the ability to polarise and dismay; it was incredibly unique. She even formed a few new words of her own language, which her fans soon took into their own lexicons. Her blog, I often thought, was one of the best parts of the internet. Openly encouraging the discussion of ideas women once would have been burned at the stake for considering, her online presence was a portal of learning.

Like Alister writing a fan letter to Aldington from La Coupole in Paris, I wrote Mystic an email praising her blog, and she responded with a surprisingly generous commission to contribute a piece, posted me a copy of her newly published book as thanks, and encouraged me in my writing.

But that wasn't what inspired me the most. Mystic Medusa was the first writer I'd ever known to make an actual living as a freelancer writing on things *she* wanted to write about — not bound to an office or a company or someone else's dictates. This was as distant and magical an idea to me, in those early days, as someone having the ability to travel to the moon. The fact that she made a living from her freelance writing, with a house and family, was even more impressive.

Years later, when I was in New York, sending her regular email updates on my antics, she forwarded one of my emails to her then-publisher, pitching my rambling emails as the 'possible beginnings of a book'. The publisher had written directly to me expressing interest in the idea.

Mystic's generosity, openness, and finger on the pulse of digital media were the impetus for so many developments in my career. She implored me to come back to Sydney, time and again, connecting me with key people who would go on to influence my life and loves. Without anyone in my family or Melbourne circle from whom I could seek help for my writing dreams, Mystic became my biggest mentor.

I don't think she realised how much she inspired me. When I first went full-time freelance — after giving it two half-hearted cracks before heading back to pound the floors of restaurants — she gave me an actual, real-life model for a life and lifestyle I wanted.

Editing pays better than waitressing, she wrote. *Get your mindset right … send out a pile of story pitches and go Louisa!*

Because she so easily invited me into her circle, I assumed I had a place there. Just as Aldington had tuned the piano and invited dad to stay in Saint Clair, then suggested some writing jobs and made introductions (where dad had always been the one in Melbourne making introductions for others).

Though both dad and Aldington had been damaged by war and the diseases of the time, it was Aldington's crack-hardy attitude of not letting it affect his creative work that dad imitated, instead using it as fuel and fodder for publication.

Mystic, likewise, refused to ever play the victim. When she suddenly lost one of her highest-paid weekly columns, when Australian newspapers haemorrhaged advertising dollars in the switch to digital media, she never whinged. She just looked for a new way, quickly, to continue to do her work — upgrading her website and trying new subscription methods to replace the archaic old newspaper model of payment, where money usually arrived months after submission of an invoice to some anonymous accountant.

Aldington described the hackwork he'd once done in London for a pittance to build up his repertoire, exactly how much he was paid for his first poem, what he was paid for writing and when, who in which country was looking for certain types of translation, and ideas for stories he thought dad could pitch. He advised dad on living costs, as though making the writing life work had to be the first priority — and that's how you made your choice about where to live.

Mystic had written to me in similarly detailed ways, encouraging me to set myself up in a cheap studio flat rather than share a house that might be too distracting, and even to rent a computer when my own had blown up. *It's a business cost and you can write it off at tax time*, she wrote. When I was hired for my first editing job, she told me exactly how to set up an email contract and invoice the publisher.

As I read the Aldington letters, I remembered how I once didn't know a single other person who even *wanted* to be a freelance writer. To be able to count someone like Mystic as a confidante and a friend was a privilege and a gift, so I understood how important Aldington was to dad. Yet at important as meaningful connections were, Mystic and Aldington also understood the necessity of 'critical distance' from distractions. Much as Aldington preferred the peaceful obscurity of French provincial life to the literary establishment of London, Mystic insisted on remaining anonymous despite the enormous number of subscribers to her blog. The writing had to came first.

Sometimes bossy, always informative, Mystic was the first person who really understood and encouraged the part of me that knew — from childhood, when I was obsessed with letters — that I wanted to be a writer. In that first year I went freelance, I had dozens of confounding experiences where I'd be met with radio silence or bizarre feedback from an editor, and her swift replies with her own stories 'from the field' made my frustrations pale in comparison.

She had at least a decade more experience than me. I'd shake my head after receiving one of her emails filled with data and details that helped me make sense of a somewhat bizarre industry. She helped me find new ways to make it work, the way *she* had, opening herself up to a global model and not constraining herself to an Australian market. (In Australia, where the shift to digital came almost a decade after the British and American newspapers had already switched to user-pays, subscriber-based models, her subscription-led blog was actually revolutionary.)

Aldington, too, was encouraging and kind, with a global viewpoint and knowledge founded in experience. He believed in dad, but he wasn't unrealistic, and he definitely cracked the whip. The details in these letters were incredibly romantic and intimate, and I loved the two men's open affection, wondering if it came from living in France, where masculinity didn't involve that Australian way of men jokingly putting each other down.

In one letter, Aldington echoed advice Mystic had given me, warning him to have a clear commission before he worked for too long on writing a particular story. He shifted, just as Mystic had shifted, from encouragement to detail to diary-like entries on word counts and book sales to ideas for what dad could try to work on next that might interest publishers in different markets. He wrote about life as an artist, how things had changed since he'd lived in a garret in Paris in the twenties and thirties, details of life in rural France in the 1950s, and what was happening in the publishing world in England and the USA and how that might be affecting dad's story pitches. From Mystic, such expansive information always blew my mind wide open and dusted out the cobwebs of clichéd thinking. I was immensely grateful for her generosity, just as in reading Aldington I saw a similar generosity of knowledge and connection.

In between Aldington's descriptions of the changing seasons in France, gossip about mutual friends, bizarre health complaints (with what sounded like medieval treatments), and, always, talk of which books to read and why, he would offer news of the latest poetry anthology he was compiling, a quick request for dad to do some paid research or translation work, and sentimental sign-offs begging dad to return or visit.

And Gisèle, Gisèle, so many references to Gisèle.

She had met Aldington, too.

I learned that dad was supposed to drive with Gisèle to Montpellier to spend the Christmas of 1953 with Aldington, but couldn't come because petrol was too expensive to leave Paris. Aldington implored him to look for a place to live in rural France — that way, he could live, and write, without having to take another soul-sucking job in an office, which he knew dad loathed. Dad had just completed a year's work as a Special Press Analyst in the Paris office of the US Special Representative while living with Gisèle in the 7th arrondissement; he quit to finish writing a book. He was thirty-two.

Did he ever finish that book? I was thirty-two when my first book came out.

I kept reading the letters.

In 1954, Aldington had started the search for a place for dad and Gisèle to live. He wrote that with a car, and with the cost of good food in rural France a fraction of what it cost in Paris, dad could live as a writer 'for fifty pounds a year'. How much Aldington had wanted dad to stay. How *close* they had been.

A community of expat writers in France. How idyllic it all sounded!

I remembered leaving Sydney that awful first time I'd tried to make it work as a writer. In the space of a week, I'd been sacked from my magazine job, my car had blown up on the Sydney Harbour Bridge, and I'd fallen off my bicycle (on the Bridge, again) and broken my tooth. I was back in Melbourne before the stitches were even out of my chin.

Mystic wrote to me, calling me back, telling me not to give up, calculating different costs, encouraging me to replace waitressing with sub-editing because it paid better — and because there was more work available in magazines in Sydney.

> Anyway, you're not a real writer until you've been sacked from a magazine. Ruth Park was sacked from her first magazine job. It's a rite of passage in this city. Truly Louisa.

Dad *almost* stayed in France. But a car accident took the last of his savings. The letters from Aldington, particularly those dated 1954 and 1955, when dad returned to Australia after eight years abroad, showed just how close a call it was. The car cost somewhere between 20,000 and 48,000 francs to fix.

In June 1953, dad had written:

Yesterday I received my final pay — 59 000 francs. After paying the doctor, the rent, the food and laundry, and the telephone, I have the enormous sum of 6000 francs to show for my year's work. We have survived, we have eaten, I have bought G some material for dressmaking and a book of Chinese paintings. I have a good reference coming to me and experience in guile. Nothing more.

After the car accident in January 1954, they also, it seemed, had to look for a new apartment. It was an awful winter in Paris, and the pipes in their kitchen in the Rue Las Cases froze over. They had to boil all their meals, and Paris had run out of coal to heat the place. Months of rejected job applications for work as a writer or translator soon followed — for a job at UNESCO, French correspondent for *The Sydney Morning Herald*, Paris correspondent for the BBC, translator for Australia House in London, translator for Air France ... Gisèle had even started to search for translation work, to keep them in Paris. She spoke fluent English, too.

But no dice.

In July 1954, they left Paris for London, marrying in a quiet registry ceremony before their slow journey back to Australia.

Of course: the eternal juggle of money, time, chance, love, and place ...

Aldington had done all he could to encourage them to stay in France. He had found a nice town where dad and Gisèle could live nearby — Alès, in his beloved South. With food prices 'a fraction' of the prices in Paris, which were already very little, and all dad needed was to get his car fixed to be comfortable. Dad had even asked Aldington to drive around and sign a year-long lease on his and Gisèle's behalf.

But then — the money ran out and they left. Dad and Gisèle returned to Australia, and Aldington's hopes of having his protégé close by were dashed. Dad and Gisèle made the long journey back to Melbourne via Ceylon in December 1954. When they arrived back in

LEFT: Louisa (aged four) and Denison (sixty-one) in a park in Melbourne, 1981.

BELOW: Arthur Boyd painting of Denison Deasey. (Arthur Boyd, *Man kneeling 1938*, oil on canvas mounted on plywood 69.6 x 59.2 cm. National Gallery of Australia, Canberra. The Arthur Boyd gift 1975.)

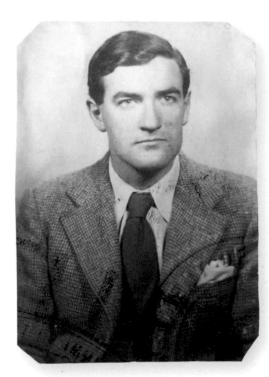

LEFT: Passport photo of Denison taken in Melbourne, 1947.

BELOW: Clémentine Poidatz reading her grandmother Michelle Chomé's letters about Denison Deasey in Paris, February 2016.

ABOVE: Siblings Kathleen, Randal, Desmond, Alice, Denison, and Louise; and their father, Reverend Denis Deasey. Melbourne, circa 1939.

RIGHT: Michelle Chomé, circa 1950.

LEFT: Denison (right) with tommy gun during Commando service in the Northern Territory, Australia.

BELOW: Denison reading beside the Commando camp somewhere in the Northern Territory, 1942.

ABOVE: Alister Kershaw with Denison in London, 1947.

LEFT: Geoffrey Dutton, Alister Kershaw, and Denison, somewhere in Europe, 1948.

ABOVE: Denison relaxing in front of Les Sables D'Or, Saint Clair, 1948.

ABOVE: Alister Kershaw and Richard Aldington working at the Villa Aucassin, 1948.

ABOVE: Denison in Saint Clair, 1948/1949.

LEFT: Denison, Catha Aldington, and Ninette Dutton. Saint Clair, 1949.

BELOW: The Villa Aucassin, March 2017.

LEFT: Gisèle reading the news to Paris at Radio Australia in Melbourne, circa 1964.

BELOW: Louisa with Gisèle in Paris, March 2017.

late January, the liner had lost all their luggage.

Dad went back to finish his history degree at Melbourne University on Saturday mornings, and soon got full-time work as a French teacher in Toorak, planning his first lesson around the word *Chez*. But he was depressed.

No Aldington, no spirit, no aesthetic, he wrote in his diary back in Australia. *Money isn't a means of exchange, here. It's an infection.*

Aldington's letters became more and more intimate and affectionate after dad's return to Australia. He dreamt of dad; he heard locals calling to each other and mistook them for dad. In one letter, he wrote that dad had belonged in Europe and he couldn't imagine him anywhere else. He seemed to be calling dad back.

Aldington, by then in his late sixties, and battling a host of ailments, must have known he'd never live to see dad back in France again.

In January 1955, as dad and Gisèle waited on their lost luggage and started the slow rebuild of life back in Australia, Aldington's book *Lawrence of Arabia* was released.

The book that had given dad his first research assignment. The research that led dad to exclaim, in the margins of his notebook, *working here and writing is the only time I feel I shouldn't be anywhere else, doing anything else*. The writing that showed him what he was capable of, and what brought him the most joy. Aldington had appreciated his swift transcription and summaries of hundreds of letters over the Channel in London, for they'd helped him build the new 'story' of T.E. Lawrence and know it was based on fact.

Lawrence of Arabia sold 30,000 copies in its first week, an instant bestseller on account of the scandalous new view it represented of the Lawrence legend. Aldington revealed Lawrence's illegitimacy and his homosexuality, but, more importantly, argued that Lawrence had fabricated or exaggerated many of his wartime exploits. The methodical research dad had completed in 1951 at the British Library, examining and copying the correspondence between Lawrence and Charlotte Shaw, wife of George Bernard Shaw, letters that the public had never seen, had enabled Aldington to prove many of the assertions he made in the book.

Aldington became notorious almost overnight, and was called up at and out of the pensione where he now lived in Montpellier to give radio and press interviews across the United Kingdom and Europe. Newspapers and radio went wild for the story, with Aldington counting over 200 newspaper clippings in the first month in one of his letters to dad.

Aldington had lived as a writer for decades, and already published numerous books, including the bestselling novel *Death of a Hero*. But even as a well-known poet and author, he'd never had notoriety like this. It was one of those peculiar cluster bombs in publishing that can't be predicted: the political and social attitudes of the time and the attachment the public had to the mythical legend of Lawrence meant that the book was met with furore.

(Eventually, when the film *Lawrence of Arabia* was made in 1962, some of Aldington's research and the references to Lawrence's homosexuality in the book were used in the script. The film was nominated for ten Oscars, and the British Film Institute called it the third-greatest British film of all time.)

And dad's research in the British Library had been so important to the creation of the book. It burned me up to know dad and Gisèle were back in Australia by the time it came out.

Wanting to share the spoils of publicity and knowing it would have raised dad's profile in both French and London literary circles, Aldington's letters show how devastated he was that dad was so far from the action. Three thousand miles away in Australia, living in a time when radio interviews could only take place in a studio, dad was cut off. The few Australian radio stations dad had to choose from paid no attention to his pitches, and he was met with apathy and rejection. Aldington was appalled, exclaiming that dad was the only one in Australia who knew the truth, because he'd been the first member of the public to view the letters from George Bernard Shaw.

Dad wasn't just physically far from Aldington, but a complete world away in the land of gum trees and *wide vacant spaces in the mind*, as he described it in his diaries. Dad's copy of *Lawrence of Arabia* — which Aldington had generously fought for the publishers to send him, *gratis* — took three months to arrive, by boat. Bookshops in England and Europe were ordering the book by the hundreds; dad reported to Aldington that Collins Booksellers in Bourke Street, the biggest bookseller in Melbourne at the time, ordered a single copy, and only after he badgered them.

If dad had only stayed in France a bit longer …

Hundreds more reviews came out in England as the scandal was discussed and dissected. Sales continued to grow, and anyone affiliated with Aldington and the book was called up to write and speak on radio. Alister and Jacques Delarue (the 'well-read police inspector' who dad had befriended in his time at the Hotel Floridor) performed a number of radio talks. Radio France gave each man a forty-five-minute slot, and Alister was paid for a number of freelance newspaper features, launching his writing career in France.

Aldington continually begged dad to pitch the story to the press in Melbourne — he'd done the research, and could argue its truth in detail. Aldington knew of dad's financial struggles and search for journalism work, knew how much writing made him happy. But dad might as well have been on another planet. He pitched the story to ABC radio in Melbourne, who rejected it and sent him to write about a sewerage farm in Werribee instead.

Dad must have felt he'd left his career behind in France. Everything he'd learned about the world and himself, all the connections that had taken eight years to create, was now in the past.

Australia was so very far from France. He'd returned to a Melbourne that boasted rows of new 'suburbs' of identical houses, talked more of money than anything else, and showed little-to-no interest in what was going on in Europe, let alone France.

When Albert Tucker returned a few years later, dad wrote that they shared the same sense of *the spiritual poverty of Australia, which was an intellectually and culturally arid wasteland in the 1950s.*

The French-Australian Association ran a fete for Bastille Day in Melbourne, and dad and Gisèle went along, hoping for some sort of Gallic reunion with like-minded kin. *They served beer and sausages,* dad wrote in his diary. *We returned home, depressed.*

Barry Humphries was one of the first to make light of this sense of Australian complacency and insularity in his comedy sketches. Dad was thrilled when he discovered Humphries' work, feeling an affinity with Humphries' entertaining theatrics and digs at Australian inertia: both had played similar surrealist pranks on Melbourne trams.

In 1958, when Humphries brought his comic characters to a wider audience on the *Wild Life in Suburbia* EP (a collaboration with Arthur Boyd's cousin, Robin Boyd), dad played the record to all who would listen. Geoff Dutton, returned to Australia by then and editing the literary magazine *Australian Letters*, listened to the recording with dad and Gisèle over dinner, and commissioned dad to interview Humphries. Dad's interview with Humphries about Dame Edna was published in 1959, the first article to explore this unique act. Until then, most Australians had seen Humphries as someone who 'dressed in drag'.

When I took a break from the Dutton and Aldington letters to make my way across from the library to the National Portrait Gallery for lunch, I caught sight of a giant portrait of Humphries in the gallery's main area. That same portrait, by Clifton Pugh, had run alongside dad's article.

I already knew about dad's connection with Barry Humphries. I'd discovered it while travelling around Australia in 2006. I had just seen his show in Perth, and I'd been so awestruck I pitched an interview to *Sunday Life* magazine, not knowing how or if I could even get to talk to him. But within forty-eight hours I was on the phone to him, and the first thing he asked was if I was any relation to *Denison Deasey*.

Aware that we had limited phone time, I didn't want to press him, but the question gave me a surge of emotion. I told him that dad had died when I was very young, so I didn't know much about him.

'You *must* look into it,' he said, emphatic. 'It's your *history*.'

I was living in Fremantle at the time, far from dad's boxes in the library, and it was only a year or so after that awful first attempt to read his papers. Humphries talked about dad for another few minutes, about how he'd made some introductions in his life that had proved important, before giving me what I needed for the magazine story in our remaining ten minutes: his impressions of arriving back in Australia after three years in England.

'My assaults on suburbia were my only defence against the creeping boredom that Melbourne in the fifties seemed to exude,' he said, echoing reams of dad's diary entries.

I worked my way through the remainder of the Aldington letters, forming a clearer picture of dad and Gisèle's return to Australia.

Returning in early 1955, dad and Gisèle moved onto land in the scenic country town of Warburton that dad had bought back in the war years. His sister Kathleen invited them to live in her suburban Armadale house the following year. Kathleen travelled regularly during this time, living in the USA on a Ford Foundation grant and teaching as a fellow at New York University in 1958. After returning to Australia herself, she secured a position at the University of Adelaide, leaving her Armadale house for dad and Gisèle to make their own.

In 1955, dad took thirty-three 'sixth-forms' in his first teaching class. On Saturdays, he'd go to his history lectures and work his way through the remainder of his unfinished degree. Gisèle sat a librarian exam at the State Library and then worked as a French correspondent for Radio Australia's telecasts to Paris. Dad continued his role as black sheep of the family by allowing Gisèle to occasionally work on the sabbath. Neither were deeply religious.

In one letter to Geoff Dutton, dad described a visit from George Bailey, the American journalist he'd befriended through Aldington in Saint Clair, and spent many years visiting in Vienna and Berlin. Dad was devastated that he couldn't shout him to dinner — his teaching wage unable to stretch that far. The cost of living, particularly the cost of 'treats of culture' such as fine wine and theatre, was comparatively high in 1950s Australia. He returned to drinking beer over wine, purchasing Gisèle small bottles of champagne so she could have a glass by the fire when they met with friends.

Meanwhile, Adrian Lawlor, the artist whose book dad had published when he'd been flush with funds, unexpectedly turned on dad, demanding dad return all the unsold copies. Dad had lost thousands publishing the book due to printing costs, mostly because Lawlor had aggressively resisted any edits on the manuscript, which was way too long, over 500 pages. Of a limited print run of 300 hardbacks, dad had managed to sell less than a hundred, and most of those went to a small group of artist friends. Despite taking out a paid advertisement in the literary journal *Meanjin*, it seemed no one in Australia wanted to read about other Australians, artistic, bohemian, or not. Lawlor's demand that dad return the books wasn't just ungrateful, it bordered on the insane.

At the same time Lawlor was demanding his book be returned, dad was searching for a publisher for his *own* book, a travel book about France, apparently. Where was this travel book? Aldington kept referring to it while he consoled dad over the Lawlor situation.

Dilettante, failure ... The words were becoming less significant, for I saw they were factually untrue. Dad was a *battler*. He didn't just work hard, he was a generous friend, though not everyone reciprocated or appreciated it. And through it all — the full-time teaching work, the lectures on Saturdays, pitching and writing articles at night, clearing the land and building his Warburton house on weekends — he was also very often sick with sinusitis and painful arthritis. Aged thirty-four, he probably still had remnants of the tuberculosis.

The details in Aldington's letters helped me to form a picture of dad and Gisèle, their life together. How close to France dad would have still felt, with her by his side. Although Aldington clearly missed dad, he approved of how happy Gisèle made him, affectionately offering to post her the French magazines, while imploring dad to use his newfound sense of calm from their relationship to keep writing consistently.

After settling in back in Australia, things seemed to be looking up for dad. He'd sold a radio play to Melbourne station 3AR's *Armchair Chat* show, *The Koepenik Affair* (after the famous German imposter Hauptmann von Köpenick), and a biography — a translation and study of the nineteenth-century artist Vivant Denon — had some publisher interest.

Every few weeks, there would be another letter from Aldington, detailing how many words dad should write each day to finish the 'travel' book, after the Denon biography. But what was this book? I'd found the Australian memoir, which talked of his family background and those early years back in Melbourne, but it had read much like a first draft, and couldn't have been longer than 40,000 words. Certainly it wasn't something you'd send to a publisher, which was what Aldington was referring to. It wasn't a 'travel' book, and it wasn't 90,000 words, which Aldington had written might be too long and need to be cut.

In April 1955, Aldington wrote with pride at dad's literary career being about to launch: the situation was 'licked' because dad's 'travel' book was about to be launched to the world. The Denon book had been rejected, but Aldington said he might have better luck pitching it after his 'travel' book came out. (A piece of Aldington's advice was an exact parallel to something Mystic had written to me: *Send a new story out the day you get a rejection … Let them know that's not your only idea.*)

Alister Kershaw and Geoff Dutton were about to have *their* first books published, so it must have seemed like the Australian contingent of those summers at Saint Clair were all launching their literary careers. Aldington's tone was that of a proud father.

Another letter appeared dated 1955, giving dad some feedback on the 'travel' book, all complimentary. Three more letters were dated April 1955, commiserating over shared money troubles and bolstering him like a father: *Work, my boy, work.*

But by September 1955, something had happened. The publisher had either pulled out of the deal or rejected the 'travel' book; it was hard to understand.

Aldington's letter was full of consolation and commiseration. *Fear not, there will always be France*, he wrote, saying he missed dad more than ever. He wrote that if dad had still been in France they would laugh all night like they had years before in Saint Clair.

But where — and what — was this travel book?

The letters from Aldington produced a sort of revolution in how I saw dad.

He wasn't a failure.

He had completed not just one, but two books in his early thirties, just as he'd promised to do when he quit the job in Paris. The Denon biography and the travel book. Along with all the articles and plays. As well as the two books he had written in the 1970s — that made four complete books.

Dad wasn't a failure.

He'd also translated an entire book to French as a 'favour' to an Englishman, I later discovered. He'd pitched radio scripts and stories — and more. But the tyranny of distance and timing, and the casino wheel of fortune that is the publishing game, had seen him take a few knockbacks. How could he consider that he'd failed?

I thought of my own wheel of fortune. Of pursuing publication with the zeal of a bloodhound in my late twenties. Would I have done that if I'd known dad wasn't a failure? That he had, in fact, *finished* things? By thirty I *had* to have a book published. Like it was a test I needed to pass as single-mindedly as Dec had passed SAS selection. *Be ashamed for the rest of your life if you don't finish this*, some cruel part of me whispered, a ghost I thought publication would vanquish.

Not just any book, but a book on travel, on love, on the risks we take in life. How I poured myself into that book — setting myself insane deadlines, like a first draft in six weeks, because I felt I was surfing an uncommon wave of publisher interest after what Mystic had done for me and I needed to make the most of it, to thank her for her generosity by succeeding.

I was *obsessed* with making the most of it. Of extending all opportunities. I'd fly to Sydney at a moment's notice just to have a face-to-face coffee with Mystic's publisher friend. *Just as dad had apparently flown to Sydney to meet the publisher from the Richard's Press who was interested in his travel book.*

Then, after I had drafted and redrafted my manuscript and thought it was acceptable enough to submit, I found the publisher had contracted cancer and left the company. The publisher who'd encouraged a whole book out of me — who'd had me thinking I *had it made*. And now, just as quickly, was gone.

Mum made me dinner that night back in Melbourne. She looked sadly at the minted peas and muttered, *not for the faint-hearted*, like I was fighting a losing battle from the start. I didn't realise she was talking more about her own views of life than my pursuit of writing.

For some reason, her belief that getting published was impossible made me even more determined to prove her wrong.

So I rewrote the entire book after feedback from a different publisher — one I'd found on my own. I moved into a share house so that I wouldn't have to get a day job and could live on my few freelance articles a month, marking down the calendar with Xs for every day of redrafting, along with the page and word counts, like I was training for a marathon.

How I wanted to prove mum wrong. Prove that I wasn't a dilettante, and that maybe what I'd inherited from dad wasn't inherently failure. I knew, when she looked at me — especially with the way I lived freelance — she saw dad.

The determination seemed to come from outside of me — a family story I hated and needed to change. I *had* to finish it. I wanted mum to see my success and change her mind about writing, perhaps about dad. I visualised the publishing house announcing my book as an acquisition on their website, and I even saw the dress I would wear at the launch.

By winter, I'd flown to Sydney, subletting a different room in a Surry Hills flat from a friend I'd met on a travel story to Tahiti. Tahiti! Even that trip hadn't seemed to convince mum that a writing career could be something good.

I *had* to be in Sydney. I went to dinner at Mystic's house, and she gave me more advice and loaded me up with books before I left. These opportunities and connections — they don't come along twice in your life — like a lightning strike. I worked nights in a bar and spent days walking the beaches or writing in libraries, waiting on a response to the redraft I'd sent to a woman at yet another publishing house, also in Sydney, who'd promised to look at it.

Finally, after I prompted her twice (on Mystic's advice), she sent me an email, and it was so strange, I realised she hadn't even bothered to read my redrafted manuscript. I cried in the beautiful Sydney light, staring at the golden cliffs of Bondi and wondering what to do. How I would have loved to talk to dad right then. Instead I called Mystic.

On Monday, I called Allen and Unwin, where the original publisher who'd requested my work had been, and explained to whoever answered the phone that the manuscript had once been requested. By Tuesday, they'd offered me a contract.

Mystic served me a goat-cheese salad in her Newtown garden. 'What book are you going to write next?' she asked brightly. The complete opposite to mum, Mystic had expected my success all along.

Yet mum's response was so odd, so completely unexpected, so completely not what I'd thought her response to my contract of publication would be.

'Thank God. Now you can move on with your life. It's been so hard for me to watch you live like this,' she said on the phone when I called. As though I'd been smoking crack or living on the street, not *writing a book*.

She didn't seem relieved at all, just tired. It finally twigged that nothing could change the story mum had in her mind. That life was hard and good things weren't coming. I know she would have been proud if she'd been able to escape the weight of her depression.

My sister consoled me over mum's response, cheering me on for my perseverance. Dec sent me a handwritten note of congratulations.

Mum chose to leave the world the week my contract arrived.

Dad wasn't a failure. Dad wasn't a failure.

To me, a failure was someone who didn't try, who didn't finish. Who cared what others thought? Dad had fearlessly pursued his dreams, despite health and money issues, despite lost luggage and missing letters and endless nonsensical rejections, despite living on a continent separated from the publishing powerhouses that ruled the world at the time. *He still did it*. He wrote. He finished. He sent. Despite teaching full-time and studying part-time and using a manual typewriter that must have made his wrists ache and his arthritic back hurt, he finished two books. Maybe four. Where was this travel book?

I tore through the rest of the material in Canberra quicker than I'd ever worked before. With only a few hours until closing, and seven boxes to finish, I scoured hundreds of Ninette's letters until I finally saw dad's name in her cursive script from a letter to Geoff in 1942.

He's had a pretty lousy time. She wrote of his appearance after six months in the Northern Territory. *The conditions and so on ... he talks only of the war ...*

A *pretty lousy time.* How they underplayed things during the war. Camping in squalid conditions in the middle of the outback for six months with no proper food, and ulcerated legs that would scar him for life, and dengue and malaria ... Watching men shoot themselves ... A *pretty lousy time.*

I felt affection for Ninette, just as I had for Aldington, because she had been there for dad at a time he needed a friend. He'd written in his diary that her bright face meeting him at the station was a relief after months with suffering men.

I worked my way through the rest of the boxes, including Geoff Dutton's enormous collection of letters from Saint Clair. He detailed secret codes they'd use at the inn, dad's unrequited love for one of Aldington's American visitors who was already married, and how the three Australian men — dad, Geoff, Al — were as close as the Three Musketeers.

When the library rang the bell for closing, I was the last to leave.

I ordered an expensive glass of French wine in front of the open fire downstairs at my hotel, and posted a photo of one of the beautiful Saint Clair envelopes on Instagram. Clém and Coralie 'liked' it from Paris at the exact same time as Ayala in Melbourne.

Chapter Thirteen

Paris

Louisa
I feel bad that we never found Gisèle ... Are you still coming to
Paris?
Coralie

That summer, when my cat was seeking shade under mum's planted succulents in the garden and the crickets started to sing, it finally felt as though things were breaking through.

My old neighbours Jason and Deanne came down to stay in the apartment upstairs, and I found myself more confident articulating dad's story. Curious about modern art and Australian history, they asked questions that had me proud of my new knowledge and dad's connections, yet aware there were still large gaps.

I started to compile a chronological book of dad's life, and ended up giving it to my brother and sister for Christmas. It was the PhD I'd been researching all year — putting his life together. It felt good to have something concrete for all the inner work.

I returned again and again to the cathedral-like room at the State Library as the days grew hotter. I juggled freelance assignments and short-term contracts to continue working my way through another six collections while planning and saving for Paris. The more I discovered, the clearer the story of his life became.

But the artistic connections still confounded me, and I wondered about the Nolan painting. I emailed a woman in Sydney, whose father's correspondence I'd found in dad's papers. He'd been a painter in Melbourne and possibly friends with Nolan, so I wondered if she might have further clues to that mysterious photo. I flew interstate to meet her, but came back none the wiser.

Despite everything I had learned and confirmed about dad, about what mattered in life, I still couldn't help feeling that if I could find this Nolan painting, prove that it was a portrait of dad, then I could prove dad was of value, too.

Coralie's name reappearing in my inbox was a perfectly timed reminder of true value. A reminder that I should forget the Nolan painting and all the other things I couldn't find. That I should get back to *the French Sisters* and the people who did matter. Remember to chase what gave me joy.

Paris.

How sweet that Coralie cared about not finding Gisèle.

I bought my ticket to France after she sent me that email, first just googling prices out of curiosity, then seeing the sum fly out of my bank account — and gulping at the horror of the exchange rate from Australian dollars to euros. After a moment of panic, my energy shifted to excitement. *This. This was what life was about!* Planning adventures when you had the means and the desire!

I breathed out with a feeling of looking *forward*, at last. France was a glorious dangling carrot, reward for all the library research, the endless months spent hunched in that cold room, and the contract I'd just accepted editing automated emails in an office in the ugliest part of Melbourne.

The excitement of an adventure to plan for gave me renewed vigour for dad's boxes. I didn't care anymore about the Nolan portrait and who had painted it. The only secrets I still wanted to uncover seemed to be waiting in France. Coralie and Clémentine were living and breathing, and though I hadn't met them, I felt connected through a shared journey. I downloaded my ticket receipt, and sent the sisters the dates.

I wanted to meet Michelle's family, but I had no idea how much time they would have to spend with me, or even how much they were interested, because I'd never actually found any meaningful references to Michelle in dad's archives. Did they really care? It had been almost a year since the initial email from Coralie — perhaps they'd all moved on?

Clémentine was possibly shooting a film somewhere else, Coralie had a new job that took her to London quite a bit, and the only other member of the family who'd messaged me was Edouard, their uncle. Yet as soon as he heard of my upcoming trip, he emailed me, as if to reassure me.

It will be so great to meet! I will take you on a tour of Paris on my Harley Davidson motorbike.

A motorbike ride around Paris!

A giant slip of light, just to think of that.

I bicycled down Brunswick Street to Fitzroy and bought myself a paper map of France to pin to my wall and look at as I counted down the weeks, stopping in a French bistro next door that I'd never noticed before. The owner talked in a sing-song French to someone on the phone as I spied a photo of his family outside the venue's sister cafe in France. *Family. France.* Why did those words seem inextricably linked?

Amid all dad's pain, suffering, disappointment, and supposed 'failures', his biggest joys had come from France.

Richard Aldington, the Villa Aucassin, his beloved Gisèle.

Paris, writing, life at the Hotel Floridor in 1951 when the hotelier had cooked for him because he was *en famille* and dad was friends with everyone in every room on every floor.

After I found the news clipping about dad's arrest at the Hotel Floridor, I'd investigated whether or not the hotel still existed, which it did. A few miserable reviews on TripAdvisor confirmed its one-star status, and I was a little too concerned to book a sentimental stay within its walls.

Clémentine wrote that she'd contact them before my trip to see if I could do a tour — but I also knew she was busy, and might be shooting a film in Istanbul during March, so I didn't hold much hope of gaining access.

Instead I found an Airbnb studio apartment in Le Marais in which to stay for the entire month of March. *My fortieth birthday in Paris.* The romance of that thought made me smile. I scanned the map of France, putting a post-it on Le Lavandou in the South, knowing Saint Clair was somewhere nearby, even though it wasn't listed on the map.

The Villa Aucassin was still a mystery, but I had to find it.

It seemed logical to me, that a place where dad had changed so much, become himself so fully, might still hold a trace of him. I felt convinced that if I found the Villa Aucassin, I would find something of dad that I'd never known before. Something secret, something hidden.

I had to find it.

But the letters hadn't listed a street address, just *Villa Aucassin* and *Chez Richard Aldington*. Hundreds of letters and diary entries, and none of them had a street address.

Every night I searched again, coming up with nothing but a sad fish-dish review on TripAdvisor for Les Sables D'Or inn, where dad had stayed and which appeared not to take travellers anymore. It was unclear whether or not the restaurant was still in operation. The sad-looking fish photo had been taken back in 2012.

While the sun blazed outside in the heat of summer with the crickets singing into sundown, I drank Provence rosé in a wine glass filled with melting ice cubes on the floor of my apartment. I spaced out dad's photos, attempting to collate the only ones I knew for sure were taken in France.

In some ways, the journey through the boxes in the library and all the new books I'd found had been about collating dad's photos. I just wanted a simple album, a neat and tidy chronology. To be able to say, *dad went here, then, and this was him here, when he was doing this.* I was envious of people with family albums someone else had arranged and annotated. The level of research just to uncover the location of one of dad's photos — and to find new ones — had taken me a year.

One photo of dad had always struck me — singed slightly at the edges, it had escaped fire in mum's painting studio, decades ago. Looking away from the camera, he was lounging on a chair in the sunshine somewhere, wearing a vest.

In another, dad was standing in front of grape vines in what looked like Provence.

Blessedly, he'd written on the back of both of them: *St Clair, 1948.*

He would have been twenty-eight.

I fingered my favourites, the ones where he smiled differently, displayed a sense of relief, a face full of light.

Saint Clair, Le Lavandou, they all had in common. 1947, 1948, 1949.

Villa Aucassin.

Saint Clair.

While family and friends drove to the coast and swam in the blazing heat, cooking up sausages and sharing barbecues in bare feet, I spent the first few weeks of the year on the floor of my living room, working through the night to the soundtrack of the Marion Cotillard film *La Vie en Rose* while I put together my picture puzzle of dad's France.

I stuck post-its on my map anytime I found a particular photo location, just to have a visual of how and when dad had travelled, so I could try to retrace his footsteps in March.

Melbourne. Paris. London. Vienna.

Saint Clair. Saint Clair. Saint Clair.

I searched the internet, holding the nearest corresponding town up to my giant map, locating Toulon a few centimetres to the left. Buried down the bottom of France, midway along the Côte d'Azur to Nice, there it was:

Saint Clair Le Lavandou.

My next task was to find the Villa Aucassin. Letters described life in the town, the Russian innkeeper named 'Berky', the fresh mullet Aldington's wife, Netta, cooked with herbs, the local fishermen who chilled rosé in the rocks of the sea.

> Last night we put a record on the gramophone upstairs and sipped a glass of pastis with Henry Williamson.

Compared to going through the same tattered pages recounting starvation and rations in London, reading dad in Saint Clair was like entering a halcyon world.

> Saint Clair is the first time I've felt the War was worth it. Everyone else seems obsessed with restraint. Here, in France, they know how to live.

I searched the photos for more signs and clues.

Dad's TB-riddled body healing with the luxury of sunshine, slow walks around the little town, Aldington's companionship, and the quiet life in the South of France. Crystal-clear Mediterranean waters, some jolly fishermen drinking their wine by the shore. Dad napping in a beret on a boat. A picnic under plane trees with Alister Kershaw and Geoff Dutton. Ninette lounging under the same plane tree. George Bailey, who'd gone on to write dozens of books, proposing to his wife because dad was so charismatic George worried he might steal her first.

I finally knew who these people were. Some of dad's closest friends.

The descriptions of the Villa were my reference point, but even with Google Maps it was impossible to find if it still existed.

Perhaps it was no longer called Aucassin? In one of Aldington's hundreds of letters to dad, he had mentioned the Harmsworth family, a link to a famous English newspaper baron. But searching all the Wikipedia entries on that family revealed no clues, either. I messaged Aldington's literary estate.

Do you know if the Villa Aucassin still exists?

They replied that they didn't know.

Saint Clair, Le Lavandou. Just the name sounded like a line from a song. I pulled a book of poetry off my shelf, seeking some relief. It was one of the small pile of books I'd chosen from dad's collection when mum had packed up our house in the country.

Inside, I saw a now-familiar name listed as editor: Richard Aldington.

Published in 1947.

Something felt so special, about knowing not only the name of the editor of this book, but also how and where it was assembled. This was the book of poetry Aldington had been working on, perhaps at the Villa Aucassin. I had to find this villa. I just wanted to look at it, to smell it, to walk inside. It was an obsession. Irrationally consuming.

At the end of January, my sister arrived back from summer holidays with a book for me: it was a guide to the Côte d'Azur that included a paragraph on Saint Clair, which was apparently a little way from the main town of Le Lavandou. I read the pages, horrified to find hotels in Saint Clair wouldn't be open until April, and my entire stay in France was booked for March. It was too late to change my ticket.

Even the ferry, which I'd hoped to take to the island of Port

Cros, where Aldington had lived with D.H. Lawrence, and dad had travelled by boat and been fed by those gorgeous jolly fishermen in one of my favourite photos, was closed for winter.

'If you're going to catch a train to the South of France, you need to book ahead. The price goes up the longer you leave it,' she said.

But how could I book a train when I had nowhere to stay?

'It seems like the town is only a tiny hamlet,' I said. 'If I even booked an Airbnb, I'd be miles from the water. And how would I get anywhere?'

I pictured myself staying in a weird bungalow miles from the town, having to beg an owner in my poor French to drive me into town.

The maps were confusing, the task of finding the Villa was overwhelming, and the time difference from Australia meant I couldn't call any hotels in the Lavandou region to find the right information. I finally figured out the phone codes and stayed up until midnight to call the weird fish-dish place, rehearsing my terrible French to state my weird quest, but they didn't answer and had no answering machine. The internet revealed no email address, either.

I emailed two hotels, in English, and received two replies in French saying they were closed until summer.

Would I have to just knock my way up and down the town to find the Villa Aucassin? I was prepared to do that, I felt so obsessed.

I emailed Aldington's biographer, Vivien Whelpton. She was generous and friendly, sending me references to dad she'd found in some of her research, but said she doubted if the Villa Aucassin still existed.

I was too scared to book the train from Paris to Toulon, still having no hotel or place to sleep in Saint Clair.

After two weeks of emails and searching, I decided to take a risk. I typed up an excerpt from one of dad's entries about Saint Clair, and carefully chose one of the old photos I'd scanned. I included details of the flora and fauna around the Villa Aucassin, hoping someone might recognise part of the description.

I added as many hashtags as I could think of and posted the picture to Instagram and Facebook, making the whole thing public, feeling vulnerable and scared.

On seeing my post, Clémentine texted me something she found on Google in French, cheering me on for my bravery.

I shared the post with the Lavandou tourism office, which also appeared to be closed for winter.

Flies buzzed and crickets sang, and I went to bed with my windows open, tossing and turning.

Had I made a huge mistake? Who books a trip to the South of France in the off-season, when nothing is open? But I'd already paid for my ticket. It was too late.

Chapter Fourteen
L'éloge

The trip to France gave me the strength to attack one final collection. It had been on my list since I'd found a copy of the *Corian* obituary. There was a small excerpt from Stephen Murray-Smith, and I had a feeling it had been cut from a larger piece.

Stephen Murray-Smith was an Australian literary figure who had known dad since Geelong Grammar. Enlisting in one of the first Commando groups like dad, he also travelled to Europe in the post-war period; and when Stephen returned to Australia, he became the founding editor of the literary journal *Overland*. He published half a dozen of dad's essays, reviews, and stories in various editions.

Unlike Geoff Dutton's contribution to the obituary, which included the painful list of dad's supposedly unfinished works, Stephen's part noted:

> When Denison settled down and wrote he wrote well. Perhaps his diaries will some day add more to this …

I suspected there might be some letters to or from dad in Stephen's collection because they seemed such close friends. But mainly, I wanted to find the rest of the obituary — if it did, in fact, exist.

> Denison Deasey was caught up somewhere between the Celtic twilight, the South of France, and Ayer's Rock …

Searching for your dead dad's obituary during summer holidays isn't the cheeriest activity, but a vision of March in France was now there to warm me when the grief came back.

Sure enough, there were dozens of references to correspondence to, from, and about dad when I examined the inventory of Stephen's enormous manuscript collection.

As I walked back to the reading room, I noticed Stephen's portrait hanging near that of Arthur Boyd. I'd been coming to the library for a year now and only just noticed him nodding at the entranceway.

I made my way slowly and methodically through the first of the boxes, moving straight to 1984.

In the first folder, I found a full two-page letter from Stephen to the chief librarian at the State Library, recommending they purchase dad's entire manuscript collection. Without Stephen's detailed recommendation, both of dad's writing style and the historical value of his manuscripts — and offered out of concern for our welfare, for mum was then a widow with three young children — I had no doubt the library would never have purchased his papers for such a large sum.

Stephen Murray-Smith was the reason I was able to read my dad's diaries.

A flicker of affection came at the obvious care he had for my dad, at making such a gesture.

Part of the recommendation gave me pause: he implored the library to make use of dad's collection before the people and players — and the reference points they carried inside them — were all gone.

As I brushed over a note from dad thanking Stephen for a warming fireside chat, I wished I could join them both. Stephen would have understood just how difficult this past year of making sense of all the connecting threads had been. He'd predicted it, in that letter to the library from 1984.

From there, I found the full obituary: three tightly typed pages about dad. I scanned urgently, pin prickles forming under my skin in the tomb-cold room. I fell back into the sense that I was six and dad had just died.

> Denison was crack-hardy, he didn't whinge ... He was a brilliant, coruscating companion and leader ... He had a hold over [his friends], as over a divorced wife who kept sending him sweaters until his death.
>
> He was hurt at school — one incident of a particularly traumatic nature was brushed aside when he sought for sympathy and protection ... He never forgot this, nor forgave. It went to that buried heart of his which really believed in decency, justice and love ... He would not be twisted, not by external forces, at any rate. And of course he paid for it ... he retained the capacity to be an honest man.
>
> I shall think of him always as the handsome, devil-may-care rake with the sports car and too much money — money which he liked, but which he disposed of, because it too got in the way of truth ...

I thought about that sense of shame I always had about dad. How I'd read that he was constantly running away from school, hitchhiking, forming 'gangs', rebelling in ways that had him pegged as the 'black sheep'. I wondered if it was connected to the 'incident of a particularly traumatic nature'.

I searched, and searched, and searched through their correspondence, trying to find out what the 'incident' was. Had dad written about it, like he'd written about the war?

And then — dad's familiar scrawl.

All my love, Denison.

In a box of articles for *Overland*, buried under a rejection slip for one of Tim Winton's first stories, was a draft of an essay about education, presumably meant for publication. Dated 1982, dad's handwriting was immediately recognisable on the covering note.

I cannot pass that school even now without a slight memory-jar of repulsion. There was this curtained room, in the deputy head's residence, the sound of flies buzzing against the window, the dark furniture, and the surprising instruction to take one's pants down.

Beating was good for one, in educational theory of the time ... but my insolence increased in proportion to the number of beatings ... I began to develop a sort of racism against the English upper class.

The English upper class. That, in one paragraph, explained years of diary entries where he scorned anyone who was dishonest, and where he displayed a particular suspicion of English snobbery related to class.

I felt a pang of anger on dad's behalf, and nausea and solidarity when I remembered something from dad's childhood memoir:

In the Junior School he'd say 'Kiss me ...' ... the little old man with the protruding eyes ... He had his own little sleep out dormitory and as a special favour a few slept there. In the mornings upon waking it was their privilege to stand behind his bed and scratch his bald head.

But I went against it. I organized a gang, dug my nails into his head when they tried to tame me by the flavoured flattery, put mice in his bed and began to build up a reputation as Bad.

My shame at his 'black sheep' status transformed into a swelling of pride at such an early sense of self-protection. But the pride was also a sense of understanding, finally, why he was so 'wasteful' with money. *He couldn't stand dishonesty.*

It wasn't something you reported to the family, he'd written.

Certainly not when it was the best school in Australia and your family was paying money for you to board there. *Power. Secrets. Money. Institutional lies.*

The job I'd left at the University a year earlier had ended because of a similar situation with an individual. No one wanted to talk about it. No one wanted to risk their jobs. Money. Secrets. Lies. *Money.*

In a second, my own attitude to freedom, the same attitude I'd always been ashamed of, because I couldn't just be 'normal' and put up with things — 'Lou, just stay there, think of the money' — was unlocked. I'd inherited it from dad.

My lifelong recurring nightmare — that someone is attacking me and I can't make a noise — came from a fear that materialised at that University job. I couldn't speak. I couldn't be honest. *Because of money. And hierarchy. And prestige.*

When I raised the issue with workmates who had noticed, and experienced, the same thing with the same individual, I was stunned at their lack of solidarity. Eventually, when it got to the point where I felt physical fear about coming into work, I initiated a report. Only one of my workmates had come with me.

Because the University had such a reputation. If they rocked the boat by speaking out, they might lose their jobs. Their security. Mortgages and money. *Money. Secrets ... Sometimes it's better just to keep quiet ...*

Three months after I'd made the initial complaint, three months during which the vile behaviour continued, the person was finally asked to leave. Remaining on a six-figure salary for a further six months to avoid any embarrassment to the University. Everyone kept going along like nothing had happened.

I was so disgusted I quit.

No one could understand why I walked away from such a job. *Best university in Australia.* I could tell my friends and family were disappointed in me — that I couldn't just grin and bear it.

Think of the money. Think of the prestige. Think of your future, Lou. Just stick it out for another year ...
Time is such a construct.

Dad's trauma was familiar; at the same time, it was both new and unknown. Part of me felt I had always known, because I had inherited the feeling that came from it, even though I didn't know where it came from. I felt disgust at the kinds of people who end up in power, as well as those who keep them there by insisting on maintaining the status quo.

Then another part of me became angry on dad's behalf, and then another part was adding it up with all else that I'd learned so far, about his attitudes to money and religion and formality and superficiality, and it all merged with his love of France, their Gallic pride in the individual and their questioning of authority and how they weren't *afraid* to talk about complicated things.

It also explained his intense interest in French education theories, which valued liberty, play, and self-expression over the hierarchical English imperialism and insistence on corporal punishment that he'd witnessed first-hand in Australia.

That vicar deserved more than mice.

His own father sat on the school council and had his name on wooden boards plastered around the halls.

It wasn't something you reported to the family …

He was just a kid. Nine years old, maybe ten.

In moments of fear like that, even as a child, you see through it all — the esteem, the religion, how unquestioned power means some can take advantage. See the rotten core. So much so that you couldn't feel safe simply because someone had more power in the hierarchy.

He was only a kid.

I remembered another incident from one of his diaries, about how the older boys at that prep school had half-filled bathtubs, put the younger boys in, then placed wooden planks above them as they turned on hot-water taps. Torturing them in some sort of initiation.

The best school in Australia. The Australian version of Eton.

Further in the childhood memoir — that sense of fiery self-protection he believed had come from his Irish ancestors, which is why he was so determined to go to Dublin and find them.

To tell some stories, to have some real, unpretentious conversations.

I looked up from my desk, understanding why dad had always been so irreverent to authority, so comrade-like in his own career as a teacher, treating his students more like allies than subjects. He encouraged them to read books off the school syllabus, to go to the theatre and explore and create and express themselves and try new things, which had got him in trouble with the other teachers and even the school boards. He endured constant attention from the school board for initiating cultural trips to the theatre. Because thinking for yourself and creative imagination wasn't something that was encouraged in his time.

I felt sadness, but also a strange sense of relief.

Months earlier, I'd contacted dad's school, to see if they had any public record of his school days. Like his army service records, his biographical cards from the school didn't make any sense until I'd read the corresponding memoirs. When they had arrived in the mail, attached was a handwritten note:

Denison had a general record of unconventionality.

There was also a handwritten apology from the school's historian for one of the notes on the card. Below the facts and dates of dad's army service and subsequent life in France were the words:

Married a non-European. Not improved.

The words referred to Gisèle.

I remembered her olive skin, a vague memory that her family had come from the Netherlands, originally. Or perhaps Indonesia.

L'éloge

⚜

I sat with Stephen's obituary, lingering on a new detail: *a divorced wife who kept sending him sweaters until his death*.

Was that Gisèle? Dad had written of her knitting by the open fire in Warburton.

Every year until he died. This warmed me so much. How she must have *loved* him.

De Satoor de Rootas was Gisèle's surname. Spelled in so many different ways depending where I looked. Some of dad's papers spelled it 'Ruytas'; another said 'Roitas'. Even the obituary spelled it differently: 'Reitas'. Coralie had told me her surname wasn't French. Maybe that's why we couldn't find her death record.

Regardless of where she'd come from, Gisèle had represented all that dad loved about France. Liberty. Art and culture (for even after she'd returned to Paris, Gisèle wrote always to dad about the latest exhibition she'd seen). Independence and freedom of self-expression. In France, he'd been unburdened by the conventions of his repressive Church of England upbringing.

I rode home through the Fitzroy Gardens, the summer song of cicadas and a gentle breeze blowing me home. As I arrived home, I heard a buzz from my phone.

A Facebook message from a stranger appeared:

Chère Mademoiselle …

The sender's name was Raphaël.

He appeared to live in Saint Clair.

Chapter Fifteen

Trouvé

*Chère Mademoiselle, La Villa Aucassin des les fonds de Saint-Clair
existe toujours.*

 Si vous venez au Lavandou, je pourrai vous la montrer.

Dear Mademoiselle, The Villa Aucassin still exists in the streets of
Saint Clair.

 If you come to Lavandou, I can show it to you.

The distinguished-looking gentleman whose face appeared by the
side of the message had no idea that, halfway across the world, he'd
made me cry tears of joy.

The Villa still exists, and he will take me there!

Somehow linked to the Lavandou tourism board, who I assumed
had forwarded him my Instagram message, he seemed very
cultured, and I was so touched by how quickly he grasped the Villa's
importance.

I corresponded with Raphaël a little more, trying to explain the
story in English; deciphering, from his messages in French, that the
owner of the Villa was an Englishman. There was also a mysterious
gardien de la Villa, and I couldn't figure out if that was Raphaël or
someone else, probably insulting him by asking, to which he replied
that he was the Cultural Minister for the Lavandou area in the South
of France.

He soon asked me for the dates I would be in Saint Clair, so he could 'make arrangements'. I quickly booked the train to Toulon, even though I still had no idea where I would stay. But *La Villa Aucassin existe toujours* … I *had* to take the risk.

By morning, another message had arrived. It was from an Englishman named Ivor Braka.

> Raphaël told me of your journey to search for the Villa Aucassin and I'm happy to tell you I'm the owner and I'd be pleased to let you see it. My phone number is below, let's discuss your trip when the times co-ordinate from London to Australia.

It all seemed so simple! Yet it had taken me so long to get up the courage to post that Instagram message! How could this be?

Late that Sunday night, as the temperature soared to the late thirties and I had the Australian Open tennis on TV while my ceiling fan whirred, I waited until it was late morning in London to call the number he'd listed.

'Hello, Ivor? Is this a good time?'

'Yes — I'm just watching the tennis.'

It was midway through the second set, and we were both going for Nadal. I could hear the echo of the same lopped balls from Ivor's television, halfway across the world.

At the tie-breaker, he insisted on calling me back.

When we spoke, the next night, he was remarkably casual, but his English accent reminded me of royalty. He asked me to bring originals of dad's Lavandou photos to his flat in London, the night I arrived.

'We'll go for a late dinner after.'

He was as interested in art as he was in history, which explained why he was so curious to see dad's photos and hear of the Aldington links to his villa. But he was a busy man, and had a lot of plans already booked, so the only night we could coordinate meeting in London was the night I arrived.

After twenty-four hours of travel, I'd be going to dinner in Sloane Square.

Ivor immediately emailed the 'gardien' — the Villa's caretaker. It wasn't Raphaël, but was in fact a woman named Josephine.

> Please show Louisa inside Aucassin, and take her up to the upper areas, and the back part which overlooks the town.

Josephine sent me a cheery email in English, and I immediately asked her if there was anywhere to stay. She suggested a hotel, one of the only ones that was open in the off-season, just a short walk from the Villa. I booked it immediately.

In the space of a few hours, I'd arranged meetings with strangers on the other side of the world to see a place I'd wondered about my entire life.

Aucassin.

Saint Clair.

All that was left to organise was Paris.

As January turned into February and my France trip was only weeks away, I became more determined than ever to finish working through dad's France material at the library. I wanted to be able to walk the streets of his *beloved Paris* as he always referred to it, to see the same buildings, to map out my own retrace of his favourite paths. I searched for addresses and clues in old letters.

Even with Gisèle gone, I could use his previous addresses as a sort of time-travelling map while I explored the city.

I circled everything on the forty-four page itinerary of dad's library collection that related to France — and one folder that didn't. I double-checked which files I'd opened and which ones I might have missed, booking to see one final box with a memoir named *Landscape with Australians*, apparently written in the 1970s.

I rode to my sisters to see her childhood photos. Perhaps there were more of Saint Clair, perhaps there were some clues about Paris … I still didn't have the collection in complete order.

My sister and I tried our best to figure out where they were taken, but she had been too young, and it made her sad not to know — or even have anyone to confirm. I noticed all our photos of Gisèle, who seemed to be with mum and dad and Ayala across France, England, and Germany in the 1970s. I wondered again at that curious relationship. In one beautiful photo, Gisèle was stooped in a white dress suit, talking to little Ayala. She treated us — dad's children — as though we were her own.

Back in the library, whipping through the last of the boxes, I stumbled across a series of poems written in the 1970s.

Four Seasons in the Berry was my first experience of mum and dad romantically entwined. Watching the Tour de France together with Ayala in Saint Satur, having a picnic in Sancerre. Touring the Berry region … Mum's handwriting mixed with dad's, as though they'd written these poems and stories together.

After seeing those photos at Ayala's, I could even picture them. Mum had been smiling as she patted a little goat.

Happy.

My sister caught the tram into the city as soon as I texted her. She trembled and smiled as she read the poetry collection, rebelliously photographing the entire document there and then with her phone without even bothering to turn the noise off.

I moved a box to protect her from view.

I realised, with a pang of solidarity, that just as I felt upset when people used to ask me about dad — *who was your father?* — Ayala felt upset when people asked her about her childhood in Europe, which started at six months and lasted until she returned to Australia at age six. It sounded so exotic, but she'd been so young she had only a few memories. With this newfound box, and its series of poems, she could now annotate her own childhood album.

With my sister beside me, I worked through the rest of the folders in the 1970s. A Hotel Floridor receipt from 1973 was jumbled in with a page from a folder marked 1981. I recognised a name: *Michelle Chomé*.

In cursive pencil, underneath a list of music-history books, was Michelle's address, in her handwriting. The page was from 1949, mixed up in the wrong box.

Ilchester Hotel, Holland Park, London.

The same diary he'd held when he caught the train back from France to London in 1949 now sat in a box of folders of writing from 1981. He'd kept her note for more than thirty years.

That's Mam's handwriting! Edouard immediately messaged, light years away, from Paris.

I had no idea why dad had held onto it for so long. It felt planted especially for me.

Newly encouraged that something from 1949 might be in one of the 1970s folders, I kept reading. And there, in a mislabelled box buried deep in the library, was the 'travel' memoir Aldington's letters had described.

The book chronicled dad's life in France with Australian expats and bohemians who'd also escaped Melbourne, from that first day arriving in Marseille to meeting Albert Tucker in a laneway in Saint Germain. It spoke of his travels with Gisèle, his love of the French, the conversations in all the places still tattered and scarred from the war, and that glorious casual simplicity and luxury with which even the poorest and humblest French treated life. It was a love story and a travel tale. Historical references mingled with lively anecdotes about people I'd only ever heard of in gallery catalogues.

There was a chapter on the Hotel Floridor, a chapter on Saint Clair, and so much more — descriptions of dad's life and friendships in Paris, the history of certain streets and how that played into his own experiences, anecdotes and insights about little towns in France in the 1940s and 1950s, and descriptions of dishes and specialties from the different regions of France. Encounters. Dialogue. Funny references.

The manuscript was typed and bound in a beautiful black spine, ready for a publisher: 300 pages, 90,000 words. *Must cut by a third*, dad had written in a margin near the start. Presumably after Aldington's advice.

France in the 1950s, it was originally titled. He'd *updated* it to *Landscape with Australians* in the 1970s when he'd gone back to read it, and that was somehow why it wound up in the 1970s box and not listed properly.

Finished in October 1955, the year of his return to Australia. Just as Aldington had advised him to get another book underway, after the Denon translation.

I felt triumphant, like I'd unearthed the most sacred manuscript of all.

Dad's writing carried me to France and through the cast of characters I'd spent a year deciphering and uncovering in his letters and diaries. But this was a polished book — the characters he described jumped off the page. Mostly, I felt dad's happiness in the book; he was touring me through France in the late 1940s to the 1950s. *What a gift*.

If the purpose of publishing is to make something that people can read long after you've gone, then dad had achieved that. The library had preserved what a publishing deal had not, just as the National Gallery in Canberra had saved his Boyd portrait from a family fire.

With Ayala reading alongside me, I tore through the first chapters of the book, reluctant to bury it back in the box.

When at last we had to go, I booked in to photograph it in its entirety the next day. I printed the whole thing at Officeworks the next night, grinning the whole way home to think of the treasure I now held in my possession.

A love note to France, a long letter to me, a guide I could take on my journey.

I stayed up late reading the chapter about a trip through a haunted village in the Pyrenees with Gisèle.

Impulsively, I emailed Coralie.

I know you already looked through the French phone book for Gisèle, but I was just wondering if your cousin found anything else — a death certificate, anything — just so we can know what happened.

Within minutes, she replied:

Attached is Gisèle's school record with her mother's maiden name and her birth date. I suggest you message anyone on Facebook with the surname Satoor de Rootas … I'll write to her school, to see if they know anything. Perhaps, like it did with us, Facebook will connect us to the right people?
Bonne chance, Louisa xx

I looked at Gisèle's name on the school record. I'd been spelling it wrong all this time. It was *Satoor de Rootas*. Not *de Satoor de Rootas*.

I found only four people with that surname on Facebook, and they were all located in the Netherlands. Less than an hour later, my phone started to ping with Facebook messages.

Gisèle is my great aunt … the last we heard from her was in 2014 …

2014?

There was an address, a nursing home outside Paris. I shook as I pasted the information in an email to Coralie, begging her to call the place.

Clém, who had by now become emotionally involved in the hunt as well, messaged me as I was sitting by the computer endlessly pressing refresh on my emails.

Coralie is on the phone to the residence right now … hold tight, Louisa!

Twenty minutes later, Coralie replied.

LOUISA — GISÈLE IS ALIVE

Part Three

Kin

Chapter Sixteen

Par avion

Gisèle is in an old people's home outside Paris. She's been there for the last nine years. She is very old and isolated (no family around) and is losing her memory. Apparently, she was always looking perfectly made up, going into Paris weekly, until just last year, when she had a stroke.

I explained the story to Sandrine the receptionist, and you are welcome to see her anytime … I suggest we call them the day before you arrive, so she's more likely to remember, because her short-term memory isn't very good.

When would you like to visit? I will call them to back to arrange when you let me know.

Coralie

I felt sick with emotion, so grateful to Coralie, so shocked, that I had to call her, despite it being late and hot in Melbourne and who knows what time in Paris.

'Is that you, Louisa?' she answered in perfect English, and I marvelled at the miracle of the phone.

'Oh, Coralie, I had to call you! This is amazing.'

I was sobbing in gratitude, but trying not to let the sniffles escape down the line. I asked her to explain how far away from Paris Gisèle's residence was. On Google Maps, it had confused me, and I had no idea which Métro train to catch. Perhaps Orsay was considered the country.

'Don't worry, Louisa, Clém is going to go there with you. See you next week in Paris!'

I wondered if I'd misheard her. I thought Clémentine was shooting a film?

Clémentine texted me, as if reading my thoughts. *Don't worry, Lou. I'm not going to let you catch the train out there alone. We'll go to Gisèle on Friday!*

To think that Gisèle had been sitting there, across the world, living, breathing, talking, *all this time*. I couldn't sleep.

My godmother had been *alive*, on the other side of the oceans it took me to find her. More, the French sisters were so caring that they took the search on as their own.

It was unreal. Finding dad's French memoir was a buried treasure, but Gisèle was a direct connection to dad. They'd met in 1949 or 1950, she'd knitted him jumpers until his death, she'd always sent us cards … She was *family*.

Gisèle is alive. Gisèle is alive. I kept repeating the information in my head, thinking of how strange the timing was, turning the events and information over and over. She'd been there *all this time*, as I searched in the library.

A stroke, just a year earlier …

But perhaps if I'd known earlier, I wouldn't have opened those boxes … ?

Ayala was speechless and Dec dropped his head to his chest when I told them the news. None of us knew what it all meant.

As the days drew towards my flight to London, excitement turned to anxiety. I scanned the list of names and addresses I'd typed into a document that my sister had turned into a printed itinerary. Strangers, really, but they meant so much in my journey:

Clémentine, Coralie, Edouard, Gisèle, Raphaël, Ivor, Sylvain.
Places on maps I'd only ever traced on paper:
London. Toulon. Paris. Orsay. Saint Clair.

It all seemed as unreal as my godmother revealing herself to be alive, years after I'd mourned her.

Stay alive, I whispered in the dark, imagining Gisèle could hear me. A year was a long time for someone aged ninety-one. What if she was gone before I got there? I'd lost so much already, I couldn't accept this possible new reality. *Alive.*

The temperature didn't drop below the high thirties the night before I left Melbourne, and at 4.00 a.m. when my taxi arrived to take me to the airport, it seemed almost insane to pack a scarf and jacket in my carry-on bag.

Once on the plane, knowing I was at least travelling towards Gisèle, but panic-stricken that she might go before I got there, I poured myself a drinkable bath of valium and plastic wine and stared at the stars on the roof of the plane until I fell into a kind of half-sleep. Somewhere above the Pacific Ocean, in between two continents, I woke up and reminded myself to drink lots of water, for the upcoming dinner with Ivor was approaching.

By the time we finally touched down, twenty-four hours and a humid stop in Dubai later, I'd made it to London.

I thought of dad's boat ride in 1947, how for five weeks in a tiny cabin with no windows he crossed the same oceans that took me a day. As sick as he'd been, and as little as I wanted to trade places, I did think, for a moment, that enforced duration of time between countries must have given him a better idea of the monumental expanse of space he'd crossed.

Walking through the many checkpoints to enter Britain from the plane, I turned on my phone to call Ivor, disorientated by the queues and calling codes. I found the line for those without a British passport.

'Wonderful that you made it, Louisa!' Ivor said, answering quickly, like we were old friends. He confirmed he'd be 'home' by the time I got through customs and made my way to his flat, giving me a rough idea of how long it would take from Heathrow in a car.

I collected my heavy luggage and walked through the airport, thinking there must be some sort of customs queue to check my bags, but, when I found myself outside, it seemed apparent there was none, and I'd missed my chance at using a luxurious indoor bathroom to get changed. As it poured down with rain in the dark outside a public bathroom, I got changed for dinner in London in a toilet cubicle next to the bus stop. I coated my face with make-up and sprayed all sorts of products in an attempt to disguise my jet-lagged stupor, then went outside and hailed a lovely old-fashioned London cab.

'First time in London, love? Let me guess — Australian?'

The black cab was so shiny and elegant, I must have said something about how old it looked, because my cabbie started telling me how many London city history tests he had to pass to drive a cab. He was very proud of his profession.

'Nah, nah, can't speak, mate, I've got an Australian in the back who's never been to London before,' I heard him say to his phone, before commencing our forty-five-minute history tour from Heathrow to the city of London.

Getting out of the airport, we passed what looked like housing-commission estates and hit a freeway full of traffic, which got thicker and thicker until we were in the sleek streets of Earl's Court and the City of Westminster.

'That's the Victoria and Albert Museum, love ... Alfred Hitchcock the film director, you know? That's his old house, oh and Lady Diana had her dresses made here ... some pretty posh fashion places, if you will ...'

It was dark, but I could still see the streets and the architecture, locations I'd only ever read of.

In Sloane Square, finally, we entered what seemed to be a court of red-bricked houses overlooking a tidy square.

'Very posh area, love, very posh. Staying with family, are we?' He turned to inspect me as he slowed down the car.

I mumbled something indecipherable in reply, not sure what to say.

'There's your man in the window,' he announced, as though Ivor was a waiting uncle. I looked out at a huge corner building, where Ivor waved from his desk.

The old building looked so elegant and inviting with its glowing lamps in the London dark, like a library or a gallery being opened up to me for a private tour.

'Louisa! Good to meet you!' We kissed on the cheek and Ivor waved me in, grabbing my enormous suitcase and hoicking it up the steps to the hallway. 'Come in, come in!' he said warmly, guiding me inside, a little distracted by something on his phone. I gathered he'd just come from an art auction and was tidying up some paperwork.

The ceilings were so tall, and the entranceway flanked by such an impressive gothic painting, I felt I could finally exhale after enduring the confinement of that pressurised air cabin for twenty-four hours.

Thin, wiry, intelligent, Ivor was friendly and open and busy and unformal. He obviously loved his work. I felt comfortable with him immediately, despite the fact we'd never met before.

His son wandered in and we were introduced, but then he quietly disappeared upstairs.

'Let's have a glass of wine in the kitchen. You can show me your photos.'

He turned to look at me as I followed him out of the study, apparently concerned by something in how I moved or sighed.

'Oh, you didn't fly coach did you … ?'

He looked nauseous just contemplating it.

'I've invited an old friend to join us for dinner. He's Australian, you'll like him. He'll be here soon.'

He led me to the kitchen, with a nervous whippet tagging along behind us both, and we sat at a large wooden table. Oh, it was so nice to be in a kitchen within an hour of landing in London, the ceilings as high as a church, soft light and natural air relaxing me after the fluorescent artificiality of that twenty-four-hour flight.

I pulled out my precious box of photos. I'd been so paranoid about losing the originals, I'd kept it in my carry-on luggage, every so often checking it was still there during the flight.

Each of the fifty or so photos was in a plastic archive sleeve with a slip of paper detailing the source, possible date, or at least possible year on the back. It had taken me all year to create that box — and still, many of the slips of paper had question marks.

Ivor poured us generous glasses of wine from a bottle of something French, eagerly scanning the photos. I learned he bought the Villa Aucassin because his own father had taken him to Saint Clair for holidays as a child in the 1950s and he had his own sentimental attachment to the town. He'd even bought some area around the Villa to protect it from overdevelopment, in an effort to help the town retain its original tranquillity. He was particularly keen to see if I had any photos of the garden or the town's flora and fauna from 1948, because he wanted to preserve the gardens as they had been originally intended.

As he looked, I pulled out a photocopy of one of dad's diary entries from Aucassin. I'd impulsively packed it, thinking Ivor might like to know Henry Williamson once drank pastis in his holiday house.

The speed at which Ivor flicked through the photos was breathtaking. I felt a pang, and wished we had more time to discuss them one by one. 'Oh, that's the fishing wharf in Saint Tropez,' he'd comment on one that had a question mark, before speeding on to the next one, suggesting it was taken in Nice or Cannes, before I had the chance to write on a post-it to stick on the back. In less than fifteen minutes, he worked through all fifty or so photos.

In the end, only one or two were actually of the Villa Aucassin.

Only two showed him the layout of Saint Clair as it was in the 1940s.

Some others, he said, were taken at the inn. Les Sables D'Or — Berky's. The restaurant with the tired fish-dish on TripAdvisor. The inn where dad had lodged when Aldington had no room at the Villa.

'Oh, God. I'm sorry, Ivor.' I felt terrible. Like he'd welcomed me to his home — and was letting me visit the Villa Aucassin — under false pretences. 'Would you like copies of those two photos of Aucassin?'

'Yes, please,' he said cheerily, before topping up my wine and his, and jumping up to get the doorbell.

Another man, Richard, joined us in the kitchen, casually shedding an extraordinarily elegant scarf and coat and dropping both on the chair beside me.

'Louisa's dad lived at Saint Clair in the 1940s! We're going to dinner soon, but let me just read this document …'

Ivor eagerly moved on to the Henry Williamson printout from dad's diary. As he held a glass of wine in one hand and read aloud from dad's memoir in his Sloane Square accent, while Richard listened and chuckled at certain moments, I felt as though dad was there, sitting with us at the table, giving a performance. Ivor seemed to understand how important dad's writing was to me, and he appreciated it, too.

A car arrived and we all bundled in and went to dinner.

'Leave your suitcase here, we'll come back after dinner and I'll order you another car,' said Ivor warmly. My London adventure had begun.

Dinner was in a nearby bistro in a place I learned to be Victoria, named after the queen, because we were just around the corner from Buckingham Palace and Westminster Abbey. I didn't have the energy to feel anxious anymore, and Ivor and Richard were so friendly, I didn't want to waste the occasion.

A waiter took our coats and shuffled us to a table at the back of the room. As we sat down, Ivor mentioned some 'appalling new developments' in the South of France, and I loved that he was interested in preserving history. It was everything I'd been working on for the past year. I had an unlikely comrade — a complete stranger who was interested in both France, and Art with a capital 'A'.

A bottle of red wine was delivered, followed by entrees, and I forgot to ask what I was eating because Richard and Ivor were busy discussing a Klimt painting that had apparently sold for 'too much' at an auction they'd just attended. 'Just because an artist is famous, doesn't mean what they've created is automatically worth millions,' one said, and I ate my mysterious entree, deliberately drinking more water than that beautiful wine in an attempt to stay awake for the duration of dinner.

Ivor, sitting across from me on the booth side, kept looking over at me every once in a while and saying kindly, 'You're doing really well,' or, 'This must just seem surreal.'

We talked about our dads — all born in the 1920s — and what they'd lived through. World War II, starvation, rationing, the mass migration to and from London after the war. I mentioned dad's tuberculosis and malaria, and Ivor suggested the enforced starvation from the war rationing may have been a factor in why they all survived such maladies back then. While dad had died aged sixty-three, Ivor's and Richard's fathers had lived to their eighties and nineties, despite similarly harrowing and ancient diseases. I agreed with Ivor's theory about enforced starvation. It would have really made them appreciate their butter and wine.

'They think a bit of induced fasting helps longevity …' We happily drank our wine and ate our bread, aware that all our fathers had struggled in nearby streets just to find these very things.

We talked of Art, and history, and value, and Australians in London in the 1940s and the present-day, and at some point an enormous plate of crab spaghetti was delivered to my place at the table. A little while later, when I hit some invisible wall and couldn't even raise my cutlery to eat, Ivor loaded up his fork and ate the rest from my plate, like he was finishing off his son's meal at the table.

Thinking of dad in his miserable wallpapered room in Edgeware Road, seventy years earlier, during those first weeks in his glorious first trip 'abroad', I felt like some kind of balance was being restored. That Ivor, a man connected to the art world, too, was buying me a delicious meal at a beautiful restaurant straight off the plane, gave me a peculiar sense of rightness.

The conversation went back to Klimt, and Art, and the names of artists whose work I'd only ever seen in the National Gallery of Australia were tossed over the table along with prices and monetary values that made my head spin.

'I mean, not everything Picasso did was amazing ...'

Ivor regaled us with some funny stories, playing different accents perfectly.

Perhaps stories are the only thing whose value doesn't change over time, I found myself pondering vaguely.

For the first time since I'd begun the whole mad journey back in Melbourne with the library and the letters, I felt like I was *experiencing* dad, how others might have experienced him in London in the 1940s.

This — what Ivor was giving me — was what dad gave to others.

I knew dad had loved to take people to dinner, when he had the money, and bugger the cost. He adored good wine, witty conversation, history, and stories, to teach through theatrics and imagination.

It's what he'd done for Michelle in London in 1949, gaining access to the Coronation chair at Westminster Abbey not because a friend played the accordion (which she'd assumed), but because he was bold enough to introduce himself to the man and ask (I'd since found in his diary).

Dad had dared to play a bigger game.

And that's why Michelle had been inspired to do the same. No wonder she hadn't forgotten him, I thought sleepily, London cabs honking outside the restaurant. Just as I would never forget the humour and ease Ivor showed with his warm and fun company to a stranger straight off the plane from Australia, swooping me into his world.

Money and access to privilege don't automatically make someone good or kind, but when you combine the two — like Ivor did, with me, being so warm and easy and welcoming and fun — it just makes the big wild ride of life make more sense.

Back at his house, Ivor ordered me a car to take me to my hotel. Bundled into this third new London car with warm farewells and wine-infused jokes, I pulled out the address of my hotel to give to the driver. I'd booked it because it seemed to be located directly across from Saint Pancras station; my sense of direction is terrible at the best of times, and I needed to find the Eurail to Paris first thing the next morning.

The driver seemed disbelieving. 'Never heard of that place, love. Sure it's a hotel?'

I showed him my printed receipt, an act that took a lot of energy as I'd been awake for two days, and was now also drunk. He put the address into his GPS, and seemed even more suspicious when we got there.

'Hang on, just let me have a look, love.' He slowed the car to a crawl, peering out the window. 'Don't want anything to happen to you, love.'

He drove around the block once more, eventually coming to a stop.

'You'll be all right, girl. Only one night,' he said, as if to reassure himself as much as me. He got my suitcase out of his trunk.

I made it up the stairs while he sat there, not moving the car. As I turned to wave, imploring him to go, he shouted again, 'Lock the door, love!'

My room was small, but it was fine enough. The carpets were a little sticky, but I couldn't see anything else wrong with the hotel. Was it because he'd collected me from Sloane Square … the contrast?

I fell asleep in another world to the one I'd left. A world of cold air and long-sleeved jumpers, a world of Art and Buckingham Palace and Sardinian wine that tasted like nectar and warm strangers who were letting me visit their villas in the South of France.

The next morning, when I walked down to reception to enquire about check-out procedure, they offered me free breakfast in the downstairs restaurant.

A TV blared from the entranceway: '*Last night, a Klimt painting sold for forty-eight million dollars at Christie's, making it the third-most expensive artwork ever sold ...*'

I poured myself a coffee from a freshly steaming jug in the restaurant, and looked for some butter for my toast.

'Sorry love, we're all out,' said a woman behind the fruit tray.

Chapter Seventeen
Passage de l'Horloge

So eager to get to Paris, I arrived at Saint Pancras station an hour early. People from all nationalities bustled about me, and without a second glance at my suitcases the customs officer stamped my passport, and I was on my way, like popping over to Paris on a two-hour train wasn't something I'd been dreaming of for years.

As I found my seat on the train, I spied my first Frenchwoman. Slim, elegant, and gliding gracefully on her pin-thin heels, she wheeled a small suitcase to her assigned seat and took out a magazine from her bag. While passengers scrambled and panted, some bellowing loudly into phones and at small children, she maintained a self-contained air of exclusion. I tried not to stare, enchanted.

The whistle blew and we were off, first trundling slowly through the outskirts of England, past shipping yards and brown squares (what I assumed to be council flats) blocking the grey skies, until we were underground, speeding through the English Channel. As though I'd taken on his ghost in the past year, I felt the peculiar sense that dad was enjoying this trip.

I tried to connect to the free wi-fi that had been advertised everywhere as I boarded the train, but there was no signal, even when we did make it out of the tunnel.

'It's actually a lie,' someone said dramatically. 'The wi-fi on the Eurail is a complete lie.'

The Frenchwoman looked up momentarily, as though a fly had

buzzed nearby, then returned to her magazine.

When we emerged from the Channel into Calais, it was like entering a sort of dream world. I had a feeling of homecoming, and I stood up to look out the windows between carriages, finding it hard to sit still. It was the most peculiar feeling. Excitement, despite my intense jetlag. Relief of return, and an unexpected sense of security. All the anxiety of being so far from Gisèle melted away as I sped towards her.

Like a sense memory that lingers, like the feeling of déjà vu, beyond thought or logic, from that moment we entered France I felt I was living in two times at once — reliving something from a previous existence, but also starting my own new story.

At Gare du Nord, my mind started calculating translations. I'd forgotten the mental energy required in translating a new language. *Bonjour*, *Je cherche*, and *Merci* were easy, but I had to start saying 'Parlez-vous anglais?' to figure out how to catch the Métro.

When I did finally make it to Le Marais (four wrong stops and six flights of stairs, with helpful people insisting on carrying my suitcases, later), my Airbnb host, Bernard, was waiting politely by the door. He couldn't speak much English, but just as Ivor had seemed to sense my dislocation the night before, he was particularly understanding about the lengthy flight from Australia, and looked at me kindly, if a little pityingly.

Bernard showed me the door codes and took me upstairs to the *deuxième étage*, and the apartment was perfect.

Near the old Jewish quarter of Paris, Le Marais held so much hidden history from World War II. The apartment I was staying in had been renovated, but it adjoined an ancient square. The cluster of six-storey buildings were called the Quartier de l'Horloge, and from my little shutter windows I could see the Passage de l'Horloge. *The passage of time.*

Bernard tried to explain there was a *supermarché* nearby, but as much as I tried to understand his directions, my brain was mush. Happy and relieved mush, but mush.

He left, and I put down my suitcase and sat at the window. *Mon appartement.* For an entire *mois.* It seemed a miracle.

I'm coming, Gisèle, I thought deliriously. *One more sleep and I'll see you.*

I'm here.

The Quartier de L'Horloge is centrally located, in the 3rd arrondissement; twenty minutes' walk north of the ancient Île de la Cité and Notre Dame, twenty-five minutes east of the Louvre, and close to so much more besides. Faced with the overwhelming question of what to do first in Paris, I decided to go to the supermarket, but as soon as I went downstairs I got lost again.

The first thing I saw when I stepped out of the Quartier was an elderly man with a hunchback quietly feeding pigeons in front of Centre Pompidou, the famous inside-out museum, seemingly draped in gantries, pipes, and wiring. Why did even that sight seem so familiar? Every step was like walking through pages of my own diary. The sounds and smells — '*Bienvenue!*' from a man selling Nutella crepes in a van nearby, a pigeon cooing, chestnuts roasting, the long queue to the archly modern Centre Pompidou in the late winter sun — it was all so perfect, so right.

I wandered around and around narrow streets amid Beaux-Arts apartment buildings, withdrew my first French banknotes from an ATM, and bought a little Eiffel Tower key ring for my apartment key from a nearby vendor. It all gave me the eerie feeling that this was *my* currency, this was *my* language, and I'd remember it in full, soon.

Like I had to scratch off the resistance to memory that I'd built up over the years. Even the words on shops, *magasin, banque, bureau,* were a language I'd always known. Remembering childhood

French lessons, I felt I was back at school with my favourite teacher: Madame Bozyk, who refused to speak English as soon as the bell went, nattering in French with a cheeky smile, her hair in a tousled bun.

The most unusual feeling of that first day walking Paris streets was that with every step, I felt I was shedding a mask I'd worn for decades — perhaps my entire life. I was finally coming back to being *me*.

At four in the afternoon, the bistros that lined the streets were full of diners, drinkers, smokers. Ten years as a waitress in similar European-style cafes in Melbourne came flooding back. Perhaps I'd been searching for Paris my entire life — in books, places, people, exchanges. Maybe even in the little French restaurant in Fitzroy where I scraped hundreds of empty plates full of oyster shells into the bin.

I wandered into shop after shop: first, a museum for poetry, then a pharmacy, distracted at every turn by more and more beauty. I was in a jetlagged delirium, but I didn't care, taking turns turning up and along cobbled side streets. Finally, I spied a pretty little restaurant that looked warm inside, worthy of my first meal in Paris.

'*Bonjour!* Is it *jeudi* today?' I asked the gentle waiter, an older, bearded man whose face, like that of most of the Frenchmen I'd noticed so far, had a lot going on under the surface.

'*Oui. C'est vrai,*' he answered, looking at me curiously while handing me a menu and pointing to the chalkboard of specials.

I translated *nos vins du moment* as *no wine at the moment*, and when he returned I asked why they'd run out.

'Where are you from?' he asked me slowly, in English, after delivering a glass of red wine because, thankfully, *nos* doesn't mean *no*, it means *our*.

'Australia,' I answered.

'Ah — but it is too far,' he said, shaking his head and making a move with his hands to signify the plane. He was decisive on this point.

Yes, yes it is.

I ordered the *plat du jour*, which was pot-au-feu, and the chef delivered it in his apron, pointing out particular ingredients in French with a flourish, like I was eating in his family kitchen and he wanted me to cherish every bite. A meal like that, after such a long journey, is almost a religious experience.

I was a millionaire, I was royalty. I had everything I wanted in that meal, in those strangers, in that little restaurant with an open fire blazing in the corner and cold Paris outside. No one hurried me, no one rushed me; two men sat talking nearby, sitting on a simple espresso and turning over what sounded like poetry but was probably something banal. The wind had started to kick up as the last of the afternoon light fell outside, but in that little bistro every bite of the slow-cooked lamb, every exquisite sip of the Beaujolais, warmed me spiritually as well as physically.

After paying the bill, I glided out of the restaurant to search for a bath plug, but with my poor French mixing with jet lag all I managed to say was *salle de bain* and shop assistants kept trying to give me soap. It took me an hour of *cherch*-ing and queuing to find they actually sold bath plugs at the supermarket, and I returned to the apartment just as the rain started, loaded up with bread, cheese, coffee, and fruit. And, thankfully, a bath plug.

'LOUISA!!!!!! WELCOME TO PARIS!!'

Lying on my bed looking out the window, I had been startled out of my reverie when the phone rang.

'Do you need anything? I have pillows, I have a hot water bottle, I have tea … Are you okay with the supermarket? I know it's hard to know what to buy when you don't speak the language … I bought lentils in Turkey last year instead of rice …'

Clémentine's kindness overtook me. Ready and waiting for my arrival, she'd called me as soon as she finished work for the day. I couldn't believe how familiar she was — taking ownership of my wellbeing while I stayed in her city.

'I'm okay! I found a bath plug, and there is even a heated towel rack ...'

We chatted for over two hours. I was propped up on the bed as the lights flickered on in the little apartments across from me in the square; Parisians appeared by the windows of their little spaces, some pulling books off a shelf to read underneath a lamp. One lady, in a beautiful dress, draped herself out the window to smoke her cigarette, while someone else played a saxophone in a room nearby. Each was alone, and none of them looked lonely.

'We're all very emotional that you're here,' Clémentine said, the narrator to this beautiful symphony. 'It's just huge, Louisa. You've flown across the world for this. We are all so excited! But, at the same time, we don't want to overwhelm you ...'

Sitting in the little Paris flat with Clém on the phone talking about the highs and lows of her acting life and all the creative risks we took that we had in common, and soon explaining how she was going to take me on the train to visit Gisèle in the morning, how she'd organised all of it and had the whole day for us to spend together, I felt something come over me, a sense memory.

It was 2009, a month after I'd signed the contract for my first book. That book, which had taken everything out of me, stretching me further than I'd dared to dream I could go. To complete it meant I sacrificed time, energy, humility.

To risk failing, to write and rewrite, to get it to a state where I could even think of showing a publisher. The book I'd written and rewritten in over forty different houses over the course of a year as I looked after cats, dogs, fish, and plants, intent on this huge gamble that mattered to no one but me.

When it was accepted, and I was given an editor all my own, she sent me the huge document back, marked-up, re-arranged, with two pages of her thoughts on what moved her and what she thought could be changed. The carefully written notes and marked-up symbols across my text implied all the care of someone taking ownership of a story I'd carried alone for such a long time.

This was Clém, with my story. Clém *understood* why I was in Paris, and I wasn't alone in the journey anymore. A relative stranger from a foreign country understood all that this meant, and I didn't even need to explain. I could hand over the manuscript now, and we would make it beautiful *together*.

And not only was she intensely interested and personally invested, but also she had the intellectual and creative skills to handle such a task as visiting Gisèle in a nursing home when we didn't even know if Gisèle would remember how to speak English.

We talked of writing and acting, travel and contrasts. My rags-to-riches tale of dinner in London after twenty-four hours in economy and a toilet cubicle outside a bus stop was met with a similar Cinderella tale involving a designer dress worn to a film premiere left in a toilet cubicle at Los Angeles International Airport. We talked about my first book, about the need for creative companionship and how Clém had once lived on a boat docked by the Bastille with no hot water and how I'd once lived in a car touring outback Australia and how both experiences made us really appreciate washing machines. She made me laugh, despite my delirious jetlag.

My head spun as I swung between the comfort of Clém and the resurgent anxiety of my impending trip to Gisèle. Would she remember me? Would she even remember how to speak English? What physical state would she be in? At ninety-one, did she still have her eyesight, her hearing?

Before we hung up, Clém checked again that I had food, that everything in the apartment was okay.

'Actually, Clém, my tea is confusing me. It doesn't smell like peppermint. It says *tilleul* on the box.'

'Oh, you bought lime tea. No worries, we'll get you some *menthe*. I'll come to your apartment at midday tomorrow. We can have lunch before we go to Gisèle, okay?'

Tomorrow. I couldn't even comprehend tomorrow. I couldn't comprehend anything except needing to sleep. Yet there was deep relief that someone with a heart like Clém's was there to help me on my journey.

'Thank you so much, Clém, I can't wait to meet you. I know you're busy ...'

'We don't really have very long,' she replied, sounding a bit worried. 'We have to make the most of every day you're in Paris.'

Like a *sister*.

Chapter Eighteen
La fille de Denison

I slept fitfully, waking at nine in the morning to French children singing nursery rhymes from a kindergarten downstairs. I fixed coffee and boiled *un oeuf* on my little stove to have with *une pomme* that I'd bought the night before, trying to concentrate long enough to write in my journal. With Paris around me, pulling my attention, I could barely stay still enough to write.

I set out to find my first park.

Walking was a balm, as I was so deeply anxious about seeing Gisèle. Would she know who I was? Would she be lucid? Would she even remember dad?

But then I somehow stumbled across a mathematically symmetrical park, and it all felt okay. There's something so visually soothing about the symmetry of Paris, the parks so self-contained and civilised. The organisation of the city and its green spaces is so opposite to the rambling, rowdy, parched-yellow or green fields of Australia, where you're just as likely to have a football kicked in your face or be bitten by one of sixteen possible bugs, spiders, or bees.

Noting a sign on the gate with the park's opening and closing hours, I remembered Ayala saying how she remembered returning to Australia because she could finally take her shoes off in a park. Boundaries seem strange to Australians, used to wide-open spaces unencumbered by paths, let alone gates and rules like having to wear shoes outside.

But it was calming, almost luxurious, to have all the order around me enforced, as though someone else would take care of maintenance; all I needed to do was turn up and look at it. To appreciate that something as wild as nature could be planted in rows, kept to a line, made to look ever-so-beautiful in a circle.

I sat on a little bench and stared at one of the stone sculptures, a naked woman facing a naked man laid out like balanced scales in their evenness. The beauty in all the details in Paris filled me — little shutter windows, sculptured fountains, carvings of stone.

I took a photo of the square and posted it to Instagram: *My first Paris park.*

Coralie immediately sent me a message. Of 400-and-something parks in Paris, the first one I'd stumbled into was Square Émile-Chautemps. Named after Michelle's great-uncle.

By quarter-to-twelve, I was back outside my apartment, pacing around the *Le Défenseur du Temps* mechanical artwork of a man wrestling with the elements of time. I took turns fighting the urge to scream in excitement or cry in terror, and I must have appeared confused, because two separate Frenchwomen walking tiny dogs through the square asked me I was lost.

Finally, a brunette rounded the corner to the Quartier, galloping towards me. Pin-thin, like my favourite woman from the train the day earlier, she was the epitome of a Parisienne. Clém grinned.

'LOUISA!' she shouted, fluttering apologies for being ten minutes late and something about the Métro. We kissed and hugged, and I noticed she was wearing exactly what I expected her to wear: black pants, boots, jacket, and a scarf tied just so. Her eyes danced as we repeated our ludicrous story, shaking our heads in wonder. We kept talking over each other.

'I mean, my God, it's just crazy … Gisèle … Gisèle is *alive* …'

Clém steered me back through the lane, and I hastened to keep up alongside her pace, relieved to be with a local so that I wouldn't have to remember what street went where. Returning from the park that morning, I'd walked the same block four times until I eventually spotted the outer pipes of Centre Pompidou and found my way back to the Passage de l'Horloge.

From midday that Friday, Clém's month-long role as my guide, translator, emotional cheer squad, and supportive and amusing friend had begun. I felt as protective of Clém as soldiers must feel about their non-combatant allies on the battlefield. She was my on-the-ground intelligence; without her, I would not have found Gisèle.

As we walked up Rue Rambuteau to the Haut Marais neighbourhood, I told Clém how beautiful it was to be in Paris, how much history seemed preserved on every corner. 'The oldest building in Australia would be maybe 200 years old, if that,' I explained, the shock of European architecture reminding me how far I'd come.

She tut-tutted, a little huffy. 'But Paris is like a museum! Everything is stuck, stuck, stuck. France is very much in the past.'

'But — all the buildings dad described in his diaries, from sixty years ago — they're still here! It's exactly why I'm so happy to be here! In Australia, we don't have history like this on the streets. Everything is so new.'

'Maybe I'm a bit Australian, then. Also, I really love Vegemite on toast with avocado,' she said and we laughed.

We lunched at Café Pinson, ordering twin bowls of salad and juice, surrounded by the singsong of a chattering crowd. Clém's phone kept buzzing with messages, and she held her phone up, to explain. She had a WhatsApp message group called *Famille*, and various members were urging her for photos of me and an update.

I had barely registered this when she handed me a gift, hidden from view until we'd settled into our table. 'This is from Coralie and I.' The bag was from a French boutique called Soeur — 'French for *sister*,' she explained.

With Clém smiling in front of me, I unwrapped the delicate

tissue paper, uncovering a beautiful scarf. I dabbed away a tear.

'Don't worry, Lou. I know jetlag makes you sad. Let's have a photo so we can send it to the family!'

'I have a huge DVD collection, Lou, do you want to borrow some to watch in your apartment tonight?' Clém said, as we passed a DVD shop on the way to catch the train.

'Ah, they have my favourite film ever, by Krzysztof Kieslowski,' I said as she flicked through the cases. She turned to look at me, and we both said at the same time, 'That film is a *masterpiece*.'

I had this surreal feeling of dropping down a portal with Clém by my side, just as I had in the library. *The Double Life of Veronique* is about two unrelated girls with the same name — one in France, the other from Poland. In the film, French Veronica mysteriously quits her singing career at the moment of Polish Veronica's death. The whole movie is a meditation on art, beauty, the nature of death and existence, parallel lives. The intimacy of strangers, the strangeness of friends, the poetry of the smallest movements in the everyday. Every time I'd watched the film, I'd yearned for Paris.

The feeling of meeting Clém that day, of walking through the streets of Paris and talking like sisters, spooked me in a beautiful kind of way as we walked towards the oldest train system in the world to make the long journey to my godmother Gisèle.

When we got to Les Halles station, Clém turned to me. It was as though she already knew everything that might upset me; she was deeply concerned for my emotional welfare while I stayed in her city.

'Just so you know, things are going to get quite intense in here,' she said, before a security guard asked us to open our handbags, while other armed guards moved around the packed station, reminding me that Paris was still in a state of emergency after a recent terrorist attack.

Down we went to the lower levels of the underground station, and with a determined '*Non!*' she fought off my attempt to pay for the train ticket, punching buttons on a screen with the speed of a local.

'We need to catch the RER,' said Clém, pronouncing it with a roll of the tongue that made it sound like an exotic song, not a train line I'd heard the French mention with a dismissive snicker. We waited at the platform and Clém got me to read the screens to show her I wouldn't get lost when I went back to Gisèle on my own.

'Coralie called the home yesterday to tell them we were coming,' she reminded me, and I put my hand back in my handbag, touching the small box of photos I'd brought on Coralie's advice. The ones I'd found in the library. I'd blown up the matchbox-sized passport picture of dad and printed it out. Perhaps, like Coralie suggested, Gisèle would find it easier to remember the 1950s than the present day. She said that's how it had been with Michelle.

We sat near the door on the train to Orsay. We passed the outskirts of Paris, the streets got wider, and eventually I saw some mountains. After the tenth or twelfth station, the train emptied out. We sat huddled together, and Clém kept protectively moving my bag, which I'd forget and let flop on the seat beside me, having to remind myself I was no longer in Australia.

We talked of everything, in detail. The story of researching dad, of my journey over the past year, found compassionate ears in Clém, who took it all very seriously — neither intrusively probing nor casually dismissive, Clém was genuinely curious and kind. There was a sense that my quest was not a hassle, that complicated stories were okay. Her generosity of spirit was extraordinary.

It was midafternoon when we arrived, after half an hour or more on the train, in Orsay. It looked like a semi-rural village, with only a small *tabac* and a scattering of shops that appeared to be closed, and I was more grateful than ever that Clém had insisted on taking me there.

It felt like a pilgrimage to a gravesite. On some level, I didn't really believe Gisèle was still alive.

Terror struck me as we rounded a corner and I saw the Residence, but Clém marched ahead, catching the door to the entranceway just as a woman walked out.

A letterbox in the foyer held Gisèle's full name. A letterbox. I could have been sending her letters all this time! I felt so guilty about all the lost years, so apprehensive.

Clém coaxed me into the lift.

'I'm going to talk to her in French, and then we can see if she understands English. I'll tell her you're Denison's daughter.'

I nodded, feeling sick with anxiety.

We knocked at the door and stared at each other nervously, listening for footsteps. Eventually, a creak, and the door opened a crack. A little woman appeared: *small, dark, and very French.*

It was Gisèle.

'*Bonjour, Madame.*' Clém spoke in a flurry of French. Her soft voice and unthreatening demeanour had Gisèle opening the door and waving us in.

Gisèle. It was Gisèle. Tiny, little, fragile Gisèle. *Those eyes.*

For a few moments, Clém kept speaking in French, with Gisèle saying what I gathered to be something like 'Why have you come?' It appeared we'd awoken her.

'*Je m'appelle Clémentine, et c'est Louisa ... La fille de Denison ...*'

Gisèle didn't know who I was.

'*... d'Australie ... La fille de Denison Deasey ...*'

Something shifted and Gisèle moved towards me.

'Deasey? ... LOUISA?'

Then that smile. Her beautiful smile.

'Little Louisa!' She shook her head in disbelief and embraced me.

I hugged her tiny body and we both cried in a physical moment that took away the tyranny of decades. The woman who had loved dad, who had known him thirty-five years, who held all the keys to my heritage in the stories in her heart — stories that were just as meaningful to her as they were to me. No need for explanation as soon as his name was mentioned. We couldn't let each other go. To touch her living, breathing body, so warm, so fragile, so strong … *Actually alive*.

Gisèle was alive. *She was really alive.*

To have that chance to hug her in human form, not just read words from a different time … it was like I had a parent back, one of my ancestors, woken from the dead. Gisèle was the connecting cord between France and dad, between dad and me, all the pieces of my history I'd thought were long gone. When Clém said the name *Denison*, it was as though a lock turned, and the way she looked at me was so healing, that immediate recognition that I was a direct connection to the man who mattered so much to her life, we both felt simpatico.

Here she was, *actually alive*. Young and old and soft and strong and pleasure and pain and grief and relief were all inside her, and me, in that moment. Tucked away in a tiny room overlooking a mountain.

It was very hard to let her go. When I eventually pulled back from our embrace, I saw that she was crying, too, searching my eyes with tears and recognition.

'Den-i-son,' she said the name slowly, repeating it with a cheeky smile and looking me up and down, pinching my cheek. '*Mon mari … mon mari …*' She smiled her beautiful smile, pointing to the sky. '*Mon mari est dans le ciel …*' She held both my hands and shook her head in tears of joy. 'Little Louisa …'

We sat down in chairs by the window. She held my hand and started to talk about dad.

Gisèle's room in the Residence was really a little apartment, much the same size as her apartment in Paris must have been.

I was relieved to see she had tokens of her life and treasured objects around her. A Buddha statue, a photo from a trip to Cambodia, different dictionaries for all the languages she spoke, evidence of her incredible and well-travelled life.

Her living space, just a small square in the front half of the room that also held her bed, was a little like a library. Just as dad's house had always smelled like a library.

She had her own little kitchen and bathroom, much like a self-contained flat. The only difference was that staff could help with shopping, cooking, and cleaning. Someone even came to read to her, because of her failing eyesight, and her obvious love of books.

The windows opened to a balcony, but there were no flowers there anymore, they had been knocked off in a storm in winter, she explained.

'I thought you were coming tomorrow,' she said, suddenly aware of her dressing gown and remembering the direct past.

I noticed a stunning lemon-coloured suit laid out on one of the chairs, as though in preparation for our visit.

'Little Louisa.' She wiggled her index finger towards my face, as Clém pulled up a third chair from the kitchen to sit beside us. 'I wanted to take you to lunch,' she said slowly, annoyed with herself about something, perhaps for forgetting the date. She was so fragile, and walked so slowly, I couldn't picture her going to a restaurant. But her face — exactly the same. Steely strong. Cheeky and stunning, with eyes that didn't miss a thing. *Gisèle.*

'I am ninety-one. My memory isn't so good,' she said, explaining her stroke the year earlier.

I started to pull the photos out of my bag, one by one, and Gisèle asked Clém to pass her the magnifying glass, in French. She warmed to Clém in a way that soothed me.

'I don't have any photos of my Australian family anymore,' she said sadly, then looked up at me with those eyes, like my presence was the reappearance of something she thought she had lost.

When I handed her the photo of dad, she held it to her chest and cried, holding me with her other hand.

After a while, she said, *'Est-ils privée?'*

'No! You can keep it.'

Gisèle shook her head, smiling, tears in her eyes.

'Aren't I lucky,' she said, and propped it next to her on the shelf. A black-and-white photo of a man sat in a frame overlooking her bed, and I knew it was her father, Gerard. Impulsively, I told her that dad had given Declan the name Gerard as a middle name. I had to refer to dad as 'Denison' or she'd forget who I was.

'Denison gave him the name … in honour of your father,' I told her, looking at the picture of her dad, who had been through so much.

She took a moment, looking up at me with her beautiful eyes, and then she shook her head again and smiled, as though she was back with dad.

'Denison was so fond of my father … very fond of him …'

She wanted to talk about living in Australia with dad, about all the beautiful birds she'd never seen until she got to Australia. When I asked her how she and dad had met, she said it was in London, after David Boyd's first pottery show, in 1950. After first gaining work in London as a nanny (like Michelle), she had worked as an artist's model for Mervyn Peake. Perhaps Mervyn had introduced her to David Boyd …

When she went to the cocktail party after David Boyd's show, she discovered she and dad had bid on matching plates — she the yellow, dad the blue. He'd made a joke and cheered her up, because she was in a strange mood, she remembered.

Time fell away in that first trip to Gisèle. An hour passed, or maybe more, and it grew dark outside in the shadow of the mountain. She never let go of my hand, and examined each photo I'd brought one by one, cherishing my connection to the man she'd spent most of her life with as much as I cherished her.

I asked why she and dad had separated, and she didn't seem to know. She only knew that she'd returned to Paris because her mother had been ill, and then she said sadly that 'Denison' met another woman, temporarily forgetting how I was connected.

'But we never stopped talking …'

A pause, and then she seemed to remember my connection to dad, asking about Ayala and Declan, remembering the kookaburras of Australia and more and more details of her life with dad, asking about aunts and uncles I had to tell her were now long gone.

'Little Louisa … I've kept all your letters. You sent me so many letters …' She stood up to riffle through a shelf and find them. 'You've always been my family, even though you were far away,' she said.

I had to breathe deeply so as not to cry.

It was too special, too sacred.

When the sky started darkening completely, I told Gisèle that I would be in Paris for a month, so I could visit her again. Like a child, this seemed to awaken something in her, and she stood up and announced suddenly that we should go and get some honey.

'Honey? Why?' I asked, laughing and a little bit confused.

'Because I have stripes on my tummy!' she replied, explaining that she had a friend who lived nearby who made his own honey. She wanted to give me a gift.

As I stood up, a little confused at how we could visit a friend when it was growing dark and she was in her dressing gown, I noticed a painting on her bookshelf. Yellow, bright, beautiful, it was by David Boyd. I knew, because in my insomnia before the flight to London, I'd searched for his work on the internet, falling across that particular series of angels and cockatoos, loving the innocence and bright beauty.

'The Boyds introduced me to Denison in London,' said Gisèle noticing my turn of the head, and she took down the painting. 'Is David still alive? And his wife, Hermia?' she asked, and I had to tell her quietly that both had passed away.

She shook her head and clucked philosophically. 'I am ninety-one,' she repeated, like she had escaped death by some obscure accident. She chuckled, and then she squeezed my cheek like we were the lucky ones.

'Little Louisa.'

She escorted Clém and I downstairs and forgot about the honey by the time we got to the lower level. When we passed some of the other citizens in the reception area, she pointed to Clém and I and told them in French that today was like Christmas.

She walked outside and hugged me for what felt like hours. I remembered Mirka Mora's words, all those years ago, 'You have your daddy *in* you.'

I whispered to Gisèle that the hug was also from Denison.

She held me tightly for many minutes, smiling through tears.

I travelled back to Paris in a sort of shell-shock. Clém had to lead me onto the train as I was totally disorientated. I couldn't stop thinking about Gisèle's stories. She'd told me so much about dad. Stories I'd ached for my entire life. Of a love that spanned thirty-five years, of family, of their life in Paris and London and Australia.

And I was her family.

And she was *mine*.

I put together the fragments of what she'd told me. In London, in her late twenties, she'd just finished a *liaison* with a man who'd lost his wife in the Blitz, and despite being in a bad mood had gone to David Boyd's art show in Chelsea. It was one of his first shows, and she'd bought the plate to support him because he was a friend. After the opening, there was a cocktail party at the Boyds' nearby house in Chelsea: dad appeared, and found her sitting by the fire on her own.

'The first thing he said to me was the last thing I said to him, when we talked on the phone the night before he died.'

The night before he died. She'd spoken with dad ...

How I'd hated to think of dad all alone in his hospital bed, just before he died that February night. But Gisèle had spoken with him *on the phone*; they'd stayed in such close contact despite the miles. He'd had some *comfort*, in his final hour.

He was her *husband* — it was clear to me that dad's relationship with mum did nothing to dent Gisèle's lifelong loyalty to dad. She and dad appeared to share a very independent, unconventional view.

The last thing Gisèle had said to dad the night before he died was the very same thing he'd said to her thirty-five years earlier when they'd first met. I ached to know what it was.

Gisèle smiled so much when she spoke of dad, and it filled a part of me I'd thought irrevocably empty. He was so loved. He was *someone*. He wasn't a failure. He had been her greatest treasure; their life together in London, Paris, and Melbourne had given her her most meaningful memories. Dad had been her life.

Throughout the afternoon, if she appeared to forget who I was, I'd gently hold up the picture of dad, which set memories falling like notes on a scale you've played over and over. Her *Australian family*, her happiest souvenir.

'*Mon mari,*' she said a lot. *My husband*. Not even caring that I was his daughter from a different woman. I belonged to Denison. So I was her family.

When they came to Australia, she'd been welcomed like kin by dad's siblings. Despite some obvious racism she experienced in Australia through references to the colour of her skin, she remembered her time in Melbourne so fondly. The kookaburras, going to the races, working at the State Library 'past the Joan of Arc statue', making the news reports on early morning radio to be broadcast live across to Paris.

'My husband was always writing,' she'd also said, 'has anyone typed up his memoirs?'

I'd shown Gisèle the photo from 1974, taken in Bois de Boulogne, both of them grinning like the oldest of friends, dad looking so at home back in France. Dad and Gisèle had still been married when it was taken. My brother had only just been born.

In another photo, when mum was bringing Dec home from the hospital in Oxford, Gisèle grinned widely like a proud aunt as they all stood in the doorway. I think dad must have taken it. *Aunty Gisèle*: this was how my cousins had described her. She'd even seemed aunt-like to my mum.

The train didn't arrive back at Saint Michel until after seven, and Clém held my arm for most of the trip. All I could manage to squeak was 'thank you' over and over. We went straight from Gisèle to meet Coralie.

After eight hours together, bonded by this strange, intense, experience, I was scared to let Clém go. We travelled up the miniscule lift to Coralie's apartment, and a new French family awaited me. Coralie, her husband, and her two little daughters greeted me at the door.

'*Le kangaroo?*' said her daughter, after Coralie explained I'd come all the way from Australia. After brief introductions, followed by goodnights to the children and her husband, Coralie bundled us off and we were apparently going to dinner in a nearby bistro.

My face was a mess. I'd been crying, listening, talking, tense for most of the day. And really, I hadn't slept properly since I'd left Australia, four days ago.

Coralie, like Clémentine, was the quintessential Parisian. Blonde to Clém's brunette, but equally miniscule and elegant, she steered me towards a seat in the corner of a beautiful French bistro. She told the waiter that she had a guest *d'Australie*, which apparently meant we were to be treated with the utmost care. Wine was poured, a delicious chicken dish was delivered, and Coralie and I caught up on everything that we hadn't been able to express in our emails.

'I messaged you because your Facebook picture was the Louvre. I saw that you had a brother and sister, but you were the only one with a picture from Paris. I thought — it's a sign, maybe she's in France?'

We shook our heads at all of it. I was still having trouble coming back from the meeting with Gisèle.

'Maybe Gisèle is the reason I contacted you?' Coralie said philosophically, understanding how momentous the reunion had been.

Over dinner, we talked of dad and Michelle, dad and Gisèle, dad and mum. Coralie mentioned 'all these women' with a cheeky smile, and we talked about lovers and husbands and how open-minded it had been of mum to encourage our relationship with Gisèle. Had dad ever apologised to Gisèle for getting another woman pregnant while they lived on separate continents? We didn't know.

Like Clémentine before her, Coralie wasn't afraid to explore complex topics about relationships and history; she didn't need to dismiss complication or quickly sum things up.

She explained her own complex family intrigues, why Michelle's father had probably asked Michelle to stop seeing dad. When Michelle had started to talk of dad again, in 1984, they thought she was being sentimental, unsure if he had really existed until they found the letters.

When Coralie asked me questions about dad and mum, I didn't feel the usual pain or grief that I'd felt back in Melbourne. Everything was different in Paris. Something felt *lighter*.

After dinner, she walked me to the Métro, kissed me on both cheeks, and instructed me how to get home.

I had a whole month ahead in France, and I already had my treasure.

So much French family.

So much beauty.

So much *love*.

A Letter from Paris

Upstairs later in my apartment, I found Clém had slipped a box of *menthe* tea in the Soeur boutique bag to replace my mistaken *tilleul*.

Chapter Nineteen

Ajustement

After four days travelling from Melbourne to London to Paris and not really sleeping, that long sleep on Friday night reunited parts of my psyche scrambling to put order into my new space in time.

I woke to find Clém had sent an audio recording of the visit, in a zip file along with dozens of photos she'd taken of Gisèle and me hugging and smiling. I'd been too overwhelmed by Gisèle's presence to notice Clém silently pressing buttons on her phone.

I replayed the audio, listening carefully.

After hours watching the rain with my notebook, trying to find words for the experience I was still trying to process, I finally left the apartment at 2.00 p.m.

I went for a casual stroll, stopping from time to time to watch the tourists. The bells from Notre Dame clanged as I stood in the rain, and I felt strangely privileged, oddly like an insider.

I stepped into a Pharmacie des Archives and the big department store BHV to buy some pyjamas. Back in Melbourne, I'd packed all the photos and documentation I needed to retrace dad's steps but had completely forgotten the basics, including toothpaste and pyjamas.

In my tired delirium the night before in my apartment, I'd pressed the wrong button on the TV and messed up the whole music/internet/television system so that the only TV channel I could get was Chérie 25, a channel that played nonstop French soap operas. As I stepped out of BHV, a familiar face stepped in front of me, as if he'd heard me calling.

'Bernard!' The only man I knew in a city of over two million. 'Ah, pardon. But I'm having trouble with the TV. I can't call you, my phone is all mixed up … I think I may have pressed a button and now I can't use the music, or wi-fi?'

'Ah, *d'accord*. I can come in twenty minutes to fix for you?'

Bernard turned up, as promised, patiently taking me through the TV system again, repeating everything he'd said two days earlier.

By Sunday morning, the jetlag had lifted just in time for my birthday. There were *bonne anniversaire* messages from the French family when I woke up, but I couldn't understand if they wanted to meet me or not. Coralie texted mysteriously that she'd 'be in touch'.

I called Clém.

'Okay, so here's what's happened. We want to make your birthday authentically French, but we couldn't agree on where to take you …'

Reuniting with Gisèle was all the gift I ever could have expected, and now the French family were arguing about where to take me for my birthday!

'Okay, here's what we're going to do,' Clém said on our third call, after numerous discussions with the rest of her family. 'We'll meet in Saint Germain. I'll text you the address when we can agree. Is 8.00 p.m. okay? Not too early?'

Of course.

I loved the Parisian view of 'early'.

When I looked in the mirror before leaving the apartment, I saw, at last, that the grim, drawn look of the last year had finally left my face. I was happy to be *me* again. Proud of all that I'd inherited and all that I chose to do, no longer uncertain. Proud of *dad*.

To feel younger than I'd felt in over a year seemed the biggest birthday miracle of all.

I walked down Rue Rambuteau from my apartment towards the Seine, past Notre Dame and across to Saint Germain, heading right at Saint Michel train station towards a neighbourhood overflowing with bistros, their tables out on the streets. It was such a beautiful walk, and I was glad I'd booked an apartment so close to all the old landmarks of Paris.

Clém's sweet face, now familiar, peeked out from a cashmere beanie, with another beautiful Frenchwoman smiling by her side.

'Hello, Louisa, how are you?' Michelle's youngest daughter, Marie, greeted me just as enthusiastically as Coralie and Clém had.

We sat down at a table outside a bistro and Coralie soon joined us, followed by Margaux — their youngest cousin and Edouard's daughter.

They were all so excited to meet me, so curious about my life and my history and my family, that I felt — just as I had with Gisèle — that my direct connection to dad made me like a visiting member of their own family.

'So, do you have children? What is your work?'

Marie asked me lots of questions and I kept catching her studying me, like perhaps we were related. Her eyes glimmered with quiet intensity.

'When is your birthday, Marie?'

'October twenty-fourth.'

'Ah! You have the same birthday as dad!' I said. There was a flutter of French, *anniversaire de Denison*, an 'ooh' from Margaux and Coralie, smiles and victorious laughter.

Marie shared that she had once been to Australia, staying in a small seaside town just outside of Melbourne. *In Point Lonsdale.*

'That's where my aunt Alice lived,' I told her, shaking my head at the coincidence — she'd visited Point Lonsdale, a village that doesn't get a lot of international tourists; Michelle's daughter had stayed in that exact spot in Australia where my aunt Alice, who'd met *her* mother in London with dad, had lived. *Washing dishes. All in song.*

Why Marie chose Alice's little town on her one and only trip to Australia was a mystery. When Clém probed her, she explained it was a *liaison*.

Ah, I loved the French reference to *liaisons*.

Coralie ordered a stream of hors d'oeuvres for us all, and we drank wine and champagne, laughing and talking about numerous different topics.

In the morning I found I'd been added to a newly created WhatsApp group by Clém: *Australian-French family.*

Chapter Twenty
Histoire partagée

It's impossible to understand how the French think about life without understanding the nuances of their language. *Histoire* doesn't just translate as *history*, it has multiple meanings in the French language — *story, history, lesson, specific information*. *Souvenir*, similarly, could mean *photo* or *memento* or *treasure* or even *record*, depending on the context. Staying in Paris had me marvelling at the different meaning of French words, dependent on the other words you placed either side of them.

I pondered the French way of only revealing the meaning of a sentence at the very end, how it spoke of their whole approach to life: too complicated, not afraid to be complicated, going the long way around. Most English-speakers — and many bilingual French — consider the language too difficult because it doesn't get straight to the point. Dad adored the French language, and, in many ways, piecing together his life had been as complicated and indirect as his favourite language itself.

After I'd learned how meaningful Saint Clair had been to dad, I'd searched and found numerous more books Alister Kershaw had written, four of which had mentioned dad's life in France. Alister Kershaw's French memoirs, particularly *Hey Days*, had described the intense conformity of Melbourne in the 1940s, and the desperation he, dad, and the more unconventional of their peers had felt to get to Europe.

Dad and Al had a long and tempestuous relationship, and I guessed it was because they were similarly impulsive, creative, and hot-tempered. Deep in Geoff Dutton's collection of papers were various references to dad and Al's exploits and disagreements. Al, who seemed, by all accounts pretty wild and irreverent, called dad 'one of nature's crackpots', but also clearly loved him, because he described him fondly, telling anecdotes about dad's practical jokes, in every book he wrote about France.

It was when dad met Gisèle that Al seemed to start getting annoyed with dad, complaining that she had made him too 'tame' in his letters to Geoff. I decided this must have been because Al preferred the crackpot version of dad who initiated wild escapades, not the calm, loved, settled version. He probably felt a bit excluded and jealous when dad found such a like-minded companion in Gisèle.

In a poetically similar fate to the one that met Aldington decades earlier, Alister had died suddenly of a heart attack in his garden in Sury-en-Vaux in 1995. At the time, he'd been in charge of Aldington's literary estate. I'd found references to Alister's children in one of dad's letters, discovering that Sylvain, his son, lived in France.

I'd sent him an email. He lived near Carcassonne, in the South, and worked as a translator. When I emailed him about my research and impending trip, he wrote back warmly, in words that echoed Alister's writing style. When I sent him my dates for France, he booked a trip to Paris to meet me.

I feel I should warn you, he wrote, understanding the need for memories even before I'd articulated my need in the email, *I don't remember much about your father.*

He met me at Rambuteau Métro station, an older man smoking an electronic cigarette, the echo of the figure of Alister I'd seen in pictures. We walked together to a nearby cafe.

'Now, I'm sorry but I can't tell you much about your father,' he said again, before recalling dad and mum's visit to Paris when Ayala was a child.

'Your father was a larger-than-life character, and he mattered a lot to my father.' He handed me a copy of *Hey Days*, which he'd carefully carried all the way from Carcassonne, 800 kilometres away. I didn't want to tell him I already had a copy.

Because his gesture was significant. I'd had to hunt for all these books and references, but this man travelled for hours on a train to meet me, bringing me a copy because he knew it mattered. Because we had shared *histoire*, through our dads.

I pulled out two photos I'd printed from copies I found in the library. One was of Dad and Alister walking down a London street. The other, of dad, Al, and Geoff walking somewhere in Switzerland.

'Oh, is this for me to keep?' he said, holding it close like a treasure, examining the never-before-seen photos of his father, much like Gisèle had treasured the photos on Saturday. 'Are you sure I can keep this?' He kept thanking me, telling me how kind it was.

'I remember when your father passed away, my father was very sad. Very, very sad. For a long time …'

Sylvain went on to tell me some stories about dad and the time in Saint Clair. About how dad got so deliriously seasick on the boat ride to Port Cros he'd recited his own eulogy in the third person.

Then there was another story of dad turning up in London unannounced and sneaking into Al's room to add lines to something he'd been composing on his typewriter, hiding in a cupboard to see Al's reaction.

We sat drinking coffee in Paris, like our fathers had done decades before, and I felt such a sense of comradeship with Sylvain. He offered to help translate for me when I got to Saint Clair, and I told him about the endless searches through boxes of letters, how many beautiful ones about Saint Clair I'd found in the library in Canberra.

'Actually … I'm an idiot. An idiot,' Sylvain suddenly said in a dramatic way that made me laugh. He remembered he had a pile of fifty letters or so from Aldington to Alister that referenced my dad.

'I'll scan them for you when I get back to Carcassonne,' he

promised, as we left the cafe to walk for a while down Rue des Archives to chat a little longer at Place Victor Hugo.

'My father was very affected by Denison's death,' he repeated. I don't know why this knowledge soothed me. As we passed a particularly beautiful doorway on an ancient building, I learned Alister had actually been writing an anecdote about dad's time at the Hotel Floridor when he heard the news.

Something clicked and stirred within me. I don't remember dad's funeral, but I do remember wondering where all his friends had been, why I never got to meet any of them. It had always pained me, to think of him dying so cut off and alone. But it wasn't true — many of his friends were just tucked away in France.

After a short walk and farewell to Sylvain, I crossed the Seine and walked through Saint Germain, across to the Musée Rodin. Clém had told me earlier that day that the gardens were a beautiful escape from the hustle of Paris.

'Whenever I'm preparing for an important role, I go there.'

I found the gardens — a smooth and symmetrical walk of luxury, ancient art, and forest greens — and the quiet and calm of it soothed me. At a little chair overlooking *The Thinker*, I sat to look and listen.

Chattering tourists and passionate Italians gathered in groups across the path, pointing and talking about aspects of each sculpture. A modernist almost by accident, Rodin was rejected from art school in Paris again and again. It wasn't until he took his first trip abroad, to Italy, in his mid-thirties, that his work gained any traction in France.

How strange, the twists and turns of the social acceptance of art.

Something about that garden, and the monumental sculptures, carved over a century earlier, reminded me of the purpose of any creative act. For art to have any kind of influence or lasting power, it has to come from that part so unique you just can't change it, irrelevant of outside opinion or recognition.

How strange, to feel a sense of comradeship with Auguste Rodin. But I did, just as I felt with Clém, and Sylvain, who immediately recognised the importance of shared stories and literature and art, doing all they could to honour it. Sylvain, carrying his father's book up from the centre of France because he knew how much those words would mean to me, apologising that he couldn't remember more, not realising how just those two or three memories were so much. Clém, taking my quest to find Gisèle as something sacred, recording the interaction, and thanking me for the honour of letting her witness the encounter.

The shame and uncertainty about dad that I'd felt back in Melbourne was as unfathomable an idea as Rodin's work being ugly. Maybe art isn't about acclaim; maybe the real treasure is actually recognition by our *kin*. By the people who matter, those strangers you immediately recognise as one of your own, whether you meet them in person or just get to view their work. Those similar souls who have a flick of the eye, an untameable part that can't be held back. Something inward that's pushing them forward, that sense of the importance of individual creation. The sense of soul freedom that all art embodies: the most honest and unique part of the spirit, the part that is immortal.

I didn't leave the garden until closing time, walking in the late afternoon light back to the Seine, from where I could see hundreds of lights on the Eiffel Tower begin to flicker.

Continuing to walk, I even found Gisèle's old apartment, the one I'd visited in 2007 when the concierge couldn't tell me where she'd gone. So many people had helped me to find her, but really it was because of the French sisters. And even though she *could* die, before I might see her again, something had already been transferred to me. A knowledge, a *histoire*, that I could recreate with words, over and over. A profound healing because I had something now, which I didn't have before Paris. A sense of my own history. My roots.

The sculptures of Rodin and all the art across Paris were like this treasure within me that I'd recovered and put into words. A sense of creative regeneration swept over me, like what I put into the world was something unique and never to be replicated.

A timeless thing, recognised by kin.

Chapter Twenty-one
En famille

Each night in my little studio apartment, the shutter windows opening up to the lives across the square, I'd been reading my way through dad's French memoir. Like the figures I saw reading and sipping solo glasses of wine by candlelight, I would pour myself a glass of something delicious, and read my way through dad's France.

I was up to 'The Hotel Floridor', the first place in Paris he stayed when he arrived from Saint Clair in May 1948. It seemed his Paris story started in Montparnasse. *The first visit to Paris! What wouldn't I give to relive that experience of May 1948.*

The hotel Floridor seemed to be built over a bicycle shop, the lift didn't work, the carpet was faded and threadbare, and a strong smell of cooking arose from the patron's quarters. I liked it at once, and liked the patron, Louis Marandou, a broad-shouldered, red-faced Berrichon whose accent it was to take me four years to understand completely.

The room was large, and so was the bed, there was a small wash-annexe with a hot and cold tap. That was for the look of it only, like the lift, hard experience taught me. A window opened on an exterior square, around which the hotel was built. The sun shone down on washing hanging over window-sills, a glimpse of a woman's head, a man shaving. I flopped on the wide bed and sniffed Paris smells deeply. The patron made me understand … if I wished to save money, let me just bring back some food from the shops, and a bottle of wine, his wife would cook it for me … I was *en famille*.

Mademoiselle Moos, an elderly woman with one leg, who had hidden resistance fighters from the Gestapo, had lived a few streets from the Floridor. She welcomed him that first night because she'd once met his sister Kathleen, and offered dad cigarettes before taking him on an express tour of shops that sold food 'not at black-market prices', introducing him to people to ensure he had the best knowledge of where to source what he needed during his Paris stay.

Food infused everything, back then, because it was so scarce. Unlike London, where dad had found that knowledge of where to get food was fiercely guarded, in Paris they talked of the black market almost casually.

The Hotel Floridor had been a complete contrast to his first rooming hotel in London, where he'd lie starving upstairs looking at the awful wallpaper as he smelled the cooking food that he wasn't allowed to eat though the patron had purchased it with dad's ration book.

According to Google, the Floridor certainly didn't look like the Palace of Versailles dad had described in wonder, but I was so happy it was still there. I'd be able to get a sense of Paris in 1948 as dad saw it — for it was certainly unrenovated.

I walked up the steps of the Métro station at Denfert-Rochereau to wait for Clém on the busy Avenue du Général Leclerc, just a short walk from the Floridor. Laurence — Clém and Coralie's mother; Michelle's oldest daughter — had invited us to lunch, and she and her husband, Arnaud, lived nearby. I spied a street vendor selling fresh jonquils and impulsively bought a bunch.

Underneath my feet lay the skeletons of over six million people in the catacombs. An underground tourist attraction that had repulsed dad, since he'd learned of tour groups accidentally 'leaving' people there, it similarly repulsed me. I'd had to quickly deal with my claustrophobia to get around on the Métro, but I wasn't going to pay to see any tunnels of bodies. The entrance to the catacombs, near the lion of the old city gates, seemed appropriately named *La barrière d'Enfer*. The Gates of Hell.

Clém greeted me with a kiss and led me laughing to the Floridor, which was still built over a motorbike shop, and still had the ancient steps and carpet. I could even picture dad pushing open 'his' front door. In dad's collection of letters at Ayala's, we even found postcards from Louis Marandou, sent to dad and Gisèle after they'd married and moved out of the hotel. Dad had returned to stay in 1973!

Clém and I walked up the steps from the front entranceway, which led to a small reception area with a little landing. The first thing I noticed was the low ceiling and the tiny lift. Dad had been over six feet tall — how on earth had he navigated Parisian lifts? It didn't even look big enough for me.

'*Bonjour!*' a friendly man greeted us, and Clém immediately started telling him (in French) that I was from Australia, and my dad had lived in this hotel after the Second World War, in 1948.

'Ah! Ah!' He was smiling and friendly, not even slightly surprised that we were treating the decrepit hotel like the living museum it is.

'He's telling me there's someone in the room that you think your dad described. But if you come back on Wednesday, at eleven in the morning, they'll let you see it when the man checks out.'

The man behind the counter offered for Clém and I to walk around in the 'common areas', so we crept up the sticky stairs to the kitchen. The stairs were so steep, I couldn't help but wonder at dad's gasping lungs, still only a few months from recovery from TB. How had he managed it?

The hotel was miniscule, but perfectly situated. A stone's throw from the Gare Montparnasse and not too far from Saint Germain, there was even a little park directly across the road.

I pictured dad walking home to the Floridor the night he was arrested, unaware of what was about to greet him in the doorway. The hotel was tiny. A swarm of police — or even journalists — would have filled the stairs out to the street.

After the Floridor visit, Clém took me to a market vendor because she wanted me to try a French goat cheese. We stopped into a bookshop where a man was parked up the front with pencils, sketching. Montparnasse, as far as I could tell from walking the streets with Clém, seemed to hold the most beautiful touches of the old Paris.

We rounded the corner to her parent's apartment, where a Frenchwoman in a leopard-print cloak joined us, talking excitedly as she seemed to know Clém. Thankfully, she didn't also join us in the lift, which only just fit the two of us. The building, according to the brass panel outside, had been the first meeting place of the leader of the French Resistance, Jean Moulin, and the lift seemed a relic of that time, too.

Laurence was waiting as we creaked our way up to the top floor. Smiling and so typically French, she was familiar from the video Clém sent me of Michelle, a year earlier. The video where Michelle repeated, 'Where is Denison?' and Laurence had smiled and replied, 'in Australia … I think …'

I felt we'd already met.

'Hello, Lou-ee-sa,' Laurence greeted me warmly, smiling and kissing me on both cheeks. She led me into the studio apartment, where smiling Arnaud was waiting in a lovely pink sweater, and I received another gentle cheek scatter of kisses and greetings.

Tall and light-filled, the apartment was scattered with a few of Laurence's oil paintings in progress, a mixture of abstract and impressionist styles, while a large one hung over the living space. I had the sense that I'd entered a gallery. There was so much light, and the view reached over the rooftops of Paris. Despite it still being early

March, the sky was bright and blue.

The large windowed doors of the living space opened to a small garden with a table set for lunch. My choice of seat was apparently important, so that I'd have the best view of the Montparnasse rooftops in the sun. Arnaud had a bottle of red open at the ready.

It was a perfect, sunny day. As Laurence fussed with food, she and Arnaud fired me questions like excited cousins.

'So — when we — ah — learned about this story — about Denison, last year — we wanted to come to Australia!' Laurence said first, staring at me intently in the same way Marie had done on my birthday. 'I thought — maybe I have a sister that I don't know? Maybe we are related?'

Arnaud sat back laughing, and poured me a glass of wine.

Clém winked at me and went inside to make herself a peppermint tea.

As we talked over a beautifully prepared feast of courses — veal and salad, potatoes and more wine, followed by cheese and bread again — I got the sense that my arrival in Paris was a cherished occasion to this warm and beautiful family.

Clém kept saying *'merci, Maman'* every time Laurence put food on her plate, which triggered the memory of watching French films with my own mum. But I didn't miss mum, just as I didn't grieve dad, in Paris. I felt close to mum in this space, because Laurence was a painter, just as mum had been. Her hands even had the same shape as my mum's, earthy and square, used to constant movement. Like they always needed a brush, a plant, something to manoeuvre into a visual presentation, *just so*.

Laurence and Arnaud wanted to know all about my research since Coralie's initial email, and I realised the whole family had been talking about and invested in the story even though miles away in Australia I'd only written to Clém and Coralie. I'd had no sense that this family would be welcoming me like this, and I found it extraordinary to look back at how lonely and confused I'd felt, researching the things I was now happily relaying with a view across the rooftops of Paris.

After a seemingly endless feast of lunch, Laurence brought out the album of Michelle's family photos. As Coralie had done a year earlier by email, Laurence explained the religious and cultural constraints Michelle had been living under when she returned from London to Paris. But now I had the knowledge of where dad had been, too, and when.

Michelle returned from London to Paris in 1950, as dad had travelled to Vienna and Berlin seeking work as a translator, before returning to France. In 1951, as dad embraced Parisian life by taking a room at the Hotel Floridor for a year while he taught English (in the 14th arrondissement), Michelle married a Frenchman and moved from the 16th the 18th.

I wondered out loud, if Michelle ever saw the newspaper clipping about dad's mistaken arrest, if she ever saw him walking the streets of Paris …

Laurence looked at me thoughtfully, saying ambiguously that Michelle had always loved the film *The Bridges of Madison County*.

Clém smiled, in the corner.

'I think she was quite sad,' Laurence continued. 'When she divorced my father, in 1984, she started to talk of this man — Denison. And we never knew who that was. We didn't know he existed until we found the letters.'

I thought to myself, how different the story would have been if Michelle had known dad had died in 1984.

We talked about art, and Laurence offered to take me on a tour of ancient ateliers, intrigued to know about dad and what I'd found in the memoir, which was that dad couldn't sell his two original paintings by Foujita that Albert Tucker had given him — instead having a Parisian art dealer accuse him of forgery. Foujita had never been known to paint anything but cats before he'd gifted Tucker the paintings of Japanese girls. Laurence offered to take me to the Montparnasse apartment where Foujita had lived. *They all cared about the history, wanted me to know it.*

I lingered for hours, not wanting to leave.

When it was finally time to go, Arnaud insisted on planning our next rendezvous.

'Louisa, I am *certain* your father would have gone to Les Closeries des Lilas. We are taking you there while you are here in Paris. You are *not* allowed to go with anyone else!'

How I loved Montparnasse. The streets were wide and light and you could see the Paris streetscape down to Saint Germain. Clém left me to walk happily home from Denfert-Rochereau station.

I had a little list of addresses in my pocket of places dad had visited or stayed — including the homes of Mademoiselle Moos and another Australian artist, David Strachan. They all seemed to be along the circuit from the Hotel Floridor, down the tree-lined Boulevarde Raspail towards Saint Germain.

It was early evening on Saturday as I stopped at La Coupole in all its shiny, Art Deco glory and ordered an overpriced coffee. Well-dressed Americans posed for photos, and I visited the washrooms Alister had described in one of his memoirs. The taps he'd been graciously allowed to use due to his poet status were now the beautiful, glossy bathrooms of the 21st century, no longer holding the ancient plumbing he described.

I walked another six kilometres down the Boulevarde Saint Michel, across the Pont Neuf bridge, and along the Seine to the Egyptian obelisk in the centre of the vast Place de La Concorde, before turning back through the stately Jardin des Tuileries to the pyramids of the Louvre.

Drunk with beauty and history and shiny wet cobblestones in the late winter rain, I finally made it to my little Marais 'home'.

Chapter Twenty-two

Date de naissance

Clém, who now called me every night for hours of chatting while she walked her two dogs, reminded me how to get to Orsay with a list of instructions. I didn't want to wait until Saturday to see Gisèle again, so I made plans to catch the train on Thursday, five days after the first visit.

But things were a little tricky without Clém to navigate me through the outskirts of Paris. I'd made a mistake with my phone plan and couldn't add roaming wi-fi. More annoyingly, I only seemed to be able to call Australia, not numbers in France, unless I was connected to the internet.

After seeing Gisèle's face light up when I'd given her those photos, I'd printed more from my computer files at a shop near Place de la Bastille. I packed them up, as well as a pot plant for her balcony, for some colour to replace the ones she'd described losing in the storm.

The Residence hadn't answered when I'd called to alert them the day before, but it was a sunny day, maybe she would be strong enough to go somewhere for lunch?

At 11.00 a.m., I walked to Saint Michel to catch the train.

Once at the Residence, I was met by a Frenchwoman in a nursing uniform.

'*Bonjour*,' I said confidently, '*Je suis venu pour visiter Madame Satoor* ...'

The nurse looked confused.

12.30 was apparently sleeping time, and I had to wait until after one for the 'residents' to be woken for lunch. I waited in the downstairs reception while the nurse brought me a miniscule glass of water, and at 1.00 p.m. on the dot caught the lift upstairs to knock for Gisèle. The hallways were silent.

The nurse, by my side, made a sleeping motion with her hands and said the word *dormir*, but I didn't really believe it. I knew Gisèle slept late in the morning; to be asleep again at 1.00 p.m. just didn't seem right. Finally, after we'd knocked and said her name a number of times, there was a slow creak of a nearby door. An elderly lady crept out to the dark hall, speaking in French to the nurse.

I heard Gisèle's name, I heard the word 'ambulance', the woman made a movement to express pain in her chest and then something about *coeur* and *dimanche*. *Gisèle had been taken to hospital for heart troubles on Sunday.*

The nurse, seeing how distressed the news made me, took me down to see 'Sandrine', who apparently knew what was happening with everyone at the Residence. Sandrine had been the one who spoke to Coralie, just a week earlier, when I'd still been in Australia.

But where was Gisèle? I tried to keep my thoughts calm.

Another tiny glass of water was delivered as I sat with Sandrine and the potted petunia, which now made me sad. Because we were unable to understand each other's language, we typed, assisted with a series of mimes, on Google Translate from her computer.

Gisèle is in the hospital.

Why?

She had heart palpitations on Sunday, she forgot to take her medicine.

Where is the hospital?

Next to the station.

How long will she be there?

It's complicated. She can't return without medical care, and we don't have the appropriate piece of paper.

What is the piece of paper? Can I get your email and phone number?

More typing …

When the exhausting dance was over, and I had instructions and names, written by Sandrine, I stood up to leave. A crowd of curious onlookers banked up at her door, I hugged Sandrine impulsively, and they looked on, bewildered.

There is one more thing to tell you. She sat down and typed again in French and I saw it translate. *When I told her you were coming from Australia to see her, she looked better than I'd seen her in a year, since she had the stroke.*

I couldn't help but worry that all the tears and emotion of my visit had made her forget to take her medication.

Onwards I marched with my pathetic petunia and my poor French making me feel stunted and powerless, down the hill and back past the *mairie*, finding the hospital.

Thankfully, remembering Gisèle's full name and birthdate by heart, I was able to hand it to a woman at the emergency triage station, who looked as bewildered as the residents at why an Australian who spoke very little French was looking for a sick 'family' member in a semirural French hospital. But knowing Gisèle's date of birth seemed the vital key. I could never have found her without that precious *date de naissance*. The *date de naissance* Coralie had given me, via email, just two weeks earlier.

The woman called over a nurse to escort me upstairs.

Deuxième étage. Chambre 512.

Gisèle was in the surgery wing, which made me even more worried. Perhaps it was her time. Perhaps that was all this was for: one final goodbye, that chance to see her on Saturday, the chance to touch her, a first and final gift …

At last, I saw door 512, and gently pushed it open to find tiny Gisèle bent over a small plate of lunch on a plastic hospital serving plate.

'Gisèle?'

'*Oui?*'

I made my way over to where she could see and hear me properly. Then, there it was — a click. A turn of the key.

'Ah … Louisa!' That smile. That beautiful smile.

She called me closer to her and stopped eating her lunch. And there we were together again, Gisèle speaking fluent English, back in Australia where the cockatoos screeched and dad's brothers and sisters had welcomed her to the family.

'They were so kind to me,' she kept saying, about Kathleen and Alice.

I wasn't sure whether or not to give her the petunia, for she seemed to have only a small tray to store her things. But the room had completely bare walls and no window. She needed *something*. I pushed it towards her.

She exclaimed at its beauty, but then had a thought. Something I'd done seemed wrong. 'Don't waste your money, this is your precious time in Europe.'

Still, she held my hand and kissed it, and we sat huddled like conspiratorial sisters. She was sorry that she couldn't offer me somewhere to stay.

I pulled out the photos I'd printed and blown up so that she could see them properly, and she repeated, just like she had on Saturday, 'Can I keep it?', kissing the backs of my hands when I said yes, like she was a little child.

'Ah. Australia …' She smiled. 'The Deaseys were so kind to me. *So* kind.'

'Of course, Gisèle, they loved you.'

'No!' She shook her finger.

'Not "of course"! Not everyone would be so kind …' She left it there, and I remembered the comment about her scrawled thoughtlessly on dad's school records.

'The Deaseys treated me like family. *My family.*'

She talked of conversations from seventy years ago, of songs and events and a party where she made her own dress, which was in a photo I had brought her. She told me stories of the aunts and uncles I'd never had the chance to meet and their lives and conversations, which meant so much to her, and every once in a while she'd point at the roof again and shake her head.

'*Mon mari est dans le ciel.*'

After an hour like this, she looked at me with her twinkling eyes.

'What are you eating? Your place in Le Marais — is it okay? What do you do for the little hole in your tummy?'

She remembered where I was staying … Gisèle asked me to pass her bag, the little purse I'd seen her carry on her neck back at the Residence, the purse with all her essentials. From her bag, she slowly pulled out an unopened box of French sweets.

And suddenly, despite another patient hacking beside me in the awful hot hospital room with no window and no natural light, we were in her apartment in Paris. Her space. *Her rules.*

And I could see why she'd survived. From being sent to a Catholic boarding school in Montparnasse from age six to eleven as her parents still lived in Sumatra, to surviving the German invasion of Paris when she was a teenager, to losing her dad for four years and enlisting in the army to find him. And how she'd travelled on her own to London at only twenty-something and she had so little money she had to lie to the cab driver and insist he drop her an hour away from some sort of boarding house where young French girls slept in dormitories and had to be out by nine in the morning to go and look for work. And she had found work, as an au pair, just like Michelle, until she was fired from a job because the mother thought Gisèle had stolen a pair of stockings. So she'd become an artist's model instead, because they liked the unusual angles of her face.

Gisèle was so proud, so *determined* to be happy.

The way she behaved, even in hospital, in this torrid room, as though she were hosting me in an apartment which overlooked the Eiffel Tower. The same flat where the Australian Embassy had been built, slightly blocking her view, making her remark with a beautiful smile, 'my life has been obscured by an Australian'.

'Where did these sweets come from?' I asked, stunned by the appearance of a box of delicacies in this hospital room.

'My friend Johnny has a car. I asked him to buy me something, in case I had a visitor.' She smiled, insisting I eat four, then further insisting that I wrap more and put them in my bag for 'later'.

I marvelled at her ability to find a friend with a car who went to the shops for her. Her instinct for survival and propriety. Ordering sweets so that she'd have something to offer a visitor.

On the train back to Paris, I kept remembering Gisèle's words. *Let's be happy*. And *Aren't I lucky*, when she'd seen the petunia. Just as she'd said decades earlier, when she took mum and I to dinner. They were her orders. Her resolutions. The words that kept her alive so long, outliving dad and Alice and all her contemporaries and even my mum, tucked away in a room on the outskirts of Paris.

No matter where you are or what you're doing, you decide to be happy. You find a friend with a car who can buy some sweets that you can share with an unexpected visitor, transforming the most miserable hospital ward into the kind of exchange only you can foster, remembering songs you once sang and how pointy was Denison's chin and how that beer in Australia made the buttons on his shirt too tight and how all of that was funny and how fascinating Australia was, and how much you loved that job at the radio in Melbourne, broadcasting all the way to Paris with the miracle of telecommunications.

And you smile. And you focus on the things you want to bring in, and block out all the rest, like the hacking woman just a metre away.

Let's be happy, she'd said, and I could feel her saying it to dad almost like a memory in my own body. How her steely, beautiful strength and companionship, her warm little hands, her beautiful smile must have propped him up in his 'suffering', and made it less.

And she remembered the first thing he said to her, which was the last thing she said to him, on the telephone from Paris the night before he died.

'Why do you take life so seriously?' he'd said, when she was stewing by the fire over her *liaison* that had ended, after David Boyd's pottery show.

And she'd said it to him on the phone before he died, and he even laughed.

Why do you take life so seriously, Denison?

He'd laughed, and known he was loved, the night before he died.

She was so tiny, and so strong. Power comes from who you *are*, not what you have. And she was Gisèle. Enduring.

Still, I hated to think of her stuck in that hot, windowless room with the very sick woman beside her. Gisèle deserved better. She needed to be back with her books and her photos and her flowers.

'Oh no, Lou, I'm so sorry about Gisèle.' Clém was devastated by the news, and arranged to meet me the next day so we could make a series of phone calls together to sort out the precious 'paperwork' Gisèle needed to be allowed back to the Residence. I hadn't asked in front of Gisèle, but I'd learned she had been taking her medication at all different times and had no daily nurse to check on her in the Residence. But they wouldn't let her out of the hospital unless she had a piece of paper saying she would have that daily care.

'I'll do it in a very careful way, don't worry, I understand her pride.'

❧

At Le Pain Quotidien over cake and coffee on the Rue des Archives, Clém made four long calls to various doctors and Sandrine, to-ing and fro-ing like she was coordinating the care of her own mother. At one stage I heard her say *'ma cousine Australienne'* and she smiled at me, like it was just simpler.

I remembered, with horror, that instead of saying the French word for godmother, *marraine*, to the doctor the day before, I'd said the French word for husband, *mari*. *She is my husband. Argh!*

'Okay. So, what's happened is Gisèle signed something when she entered that Residence which said she didn't need medical assistance. And Sandrine can't give it to her unless she asks. So the doctor won't let her go back without it.'

I could just imagine Gisèle's sense of privacy and pride, not wanting a daily check-up. But she was ninety-one. And on too much daily medication that needed to be taken at the same time every day. It had to be done. The mysterious piece of paper had to come from Gisèle's Parisian doctor, for the hospital to hand over the care.

My time in Paris was passing, quickly. In a few weeks I'd be back in Australia. I hated feeling so powerless to help.

'Don't worry, Lou, we'll get the piece of paper. And even when you go back to Australia, I'll check on Gisèle,' Clém said, reading the worry in my face.

Chapter Twenty-three
Contradictoire

A series of emails and messages ping-ponged from Clém to Sandrine, cc-ing me. Clém wouldn't rest until the situation with Gisèle's paper was sorted.

On Sunday, Edouard and his beautiful wife, Catherine, arranged to meet me for lunch in front of the Marché des Enfants Rouges, the oldest covered market in Paris, and he found me swooning over the giant selection of cheeses. Gregarious and enthusiastic, he was so excited to meet, like all the family had been, taking me to lunch nearby at a bistro in Bastille. He was friendly and protective — just as Clém and Coralie and their parents and Marie had been — and decisive and funny at the same time. He was unafraid to talk about the family history, about the complicated times in which both our parents lived.

At one point, Edouard moved my bag, which I'd left on a nearby chair. 'You need to be careful with your bag in Paris, Louisa,' he said with a frown. He was telling me off, but it came from a place of care. It was like my brother was in Paris.

My salad was delivered with a giant slab of camembert, and I audibly swooned.

'You like French cheese? That's it!' Edouard pounded his fist on the table. 'We will have a cheese night, at my place.'

The WhatsApp group buzzed with messages from the *Australian-French family* over who could come and what to bring — and there: it was arranged.

Marie and her partner, Anne, were coming; Laurence and Arnaud, too. Margaux and Maxime — Edouard's children, who'd been the first to transcribe Michelle's letters — would also be there.

Cheese. Saucisson. Edouard's place. Friday night. Another 'early' night, I was to turn up at nine.

By morning, Clém had sent an enormously relieving piece of news: Sandrine said she would take responsibility for the mysterious 'piece of paper', so Gisèle could return to the Residence.

With the number of pills Gisèle had to take every day since her stroke a year earlier, she needed careful monitoring. The reason she'd been sent to hospital was because she couldn't remember if she'd taken her heart medication. She would now have a daily visit from a nurse as part of her care. In France, the cost of this extra care was a fraction of what it would cost in a nursing home in Australia.

Clémentine replied to Sandrine before I'd even typed *merci*, and as I pressed refresh I saw emails from Ayala and Dec. The two had been worried in Melbourne.

Gisèle is family, Lou. What can we get to thank Clém … ?

A little more at peace with the idea of Gisèle, I opened myself up to Paris. The next week passed in a beautiful blur of sightseeing and deliciously unique experiences. I went to poetry in a cave, and read dad's memoir at Café De Flore, underlining pages before walking off to find the locations like he'd left me a Parisian treasure hunt. I caught the train to Montmartre and retraced the steps I'd taken ten years before, finding a church dad had described and feeling so moved from my time inside that it felt akin to a séance. I drank wine in little bistros at happy hour in Saint Germain and walked myself to the Dali museum. I visited the Bibliothèque Nationale, the most beautiful library on the planet, which reminded me of a sculpture gallery where the books lined gold-flecked shelves. I bought candles and gifts from Diptyque and Buly, and browsed clothing stores that explained exactly why Gisèle had always been so impeccably dressed. The level of detail on the French designs was exquisite.

And every night, Clém and I would catch up on the phone, sharing the latest on Gisèle and my treasure hunt of dad, as well as the details and dramas of Clém's life, which had me feeling like I'd known her for years.

Laurence took me on a tour of the ancient ateliers of Montparnasse, and we lunched in the Luxembourg Gardens. Circular paths, it all felt, me and Michelle's daughters and grandchildren, dad and Gisèle, I wondered so many times if he'd seen Michelle again in Paris. It was a dream holiday, a new life, an experience of family and history and returning to myself I hadn't expected.

I discovered, to my delight, that the first writer I'd met on my 2007 trip to New York — Karen — was now living in Trocadéro, just across the Seine from the Eiffel Tower. We rendezvoused at Café Carette, where we shared tales of the madness of freelance journalism, and she told me about her new life and medical career in Paris, thankful not to be pitching for work in that exhausting roundabout that is living freelance.

Coralie had Clém and me over for pizza and wine in her apartment, and I went to the national museum of modern art at Centre Pompidou, visited the contemporary photography gallery Jeu de Paume, and promenaded the Jardin des Plantes, the largest botanical garden in France. I got lost searching for the Henri Cartier-Bresson museum, but it didn't matter, I was in Paris and every other corner held a doorway to wonder and beauty.

Early evening, when the Paris light would start to fade from 5.00 p.m., I'd find myself a spot on Boulevard Saint Germain or Rue Vieille du Temple for a glass of wine or a cup of coffee.

Over a glass of Châteauneuf du Pape sitting at the bookshop bar

Contradictoire

La Belle Hortense in Le Marais, a French couple told me of their holiday house in Le Lavandou. By the time the conversation was over, they'd offered me their phone number in case I needed a translator when I got to the town.

The French were serious, yes, but also warm and intelligent and interesting and concerned with aesthetics and contradictory about politics, and happy to discuss the various shades.

I saw the lights of the Eiffel Tower glitter at sunset, and swam at Piscine Pontoise, walking home in the rain across the Île de la Cité.

I wrote my first poem in years and queued to present it, adding my name to the list of performers at Au Chat Noir. I went for drinks with an Australian writer friend who'd moved to Paris, and took notes on how she'd done it because I wanted to return for longer.

My visit to Saint Clair was inching nearer, but those three weeks in Paris felt like the preparation for a whole new life ahead of me. Old friends and new family overlapped and intertwined, and I had the feeling, finally, that I'd found not just my family of origin, but a place I fit in. Like a book on a shelf I'd waited years to open, Paris had always been waiting for me.

Chapter Twenty-four

Fête de fromage

It was Friday night, time for *fromage*. I'd been careful to eat nothing but soup for lunch, because I knew how proud the French are of their unique rules about pasteurisation.

I hailed a taxi in Montparnasse after catching the Métro and getting lost, and gave the driver Edouard's address.

Safely inside a stately entrance, past three separate sets of door codes and up in another teeny tiny lift, Michelle's three children were all waiting with smiles and wine. Leonard Cohen crooned on the stereo, the aroma of baked apples and cheese and bread mixed in the living room, and there were cries of '*Bonsoir!*' and 'Welcome!'

Maxime took my coat and lay it in the 'cloak room' (his bedroom), and Edouard steered me towards the numerous platters at the back of the living room. He proudly explained each of the dozens of delicious French cheeses. Ooh la la. Soft goats, stinky bries, mouldy blues, this was my idea of a last supper.

Arnaud held out a plate and challenged me to try them all. I shook my head — there was a lot of cheese.

'But Louisa, you must.' He was emphatic. 'This night is held in your honour.'

I was in a French film, chatter and cheeses moving in circles around me, Michelle's children taking turns to ply me with questions. Every once in a while, if my plate became empty, Arnaud's knife would appear, Daliesque, with a large sliver of cheese, which was then moved to my plate with a quiet description of its origin.

There was an air of competition around who spoke the best English in the family, which was a relief for me, because it meant that when anyone asked me a question there would be an argument over the best way to phrase it. I didn't need to translate. Yet I loved hearing the French spoken.

I wasn't sure I understood properly, but Edouard seemed to be saying his parents sent him to a Montessori school, but took him out because he was too creative. There was no sense of shame in us all sharing our family stories, just an intelligent, passionate, high, low, open, and curious discourse.

'Louisa, what is your favourite of the cheeses?' Arnaud prodded in between an exchange I was having with Marie on psychotherapy, because cheese is just as important as the deeper discussions in life.

Then suddenly the discussion turned to me getting some good cheese back to Australia. 'It's your right!' shouted Arnaud, explaining how to get a vacuum-sealed bag of their finest *fromage* through customs in London and back to Australia.

At midnight, when I was settled on the couch in between Laurence and Marie, talking about dad, Edouard disappeared to his study. He returned, proudly brandishing a copy of my travel memoir, *Love & Other U-Turns*, calling everyone's attention to the pink-covered paperback. The book was passed around the group, thumbed and discussed, and eventually he handed me a pen for my signature while the family reverentially went quiet as I thought of what to write.

'It's a very modern cover,' Marie said, and Clém explained that in France, books are usually released with only the title of the book on the cover. No pictures. And the hardbacks in France were usually a cheaper edition printed on lower-quality paper with rough binding. My published paperback was a treasure!

Catherine waited until I'd finished signing, and handed me a slice of her apple tart.

Who were this family, where had they come from?

Laurence pulled out a slip of paper, handing it to Arnaud. It held a transcription of a piece of graffiti we'd seen written on a wall outside La Grande Chaumière in Montparnasse when we'd taken our atelier tour; it had been written after the terrorist attacks in Paris in 2015. Laurence and I had discussed what it represented about the French attitude to life. *France is the personification of what all the religious fanatics hate*, it began.

Arnaud read the translated version aloud, persevering despite numerous interruptions to discuss which English word would have been a better translation. Exhausted after the performance and all the interruptions, he retreated to the corner with a whisky.

Clém kept looking over to me and smiling. Someone took some photos and a video.

'You're doing me a huge favour,' I said to Edouard.

'What do you mean?' he replied, perhaps thinking I meant the cheese, which I did, too.

'By competing over your English. It's quite relaxing for me to not have to translate.'

He peered down from his glasses like I'd set him a new challenge.

'Do you like movies?'

'I *love* movies.'

'We will take you to the movies on Sunday. I'll find one with the subtitles in French for me and Catherine. Clém will give you directions to find the cinema from Le Marais.'

And that was that. A new appointment had been arranged.

'Thank you for bringing everyone together like this, Edouard!' I said later, but Laurence looked concerned about something and I heard her refer to a 'Benjamin'. It seemed Coralie and Clém's brother never received an invite to *Cheese Night*. Clém had accidentally put the wrong number in our Australian-French WhatsApp group.

After 1.00 a.m., when everyone started to leave, Edouard booked me an Uber ride to get home. We all walked down the stairs, and when it arrived Edouard leaned in and spoke in French to the driver before opening the passenger door for me to get in.

'I told him I'm your cousin so he keeps you safe,' he said.

I sailed back across the Seine in the rain, full of *fromage*.

On Sunday, I met Edouard and Catherine at the cinemas in the huge Beaugrenelle shopping centre. We enjoyed two hours of spoken English with French subtitles, a little breather from the constant mathematics of translation.

'Do you go to the movies very often?' I asked Catherine on the way out.

'Every weekend, sometimes twice or more.'

No embarrassed laughter, no faux guilt. That's just what they like to do — no apologies. God, I loved them.

As we walked outside, Edouard spotted someone in the crowd.

'Pierre!' It was his oldest friend, who apparently already knew who I was, because he'd heard the story of dad and Michelle many times over the last year.

We all went over the road to a bar for a glass of champagne.

As we walked inside, Edouard looked like something had struck him.

Hasard. Hasard. I kept hearing that word. And then Edouard said in English, 'This is as if from God!'

It was Clém and Coralie's brother, Benjamin, and his girlfriend. They lived elsewhere in Paris, but their nearest cinema had been sold out, so they'd made the unusual decision to come all the way to Beaugrenelle.

We kissed and talked. I'd finally met the whole family. *All Michelle's children and grandchildren.*

'That is bizarre,' said Edouard, shaking his head with a smile after they left, and I couldn't quite believe it either.

After our perfect glass of champagne, Edouard insisted on taking me home on his motorbike. Catherine gave me her pink helmet and left to go home by the Métro.

'So. Louisa. I will ride along the Seine and you will see Paris by night.'

With the Eiffel Tower flickering as we left Beaugrenelle, we passed the Musée D'Orsay, the Louvre, and finally crossed the Seine. When we'd crossed the river and I saw the familiar Métro station signs, I was hit by a sweep of sadness that it would all be ending soon.

'Thank you so much, Edouard. You've all been so generous.'

'Of course, Louisa.' It was, apparently, an obvious conclusion. 'We have been waiting for you to arrive since Coralie's email.'

Hasard. What did that word mean?

Like dad's life — full of so many coincidences. Perhaps he didn't suffer from bad timing, perhaps it was all as it should be? Perhaps his life, actually, was very beautiful?

Perhaps those moments of hazard, like they had for me, meant that everything happened at just the right time — meeting Michelle's last grandchild, quite by accident, then celebrating with *une coupe de champagne* and being driven across glittering Paris on the back of a motorbike. Perhaps the return to Australia in 1954 hadn't been a failure, but, as Gisèle seemed to remember it, just a continuation of the French story, with a different landscape and more wild birds?

Maybe dad's story was more joy than sadness? More luck than loss?

He'd once joked to a cousin that being the 'seventh son', according to Celtic myth, gave him extra powers. And maybe it *did*. Like Gisèle, he'd lived through a lot — war and malaria, starvation and tuberculosis. Even when mistaken for a Cold War spy, he hadn't been shot, but instead was handed *a cup of champagne*.

After fifty years on earth, when he'd assumed he was unable, he'd even had children.

And now here I was, seeing Paris as he did, almost like he and Michelle were directing the scene from the skies.

As Saint Clair drew nearer, I began to feel harrowed by the clattering Métro, the wailing beggars, the sleepless song of the city. I wasn't ready to leave France, but I needed a break from Paris. Like I'd needed that first sleep after catching my flight, I wished for space to knit something up in my psyche. To make sense of the patterns, to see the story from afar.

A message from Raphaël arrived in my inbox. In one line, like a telegram, it said simply:

See you tomorrow.

Chapter Twenty-five

Émue

On the spring equinox in Australia, and autumn equinox in France, I made my way to Saint Clair. The date seemed significant: a day of equal light and dark. The turning of the wheel.

A montage of French countryside passed my train window, and by lunchtime we'd reached Saint Rémy de Provence, the azure blue of the Mediterranean spinning past peach-coloured rooftops. Soon, we were in Toulon.

The South of France. Saint Tropez. Cannes. Nice.

Who did I think I was? This was a place for royalty, for *artistes* of the first order, not someone like me.

Yet here I was. The place dad had fallen in love with France, at first sight. The blue coffee cup on my perfect little train-tray held the words *coupe de foudre* in cursive script across the outside, like an inside joke.

As I left Gare de Toulon in search of the nearby bus to Saint Clair, I heaved dad's heavy French travel memoir into my handbag, rolling my suitcase behind me.

Once I'd found the stop and got on board, the bus hurtled towards Saint Tropez, and I started to let myself believe I'd see it. *Saint Clair, Le Lavandou.* An actual place, as real and tactile as the pages weighing my bag down. My secret entrance token, the key to the palace. I breathed and sighed, feeling heavy with the new pilgrimage.

The accents around me had a peculiar sing-song, and, as both

Sylvain and the members of the French family had warned in friendly WhatsApp messages the night before, it would be hard to find anyone who spoke English. The bus driver had taken my euro fare while speaking unintelligible French about what time we arrived, muttering cheerily as he loaded my suitcase into his cabin.

For two hours we twisted and churned around Toulon, through to Hyères, then finally, an hour later than I'd told Raphaël I would be arriving, we ground to a halt next to a footpath on a small street of closed shops that looked down to the ocean after the main town of Le Lavandou.

I got off the packed bus.

A Citroën circled the roundabout, the driver honking when he saw me.

Saint Clair was a dream of the South. A small bay between two rocky points, a scatter of small houses, mimosas and eucalypts, vines and olive trees half circled by low hills. There was a daily bus service along the narrow road but no traffic of any importance.

As the bus disappeared and Raphaël galloped over the road to shake my hands and snatch my suitcase, just as dad's heavy bags had been nabbed by generous Frenchman decades before, I felt a sweep of emotion.

'How was your travel?' Raphaël asked politely, and I mumbled something like '*très bon*' despite a headache that had taken over since Toulon with the fear I was on the wrong bus until I saw the sign to Saint Clair.

Saint Clair, Le Lavandou. So many things could have gone wrong on the way. To go from hundreds of pages full of dad's love and sighs, to finally be standing in the physical space, seemed too unreal a thing. Those papers, filling hundreds of boxes in both Melbourne and Canberra's chief libraries, all the way back in Australia, held the imprint of dad. But this is where he'd been as he wrote them. *The actual place.*

The papers looped and crossed time, his whole life, really, but they always came back to Saint Clair.

The poet's villa. The lost love.

Literature and war and sun and champagne and music and writing and romance and superstition and the sense that he'd found the place that he fit.

Hope, relief, kindness, and food. Rediscovery of the peace they'd lost from war's destruction …

For dad, the gentle sewing together again of a body wracked by tubercular infection.

And a nightingale who sang during the day.

May 1948

Last week I climbed up the slippery rocks of a cascade which falls the full height of the hills ringing Saint Clair. At the top I found a track, and walked along. After a mile or so, the knock-kneed invalid of early March, who could scarcely walk downstairs for meals, began to run.

That is what Saint Clair has done for me …

Raphaël had the deep tan of someone who lives on the Mediterranean coast, but the clothes of a notable dignitary. I looked down at my jeans and T-shirt, feeling ugly and casual and all too Australian. He had a kind, sensitive face, though, and studied me inquisitively, a little like Laurence had done, back in Paris.

I kept dad's heavy memoir in the bag across my aching shoulder as he lifted my suitcase into the boot of his car. Something superstitious rose within me — I couldn't let it go, as if it could keep me safe in this anxious moment.

I went immediately to the left, the passenger side of cars in Australia. Raphaël galloped again, to catch me, looking confused.

'Ah — *I* am driving …'

In his car, I could barely speak, for fear of breaking or destroying my luck, of jeopardising something I worried was too valuable to accept.

'So,' said Raphaël, looking at his watch, 'we have an appointment with Josephine at La Villa Aucassin.'

The Villa.

'I will stop just for a small time at your Hotel, first.'

Another tanned Frenchman took my suitcase and handed me a giant key for my room at the hotel, without needing my name.

As I put my bags and coat down in the light-filled room, I could hear Raphaël talking to the hotelier, in French.

Lointain papa ... après la guerre ... les poètes amoureux ... elle est une australienne ...

The mirror in the hotel bathroom showed me an anxious face gaping back, but it couldn't matter.

I grabbed my handbag, and dad's heavy French memoir, and left the room.

Once in Raphaël's car again, we drove twenty metres up a track that led to the Villa Aucassin. I could have walked, but he took his role as cultural dignitary very seriously, and I was aware it was a great privilege to be seeing this villa, which made it even more ludicrous that I'd found it through social media. It was Ivor's private residence, not a tourist attraction.

As Raphaël pulled up, I looked around at the ancient mountains of Bormes, flanking the town like a protective shoulder, the ocean laid out through the trees below.

Place of my ancestors. Once dad's home, too.

Tonight my loved sister Alice came to stay. I put her to bed in my room and walked on to the terrace for a few minutes. The cool wind blowing. Silence. The lonely fir trees on the bare point swept by this wind ... this is my land; I have become possessive about

> Saint Clair ... Yesterday I had the odd experience of having Richard
> Aldington tell me a story about my own uncle ... My old uncle
> Charlie, mother's brother, fits in ... Everyone down here loved him.
> The slow bush speech, old tanned face, pipe always in a gnarled
> fist, without pretension or curiosity, living out the years after his
> hard work finished with slow and deep pleasure.

As we got out of Raphaël's car and I saw *Aucassin* in cursive script
on the bronze gates, I wondered at the insanity of thinking I could
come here and just knock on doors. I might have found it — but
the gates were locked, and the sweeping forest that would have led
straight down to the sea had been since cleared and turned into roads
with houses.

But it was still so quiet.

Aside from Raphaël, and the movement of Josephine, who had
come to let us in, the place and the pace of my journey, seemed
finally calm.

> Events are not sudden here ... Our happenings seem to approach
> more slowly than in cities ... Hotness enough for swimming during
> many days, and now a cool breeze from the sea.

When the bronze gates opened, something came over me. I
lost my confidence and felt a wave of nausea. Fighting back tears, I
smiled instead, because Josephine was here to show me around.

'So you found it!' she said warmly, as Raphaël pulled out a camera
and started to take photos. As with Clém on our precious visit to
Gisèle, I knew I would be grateful for the record, the *souvenir*. But
still, I felt complex, like he was recording a kind of death. It felt fake
to smile. I couldn't explain my unmooring.

Inside the gates, the grounds of the Villa were stunning. There
were citrus and mimosas. A bocce court was fashioned to one side,
a cleared garden where the forest to sea would have been, and an

ancient stone step and shaded table on the side of the mountain.

The impressively large and preserved villa stood with white, concrete walls, in its original state. The blue shutter windows upstairs opened out to a verandah that overlooked the sea.

Catha goes to bed. Dusk falling. Richard goes for a bottle of champagne. I play a few bars on the piano. Netta smokes peacefully.

I wanted to sit, and take it all in, but my two guardians, those precious connecting humans who'd allowed me to enter the gates, were chattering in French, pulling me forward. Speeding the process along, where I just wanted to press pause and stop.

I couldn't figure out what to do. I knew the short visit would be my only chance, and I wanted to search for dad. I knew he wasn't there, I didn't know why I thought I'd find him, because the forest was no longer a forest and now it held new homes. I just wanted to be alone there.

Raphaël and Josephine led me up a little track to the lookout behind the Villa, and despite the new houses below we still had a view of the township. Serge Berkaloff's inn, the track to the beach, it was all still there.

A small ancient world — preserved in its beauty, I gathered, much from Ivor's influence. Thanks to him, the rows of tall, peach-painted apartments that lined much of the coastline didn't obstruct all the views in Saint Clair. He'd bought much of the land around Aucassin just to protect it.

We moved inside, walking upstairs, and I had the sense that I was standing in the room that had been dad's bedroom.

'*La chambre australienne*,' said Raphaël, close behind me, and when I asked him why he pointed to a framed photo of Uluru.

… caught up somewhere between the Celtic twilight, the South of France, and Ayer's Rock …

Standing in that room felt like return to a family home. I could almost smell dad's tobacco pipe, remember the movements of his arm and the constant scratching of thoughts on paper.

The cool wind blowing. Silence. The lonely fir trees on the bare point swept by the wind. I am in France, and for two months in a Villa. The green sea is a hundred metres away ... Richard, Al, Serge. At home in the place I love with people I love.

God, even the nightingales excite me; why need there be champagne ... ?

We walked out onto the verandah.

... the sound of steps on the verandah, some new visitor, the conversation turns to writing, art or music ... disgust with the war years ...

The sky was the same, the sea was the same, even the creaking floorboards held the imprint of dad's halcyon days.

Yet I felt so confused. Discombobulated, disorientated, juggling past and present in my heart and not sure how to behave with two strangers.

Downstairs, our visit reaching an end, Raphaël opened his car.

'If you don't have any plans for the evening, I thought I could drive you into Le Lavandou and we could have a nice drink?' said Josephine, kindly.

It was a beautiful offer, warm and generous, but I was fighting back tears, counting down the moments until I could be alone.

'I'm sorry — I don't know how to say it in French — but this is quite overwhelming,' I said, feeling guilty.

Some quiet talk, in French again. Raphaël clasped his hands in front of him, looking at the ground.

'*Vous êtes émue*,' said Josephine. Raphaël nodded, in agreement.

I felt even more *émue* as she locked the gates to Aucassin and I knew my chance was over.

As Raphaël dropped me back at my hotel, he stated in his lilting accent that he'd booked lunch the following day.

'So we will meet at *midi*, at Les Sables D'Or.'

Les Sables D'Or. *Serge Berkaloff's inn*. The inn of the thousand bottles, the Count with the long eyelashes, and twenty types of hors d'oeuvres.

After passing the owners at my hotel reception, I opened up my room and closed the door.

It wasn't until I unpacked a few things and sat outside on the balcony under a giant orange tree that I understood why I needed to be alone. A church bell rang slowly, like it was signifying the end of a hymn.

I watched the sun set pink and orange across the Mediterranean sky in silence. The backdrop of the ancient mountains slowly shaded darker, and the salty sea waved and lapped, only metres down the path.

It was finished. Something had finished. A battle I hadn't even known I'd enlisted in fighting, all that time ago back in the library.

But why didn't I feel more relieved?

I wished I could return to Aucassin, alone, to lay something down in a ritual or to whisper to dad, but the gates were locked. As the air dropped in temperature and the sun started to fade, I put on my shoes to walk the town alone.

I wandered up and around the tiny town. I couldn't hear dad, so much as feel him whisper.

He wanted to tell me the story.

A Letter from Paris

It was March 1948, and I'd been in London for eight months, Lou. Those hospitals in Dublin and Switzerland ... Grey skies and biting winds were punishing to my wretched windpipes after catching tuberculosis from the boat. My ration book had been confiscated by the patron of my boarding house, and as I lay, half-starving in that ill-patterned room, a man gassed himself in the room beside me.

The War was over, so why were we all still suffering? Al wrote me a maddening letter with tempting descriptions of Saint Clair.

The mess of the War years still lapped and waved at my memories, threatening to surface at the strangest of times.

Getting to England had been no mere matter. No one would write me a recommendation. I had to beg that bunker on the bottom floor of the SS Asturias because of my behaviour at Geelong Grammar. Over 150 pounds, and I still had to weasel my way onto that hell-ship.

Five weeks. No windows, no trips out on deck. God-awful, matchbox-sized packets of food. And a mad captain addicted to speeches.

London seemed full of martyrs and misery. It was a medieval game of power and subterfuge just to get an egg, the tradespeople behind their counters intoxicated with their newfound roles of power. Meat, fresh fruit, and more than a thumb-sized pat of butter were unavailable, as, it seemed, was cheer. I buried myself at the galleries until Al saved the day.

The price of a talk on kangaroos for Roy Campbell, who'd just landed the job at the BBC in London, got Al to Paris, and from there he wrote to Aldington in Saint Clair. His letters started to arrive at my flat in Edgeware Road. Talk of sunshine and food, books, music, and song. Aldington, an English poet who'd written the best anti-war book I'd ever read, had exiled himself from England's rations and found a hamlet of peace in the southern coast of France. There, he wrote, and Al joined him at noon each day.

'You can eat well, Dease, and rest, and talk books. Come stay with us in Saint Clair.'

There was sun, eggs, fresh fish, and bread. Even the wine was unrationed.

Émue

Londoners warned me against it, Lou. They said the French had 'failed to plan' for the War, or some rubbish. But I ignored the propaganda and caught the plane, after producing some other documentation proving the sea air would be good for my lungs. At Marseille, I tottered down the steps like an octogenarian clutching my windpipes — and was greeted by warm air and men in berets. Grunting in French through the stubs of cigarettes in their mouths, they delivered my bags to a bus.

France seemed like life again, Lou. Winter had ended — the long winters of Australia and England and the misery of the War years, people hiding in their houses ... or drinking in closed institutions with their backs to the street.

Here, Lou, I feel the War was finally worth something. You've noticed, haven't you, Lou? They make the most of things. They sit outside. They take time to discuss things, to savour different moments — in all their complicated glory. They face the sun.

For a year I'd sat hunched in the tomb-cold reading room in the library. It had felt destructive, really, unearthing dad's life and loves. Thinking of mum and dad, of all that loss. The struggle had so many times felt futile; he was gone, why did this matter?

But I'd had to get to the end of those pages. And I finally had, in Saint Clair.

As I sat on the private little beach with an ancient tugboat anchored near the lapping waves, I took off my shoes and scrunched toes in the sand, walking across and along the water, letting something reach and fall down like the patterns of the water, that same shore that had cleansed dad's painful limbs so long ago, the same limbs that held scars and hollows from infection in the war.

I made it. The pilgrimage was over. Perhaps this had been what it was about — finding my way to Saint Clair.

I walked, barefoot, up and around to the narrow rocky path that led to Le Lavandou, up to La Fossette (the hotel dad had once described under the beauty of a full moon), and the sky changed to a deeper purple. I found myself at a lookout. Instead of a stone plaque to explain its history, it held a painting, a rendered representation of the view laid out in front of me. I'd unintentionally followed the *Chemin des Peintres*, a walking path created by Raphaël honouring painters and writers who made Saint Clair their home. This particular painting was the work of Théo van Rysselberghe, who spent the last winter of his life 'hiding' in the quietness of Saint Clair.

I walked down the little hill back to the town, finding that the one and only shop had closed. But there was one restaurant that was open: Les Sables D'Or.

I sat outside under the same plane tree dad had felt 'scratch' him as he tottered in to find his dear friend Berky making numerous delicious hors d'oeuvres for his dinner. The same inn that filled our mysterious family album. Numerous black-and-white photos of dad — they'd all been taken under that very plane tree. One — my favourite — had even escaped fire that had melted steel in my mum's painting studio. I didn't know which was the bigger miracle. Still having the photo or standing where it was taken.

I ate my perfect dinner under the tree with a view to the full restaurant inside. Unlike the sad TripAdvisor review I'd found from Australia, in reality, Les Sables D'Or was a thriving, warm, and cosy restaurant, with fresh produce cooked by locals.

Far from the clatter and clang of Paris, I slept deeply. In the morning, a crack of light slipped through the bedroom blinds and I reached a toe to open it further.

Home. I'd made it. I had nowhere to be, no Métro to catch, just a day in Saint Clair and lunch with Raphaël and Josephine.

I wandered downstairs to the breakfast room, where one of the original church walls from ancient days now held up the building. Dad had written of the church in his memoir, saying that pilgrims would travel to the village to have their sight restored.

Saint Clair. *So Clear.* The words seemed the same.

I'd made it. No more fighting.

Life was *allowed* to be joy. Gisèle's words, *let's just be happy*, seemed to be dad's, too, and the feeling was finally transferred.

After breakfast, I showered and walked back up and down the streets of the town, back to Aucassin's gates and retracing the track to the inn and past the little village gardens growing vegetables in the sun. The town was placidly sleepy.

Up I walked on the road to a view of the rocky point of the sea, the rockpools below, near a camping ground. Those same rockpools in our family photos, where Aldington and Catha waded, and dad, Ninette, Geoff, and Al dipped and swam.

It was a walking meditation, travelling barefoot around the town, and the only person I saw was a Frenchman adding a new lick of paint to a shopfront near the sea.

In the little Saint Clair supermarket, I bought a bottle of Provence rosé — the same one I'd sipped on my apartment floor through the Australian summer as I tried to make sense of the photos of this town. Here, it cost three euros.

I felt sorry to have only two days in Saint Clair, remembering my state of mind when I'd booked the trip. How foreign that feeling of fear seemed, now.

Back at reception, the woman in love with the man who'd made me breakfast told me I was wanted on the phone.

Clém. She hadn't been able to get me on my mobile phone, which didn't work because I had no wi-fi. We spoke in my room.

'Lou — there is some kind of transformation in your voice. You have to stay longer. I'll change your ticket.'

Knowing my internet connection was poor, she quickly made the transaction, booking me for a train a night later than I'd planned, and emailed reception the receipt, to print.

'I miss you, Lou,' she said sweetly, and I missed her, too.

But I wasn't ready to leave Saint Clair.

Chapter Twenty-six
Les Sables D'Or

Raphaël was waiting by the entrance to Les Sables D'Or at midday on the dot, ready with another welcoming smile and handshake. We sat outside, under dad's plane tree, which shaded us from the bright sun. I passed Raphaël my box of photos, the ones it had taken the course of a year's research to put in any chronology.

Raphaël wore his glasses to pore over them slowly. 'Precious, precious photographs,' he marvelled quietly, as he held one up to examine, then another, inspecting each carefully in the light. Like Ivor had, just weeks before in London, Raphaël was able to quickly identify the island of Port Cros and the town of Le Lavandou in so many of the photos.

Without anywhere to be or rush, we sat there in the sunshine, served by a gracious maître d', who also discussed the photos — taken of Australians under her restaurant's plane tree — in French. Josephine and her husband arrived, joining in the examination. I learned which ones were taken on the island of Port Cros. Raphaël pointed to the upstairs section of the restaurant to show where dad had lounged in the sun seventy years earlier, and explained that the grape vines in my favourite photo were on the track behind us.

I felt an unfurling as I sat and ate with these beautiful yet familiar strangers.

This is what life could be like, if I wanted it.

Sometimes acceptance is harder than effort — like the train ticket from Clém, *let it be easy, Lou.*

As the entrees were delivered and eagerly shared around the table — salmon pâté, cheesy slices of bruschetta, marinated and roast vegetables, all of it fresh and full of goodness — I asked about Port Cros.

'Can I catch a boat there, like dad did?'

Serious looks around the table, and Josephine translated.

'The ferry doesn't run until spring. It's still the last days of winter.'

But how could this be winter? I thought, looking at the blue sky and feeling a warming breeze from the beach close by.

Before lunch was served, the maître d' brought a large freshly caught fish, uncooked, for Raphaël to inspect. Cooked, it came out with a similar fanfare. The maître d' deboned and descaled the fish, dishing up our individual portions and delivering a perfect bowl of salad and another of bread to the table. Wine was poured, rosé. And more water. In Melbourne, this kind of service would be called 'fine dining', but we were just in a simple bistro in a little village. A hamlet, really. No wonder dad wrote so much about French food.

I refused dessert, feeling full, but regretted my decision when I saw the obvious pleasure my companions were taking in their giant bowls of tiramisu and crème brûlée.

After lunch, Josephine had a new offer, and, free from my anxious overwhelm of the day before, I was open and ready to accept.

'Would you like to come for a drive to Bormes? I can show you the view from the mountains, and we can see the little villages. You don't have a car, and it would be a pity for you not to see down from the mountain.'

Saint Clair was so, so beautiful. Quaint. Unpretentious. A little fishing village, perhaps only busy in the summer.

As we drove up the hill, slowing down to pass what looked like a building in the throes of restoration, Josephine explained that it had once been the home of Théo van Rysselberghe. With the help of Ivor, Raphaël was turning it into a gallery as part of the *Chemin des Peintres*.

Ivor and Raphaël were perhaps the most perfect finders of my 'message in a bottle', as Raphaël had first referred to it. They honoured history, they treasured art, and they worked hard to preserve that feeling in Saint Clair that dad had felt when he first came there.

As the church bell rang on the hour (and ten minutes later 'in case you forget', joked Josephine), with La Villa Aucassin and Les Sables D'Or behind us in the rear-view mirror, we wound our way up the mountains of Bormes, the same road dad had driven in his MG decades earlier.

'I moved here with my husband, from Paris, ten years ago,' Josephine explained as we drove. 'It was a risk, moving here, but Paris was too busy, and look — it's so much better, to live here.'

It really was. Sunshine and light and peace and quiet.

'We go back for the exhibitions, of course ...'

I understood the choices dad had made, what he'd risked and 'wasted' in order to stay — and return — to France.

I will bring every penny I have from Australia and live here in Europe ... 'Oh if the heart be sick it is to old countries you must go.'

This place was *so* beautiful, it was full of the kind of gentleness and warmth that burned grief from your skin.

Australia had sunshine and sea, but this was something different. A patina of old and new, past and present, an honouring of family and a sense of personal history, which combined to form the perfect present. Being in that space, driving up the mountains of Bormes with Josephine, felt like a piano song I'd always remember how to play, an instinct, the steps to a dance — my body or my senses had been there before, and I would never completely leave.

Up we went to the ancient park and mountains, forests full of granite that dropped steeply below, stretching out to sea under a clear sky that reached all the way across to Corsica. It was a perfect day.

A crowded car of Italian tradesmen wished us a cheery *Ciao!* as we let them pass on a narrow point, and Josephine knew them, like she appeared to know everyone.

'Because we are so close to Italy, everyone says *Ciao*,' she explained.

The mountains wrapped around each other like padded cushions flanking the bigger area of Lavandou, but the view when we reached the top was forest greens and oceanic blue. Oh, the stories this land contained …

I remembered one of dad's diaries, when he'd stayed in Saint Clair the first time, for two months in 1948, recovering from tubercular pleurisy and finally being able to run.

Walked with Al through sides of nearby Gorges, passed along tracks through many vineyards — and all the workers — I'm not yet used to saying peasants — greeted us and wished us 'bon promenade' and again as we returned. On the way back another asked us to come in for a drink, and we joined him in a spotless kitchen.

Above us, a painting. He talked of Dante, being an Italian as so many are about here, and offered us a drink from a plain bottle an excellent liquor. It tasted unusual. I asked from what part of France it came. Gesturing towards the vines just on the side window he told me he himself had made it.

Apart from the vines, they grow potatoes, artichokes, beans and peas here in Saint Clair. Occasionally great lorries grind the back road behind the Inn and emerge after some time, laden with cases. I have only just realized that they are cases of flowers.

What a country.

Dipping and weaving until we got to an ancient church, Josephine pulled into an ancient village tucked into the mountains. 'Bormes les

Mimosas,' she announced, letting out her little dog and locking the car. We were apparently taking her dog for a walk.

An ancient village with its own, unique, deeper church bell ringing, this was, I soon remembered, the place dad had described coming to a Sunday dance in the square.

'So this place has music and is popular on Sundays with artists,' said Josephine, pointing to a large bistro that overlooked the village below.

I knew, immediately, it was where dad had sat with Roy Campbell, who told Catha tales in his South African accent …

> Roy in the little square in Bormes with the jazzy pasodoble music coming out of the big café behind us, yellow flags of the square, the lights of Lavandou and Saint Clair, where I'm living below down by the sea and Roy talking in his fantastic accent looking happy with his coat off and the smog of London out of his throat, telling Catha tales, saying … 'we can have another pastis and it's on me …'

Around us were medieval houses overgrown with bougainvillea flowers, and we took the little dog down a street with ancient walkways that revealed lounging cats, hidden in the archways. Peach-coloured rooftops, passageways to secret paths, shutter windows and doorways that were masterpieces in their own right. Stone pathways led to thatch-roofed houses and a hidden *maison des artistes*.

My feet grew sore in the hot sun. Strangely, I'd only packed ballet flats, leaving my sneakers back in Paris.

'What size shoe are you?' asked Josephine, wanting every little detail of my stay to be good, offering to drive home to get me her espadrilles.

But our feet were different sizes, and it didn't matter to me, anyway.

⚜

After a dizzyingly beautiful afternoon exploring the mountains of Bormes and the Forêt du Dom, Josephine delivered me back to my hotel at sundown. I remembered I'd forgotten to ask to stay another night.

'*Ma chambre* — is it possible to stay another night?'

'*C'est possible,*' he repeated back.

C'est possible. They were always saying that, to me.

I thought of something else.

'Ah, do you know if there is a boat to Port Cros ... maybe tomorrow?'

'*C'est possible,*' he replied, just as ambiguously. It seemed that was all I needed to know, for now, and he would investigate in his own time. I left it at that.

I sat on my balcony overlooking the citrus trees, writing in my journal and planning a new life, one where I could live in a place like this, one full of peace and beauty and the time to savour all of it. Where I needn't be ashamed of my obsession with writing and my own family history. One where things were *possible*, if I just let them be.

Chapter Twenty-seven

Port Cros

The hotel was quiet in the morning, and I realised I'd overslept, padding down to a silent kitchen and no background of French giggles. I wandered about the eating area, unlocking the door to the courtyard on the wall to the ancient church, feeling as though I was staying in a summerhouse owned by friends.

Eventually, the man came downstairs, stretching and full of apologies, and brewed coffee for us both to have our morning bowl.

'*Du café*,' he said drowsily, placing a large pot on my little table. But then — the loud ring of the phone upstairs, chatter in French, the woman now at my table, a piece of paper before her.

'Ah — so — I spoke with the — how you say — boat? — and there is one leaving in ten minutes, from Le Lavandou.' She tapped her watch. 'It will take you too long to walk along the path. I can drive you?'

I threw my delicious untouched baguettes and assorted cheeses in a bag, rushing upstairs for the rest of my things.

'You have cream?' said the woman as we walked to her car. 'For your face?'

Was she checking that I'd moisturised?

'And a towel, for swimming? And some money to buy lunch? And swimsuit? And a bottle of water?'

'*Oui* —' I raced back to get the towel.

We were halfway to Le Lavandou when I realised that by *cream* she meant *sunscreen*. It didn't matter. I was in France, where they still have an ozone in the sky above, and the bright sun isn't the cancerous threat it is back in Australia.

Besides, I pictured a quaint little cafe on the water, where I'd sit with my journal under the shade. I set off for my trip wearing leggings, a T-shirt, and ballet flats. A strange outfit, certainly. The woman from the hotel pointed at my 'dancing shoes' with a look of confusion.

At the little jetty, we all loaded up onto a large ferry, soon speeding across the water. Bronzed French and Italians clad in white surrounded me, and, when we stopped at Île du Levant, there were giggles and talk of the 'nudists' who lived on the island.

> Levant, which was used between the wars for naval gunnery practice, acquired some notoriety after the last war when a colony of nudists settled there. They may still be there for all I know …

Four cats languidly wandered up the jetty to greet the handful of visitors.

It took almost an hour to cross the blue expanse and make it to Port Cros, and as we slowly docked in the little port I saw a few men painting the exteriors of a shop, but no movement besides.

I'd never been to an island on my own before, but I wasn't afraid. Just excited.

Port Cros was the island where Aldington had holidayed with D.H. Lawrence for a fortnight in 1928, returning numerous times after, particularly with dad. Dad had, it seemed, travelled many times to the island with Aldington and Al and the Duttons and others in those summers in Saint Clair in the 1940s, even though he got seasick.

Raphaël, just a day before, had identified the small rowboat in many of our photos. 'Monsieur Gigonet', as written in dad's diaries, would merely examine the sky before deciding if it was safe to leave Plage de Saint Clair.

> Frieda [Lawrence's wife] and Lorenzo [Lawrence himself] had come down to the coast in 1928, searching for a climate to help his recovery. Richard asked them to stay with him on one of the islands off the coast and we went out in a fisherman's boat to see the place … Time to visit Port Cros with the good Monsieur Gigonet, whose fishing boat is housed at the end of the little bay of Saint Clair.

A fishing boat. The waters had been choppy in my luxury high-speed ferry, and I'd had to cling to the seats in front of me, sometimes, just to avoid a fall. Dad had come here in a *rowboat*. And he got seasick.

It would have taken hours.

The first thing I noticed, as the ferry docked in Port Cros, was an ancient fort, up a steep hill.

> Port Cros had been the prey of Moorish pirates for centuries, a rocky, wooded islet preserved by the government from development. We anchored in the little harbor, and Al and Richard climbed up to see the Vigie, the watchtower place where he had put up the Lawrences.

There was a post office, a tourist information office, and a strip of *magasins* being painted or built, I wasn't quite sure — but all looked *très fermé*.

The ferry wouldn't come back to collect me until five that evening. I had my notebook and pen, and bathers for a swim, and I pictured lots of nice slow saunters in the sun between delicious delicacies.

I set off to find coffee in one of the shops.

✦

My favourite photo of dad from the island, I'd first found in Geoff Dutton's memoir, *Out in the Open*. Head back in laughter, two friends across, all sitting at a wooden picnic table with two jolly-looking fishermen serving wine and soup from a giant breadboard, the background was a forest. It was a bouillabaisse picnic described in dad's French memoir.

I'd reread the passage in my hotel room the night before.

In the early morning, as we move out of the shelter of the point, the smooth sea is dotted with dark shapes, Lavandou fishermen returning from their night's work. Some have been out to the lobster pots, others have been netting all the various fish of the Mediterranean: conger, mullet, rascasse, squid, loup-de-mer, cod and the crustacean. Ah! The crustacean. On these the success of the bouillabaisse depends, and Monsieur Gigonet heads to intercept the boats ... shouts are exchanged in broad patois; a bucket of brilliant-coloured little fish is handed over the side. Sea-spiders, shrimp, scampi and prawns and lobsters ... the jewels of the colourful bouillabaisse.

I'd since found a matching set of picnic photos, almost as though photos were taken with every bite of the feast. In one, Monsieur Gigonet, with his scarf and his fishing cap just so, is grinning widely and clutching wine in a carafe, as dad dishes himself up more bread.

Bouillabaisse-s! is shouted again. Under the shade of an umbrella pine what was once a table is made to serve again with a few old boxes for seats. From somewhere Monsieur Gigonet produces a huge cork platter, over which the fish, potatoes and onions are laid; the whole has been dyed yellow by the saffron, with brilliant patches of scarlet from the little crabs. If only there had been some way of cooling the wine ... but the other fisherman is doing something with a length of cord near the old wall ... up come three bottles of wine, looped together, and fresh as if they had been packed in ice.

As I centred myself on the island, which was quiet except for the sounds of a few men hammering nails onto a wall somewhere close, I looked around for the cafe I'd hoped for. A Frenchman with a paintbrush in one hand and a cigarette in another wandered towards me, curiously.

'Ah ... *je cherche une café* ... ?'

'Ah, *non*.' He looked *désolée*. '*Tous fermés*.' He shrugged and turned as if to display.

'*Pas de magasins?*' I double-checked, repeating quietly to the growing gathering of curious and *désolée* locals now walking to meet me.

'*Je cherche du café?*' I made a motion for drinking coffee.

'Ah-ah.' A chatter of French. Some pointing. A shout.

'JOELLE!!!!' a man bellowed, shattering the quiet (for all the men had stopped hammering to look). A small, suntanned woman emerged quickly from a cottage, marching across.

'*Oui?*'

More chatter in French, some pointing and talk of coffee. I gathered I was to follow her. Soon, we were at the doors to her cottage, in her immaculate kitchen; I was ordered to *asseyez vous*, so I sat down at her table.

A plate of biscuits was placed in front of me, a bowl of sugar cubes, and a steaming hot cup of espresso.

'*Êtes vous américain?*'

'Ah, *non. Je suis australien.*'

'Ah! *Le kangaroo!*' she said cheerily, running off to answer her phone in a nearby room.

So I sat in this sweet little kitchen on an ancient island and sipped Joelle's espresso. It wasn't the cafe I'd pictured, but it was somehow better.

✤

What do you do on an ancient island all day when the ferry apparently won't be back until five o'clock and nothing is open?

I just walked and thought.

Walking alone to remote places gives one a feeling of ownership, dad had written.

I walked and walked in my ballet flats, up forest tracks and down cliff edges to secluded inlets. I swam in the ocean in a little beach on my own and ate my breakfast baguette filled with delicious cheeses from the shade of a tree overlooking the cliff edge to the deep blue. It was *my* island, that day, and I didn't meet a soul once I'd wandered a few paths away from the harbour.

I climbed to the edge of the island, which overlooked a rocky point that made me dizzy with its drama, dramatic cuts of cliff on the windy side of the island contrasting wildly with the softness of the protected bays. The vertigo I felt, standing on the edge of endless blue, feeling I'd never be found if the wind blew any stronger, had me dancing in my ballet flats back to the known path.

I followed path after hidden track to hidden path. Signs in French warned that *le forêt est inflammable*, and I stumbled upon a deep ancient well. It was a storybook walk, through a land I'd only ever imagined belonged in fairytales and picture books, and as my blisters started to hurt I saw another sign for a historic fort up ahead — a different one to the one where Aldington had stayed with D.H. Lawrence.

This one seemed more sombre, quite scary. I approached as though it was a sleeping giant, for something gave me pause. I didn't want to turn my back on it, as though a full battle of troops might start shooting me — it seemed so full of recent drama. Yet it was pre-Napoleonic, built hundreds of years ago. A castle, a moat — grown over with grass and vines, but just as forbidding — and dark, closed gates. There was even what looked to be a working drawbridge.

As I walked the periphery of the fort, unwilling to cross the moat for the strong feeling of fear, I wondered at the history and dramas that once unfolded, while the space gave me an increasing sense of foreboding. That something created in the sixteenth century, and unused since World War II, could still elicit such a powerful response in my physical body surprised me. I wondered at dad, driving across Europe a mere two years after World War II had ended, sleeping in country homes that once housed fleeing families, the Gestapo, even the Resistance.

And, even though it scared me a little, the sense of everything being so interesting and full of stories in France had me wanting to return, before I'd even left.

I wandered down from the fort to find a tribute to American allied forces during World War II.

I found a seat by the water near the ferry dock and wrote in my little notebook, sitting on the shore with my toes in the water, perhaps the same water where dad's fisherman had cooled his wine.

I didn't feel bored, or hungry, or frustrated. I filled my notebook with thoughts and phrases. I napped under the shade of a shop, and I refilled my water bottle from a tap that warned that drinking water was only a recent addition to the island's amenities.

An entire day stuck on an island in the South of France was perhaps the perfect period of integration for the momentous shifts in my world view that had taken place over the last few weeks. I took the occasional photo on my walk, but mostly I just let my eyes take it in.

Every path I took, every track, seemed to hold remnants of ages past, relics and monuments that laid tribute to all that had gone before. The French honouring of history, their sense of occasion and announcement, their love of food and life, such that a fisherman was concerned that I get my espresso and Joelle had even offered to make me lunch, demanding to know what I had to eat, only letting me go once I'd produced my stale baguette as proof.

No wonder this was dad's peace after the war.

They knew what had gone before, but they also appreciated the present day and the simple necessities of human connection, food, beauty, and service.

When I'd walked so much and for so long that blisters formed on my toes, I found a shady spot back at the village, passing the same men who had greeted me that morning.

As the ferry steamed me back across the water over the course of an hour, a familiar figure came into view at the harbour. It was Raphaël. He explained, in French, that the tourism office where he worked looked out to the ferry station.

He, too, seemed concerned by my footwear. 'Dancing shoes?' He stared at my feet. He was insistent on delivering me back to my hotel.

In my room, I peeled off my sweaty clothes and looked in the mirror. After spending all day in the sun, I wasn't even burned.

There's a word I learned in Saint Clair, because I was searching for a way to explain how I felt when I stayed there.

Nepenthe is a medicine for sorrow, literally a 'drug of forgetfulness', mentioned in Homer's Odyssey and other ancient texts that dad loved. It means: something so beautiful that it takes away all feelings of sorrow, depression, or grief.

In the depths of my grief for both my parents, I'd sometimes wondered if amnesia might be the only way to lose the pain. Amnesia of all they were to me and could have been, forgetting all the unfinished stories it pained me to never know.

But when I'd woken in Saint Clair that first morning, after a sleep so long and so deep I was momentarily unsure where I was or when, I knew the search for amnesia was over. It was like the closing of a circle. It was more than the end of a journey to understand where dad's letters had come from.

Dad was in everything that I loved about Saint Clair, and in every part of me that took the risk to search for it. The kind of person who journeys across the world because of a letter.

The kind of person who — no matter what's gone before — leaves the door open to joy.

To have that feeling of kinship — with dad, with the French, but most of all, with myself — was worth risking everything.

I remembered who I was, in Saint Clair.

Chapter Twenty-eight
La clé

On my last day in Saint Clair, I received one final treasure.

It had started to rain as I packed my suitcase, and Josephine texted.

It's not very nice with the rain. I spoke with Ivor, he says it would be better if you come to the Villa to spend the rest of your time in Saint Clair.

I hadn't expected her to leave me the key.

It was different being left alone in the Villa. When the gate locked shut, I walked the circumference of the garden from lemon tree to mimosa tree, and sat on the stone porch that looked down to the sea. I felt so content.

I wandered from room to room in the 1920s-built mansion. The floorboards, the tiles, most of the fittings and fixtures were exactly as they would have been when dad, Kershaw, and Aldington had stayed there, writing and dreaming and singing and sighing and entertaining guests from England and Australia who shared one thing in common: a love of poetry, a sense of the sweetness of life and how much it needed to be preserved, or reimagined. A protection of their precious peace, because they knew what war could shatter.

My peace here … an absence of strain and strife, it has always been peace.

I walked upstairs to the master room, and looked out the shutter windows to the ocean, almost hearing music on the gramophone, dad playing the large piano downstairs, I could even taste the sweet, dry bubble of champagne Richard might have opened from the verandah. I could feel love and peace emanating from the floorboards, coming from all who had lived and laughed here, and all the poetry they'd created from those times and in the path their lives took afterwards. The choices they had made to come here, what they'd suffered and what they'd saved.

I smelled the mist rising up from the garden, and that same Mediterranean air dad had inhaled in 1948, and I remembered his words.

Here, I see the war was worth it.

Downstairs, I returned to my notebooks, carrying dad's heavy French memoir into the living room, where I could curl up under the lamp on the couch.

I leafed through the pages of dad's memoir, thinking of the extraordinary journey he'd taken to come here, to start a life in France. The pages typed on an ancient, heavy typewriter, the stiffness of his aching back making the typing exercise a battle between awareness of pain and the desire to see something through. The desire to create something that lasted.

The memoir had been the heaviest thing in my suitcase to France, probably weighing as much as his ancient typewriter, and I'd almost left it in Australia, until Ayala implored me to use it as a guide through the French life of dad.

I'd used that memoir as a map, retracing dad's footsteps in Paris and Saint Clair. While the France that I saw wasn't still peppered with scars from the occupation of World War II as it was when he arrived, everywhere I'd journeyed held ruins from ancient battles, and doorways to medieval churches.

I lay down dad's memoir in the Villa Aucassin as a thank-you to Ivor for keeping it as it was, for letting me in.

Besides, I knew the story and I would always have it, now — the feeling of a life that held joy as well as sorrow, sunshine as well as sickness, a beauty and love that lasted so much longer than his physical pain. Dad's words had shown me the way. I'm sure he would have liked that memoir to return to Saint Clair, to the Villa where, outside, the nightingales still sing during the day, his words back in his beloved France full of people who felt like kin.

I wrote a long note and slipped it into the front page, placing the heavy manuscript on the table in the room that looked out to the sea.

After an hour alone in the precious Villa, Raphaël arrived, the man who'd bridged the divide between me and Saint Clair. He parked outside and I opened the gate.

'So — you have your key … ?' he said, and I'd been lost in thought for so long I thought he was being poetic.

'No, I mean, we need to lock the door.' I just stood there, blankly.

We laughed in a way that bridged all our language mishaps. But he seemed concerned about something — and there was a change in his face. He looked at his watch.

'Louisa — have you eaten?'

Oh, France. The necessity of food.

'Raphaël, I have to ask. You and Josephine have been so generous, so kind. Why?'

He looked at me thoughtfully, opening the door to his car.

'Because we see, the story is very *sensible*.'

'Sensitive?'

'*Oui*. Pardon …'

He stood, choosing the right words to finish.

'And — it is your *father*.'

Chapter Twenty-nine
Ma marraine

As if sensing I'd stepped in the door, Clém called before I'd even taken off my jacket. It was after midnight.

'I hope you won't be too sad to be back in Paris, Lou, but I have some good news for you …'

She'd heard from Sandrine, and Gisèle was safely back in her Residence apartment, now receiving daily medical care, apparently happier and healthier than she'd been even before our first visit.

'I have to work on Saturday morning, but I was thinking we could go at lunchtime and take her some flowers to replace the ones on her balcony that blew over in the wind.'

We talked into the night, and I could sense Clém's love and urgency, that familiar tug of attachment and separation, trying to find the middle ground. Clém reassured me, for the umpteenth time, that she would check on Gisèle after I returned to Australia. We talked into the night, laughing at my poor French and what I'd said and done in Saint Clair.

'When Raphaël asked me how old I was, he was very embarrassed, but I think none of them really understood how dad had lived there after the war, and had me so late in life. I told Raphaël *quatorze*, and he looked at me so weirdly.'

'Oh, Lou, you said you were fourteen.'

⚜

On our tour through the ateliers a few weeks earlier, Laurence had taken me to the studio where Foujita once lived. I still chuckled to think of dad clutching his Foujita paintings that Albert Tucker had given him, trying to sell them in the Latin Quarter to secure some more French francs to prolong his stay, but accused of forgery instead.

The paintings fitted easily into my suitcase, and I had taken them as an added security. I had no gold-watch to pawn, and my typewriter remained at Saint Clair.

The leading French experts on the Japanese artist's work were to be found near the Rue Jacob, I discovered, so off I went on the 68 bus, roaring down the Boulevard Raspail to fortune and prosperity. I did sums in my head and wondered how many more delicious weeks I would spend in Paris — perhaps even a month.

The expert lady pounced on the paintings with that clutching hand of the dealer in beauty. She looked from them to the cats on her gallery-walls, and then at me, as if I had painted them myself.

'Where did you get them?' she said. I told her they'd come from Foujita himself. 'Impossible!' she said. Angrily, she told me in plain language, that she could tell a Foujita when she saw one, signature or none. Did she think I had painted them? I demanded, almost as cross as she by this time. She shrugged, put them back in their brown paper wrapping. One thing was certain, Foujita had not.

I had read several books in a bistro later before the humour of the thing struck me. There was I, two late works of a known Parisian artist lying on the zinc counter beside my glass and the experts declared them forgeries!

What added to the joke was that Albert Tucker had a letter from Foujita himself, written in English, referring to the paintings.

La Closerie des Lilas was one of those particularly exquisite relics where I could imagine dad had stopped in for a drink and placed the precious Foujitas on the zinc counter. Its name translating as 'a pleasure garden of lilacs', the stately restaurant and bistro on the corner of Boulevard de Montparnasse is a Paris institution. Much like La Coupole, La Closerie had been refurbished for the moneyed set, catering to the fascination with the ancient literati who once mingled and scribbled inside its walls. Although he'd never be able to afford a mineral water by its current prices, you can still picture Hemingway sitting over his notebooks with a whisky in the corner, or Rimbaud singing over the piano in the entranceway.

French and American voices filled the entranceway to the bistro when I arrived, flanked by a wooden bar full of spirits, and white-shirted bartenders. Someone sat at the grand piano playing jazz while the Friday night crowd grew in size and decibels.

Arnaud and Laurence's friendly faces appeared as I took in the ambience of the busy bar, and we all stood up to kiss.

'How was Saint Clair?' said Laurence, keen to know everything about the trip, while Arnaud ordered little plates of croque madame, oysters, and prawns, and Laurence and I had cups of champagne.

I shared the tale of the Villa, of Port Cros, of the trip to Bormes, and there was much passing around of my phone with its photos.

'Can you send me this photo?' She pointed to one of the garden at Aucassin, holding it up and out to see it in a different light.

Surrounded by Arnaud and Laurence and now Clém, all eager to learn of my trip, sitting in that busy bar in Paris was beautiful but bittersweet. Almost as soon as I'd met this extraordinary family, it was time for me to leave.

On Saturday, the sun was shining and it was a tourist-postcard day across the Seine. I strolled the now-familiar path down the Rue de Rivoli, past the Hotel de Ville and Notre Dame, to wait for Clém on the steps of Saint Michel. A busker played Piaf's 'La Vie en rose' on accordion to passing tourists catching photos of the light across the water, reminding me of the video of Michelle. Was that really just over a year earlier?

At Orsay, reflecting our happy moods, there was a celebration in the village, and crowds of children and parents were in costume and singing up and down the main street. At the little nursery where I'd bought the petunia, what felt like months before, Clém insisted on buying four pretty purple plants for Gisèle, and I chose a large camellia.

We walked up to the Residence, and Gisèle greeted us happily, like she'd been hosting us for years. She seemed younger and healthier than even weeks earlier. It was a complete miracle.

Her smile when she saw the camellia, touching the leaves and bringing its pink flowers to her nose, made the choice even more special.

'Camellias. I grew them in Australia with Denison.'

'Den-i-son,' she said slowly, settling into the memory.

For hours we sat in her little room looking out over the mountain. She told us about working as a young French au pair in London and the Isle of Wight.

Gisèle and Michelle — both meeting dad in London. Both French twenty-something au pairs travelling with Catholic nuns. And now here I was, with Gisèle, *because* of Michelle.

After many hours, it was impossible to say goodbye to Gisèle without tears. We hugged and kissed, and I whispered that I loved her.

How do you say goodbye to people who've changed your life so deeply?

I had only been in Paris a month, but the tug and pull of two countries — France and Australia — was mind-boggling.

The Leducs were my family, Gisèle was my family, but I had to get back on the train to London, then the plane to Australia, moments after finding, in France, treasures and secrets I'd been searching for my entire life.

I wept to Clém on the phone that night, completely melting down over the course of an hour, a free call on an internet service that would have cost thousands in dad's time. How did they do it? Travelling in times when goodbyes were so final, without any of the Skype or email or video or photo connections we have to minimise the difficulties of time and space.

In the morning, I put ice cubes in a face washer and tried to restore my eyes from their piggy state, but it was no use. It didn't matter, anyway.

I'd forgotten how much power beauty has to take away pain.

Chapter Thirty

Au revoir, Paris

Edouard hadn't forgotten his motorbike promise.

> Hello Louisa
>
> Are you ready for a little trip across Paris? We will go along the Seine to the Champs Elysee to Montmartre, Bastille, rue de la Contrescarpe (Pantheon), Montparnasse, Tour Eiffel, Saint Germain then back to Rambuteau. Please wear a jacket, it's cold in the morning.

For an hour we rode, amid exhilarating beauty, all the little spring flowers coming up to blossom in the early light. Spoiled with wondrous visuals, we rode slowly along the Seine and up the Champs Élysées, along the Butte to Sacré Coeur in Montmartre. On the back of Edouard's Harley Davidson, we unintentionally recreated dad's first, endless, beauty-filled walk that night in May 1948.

Further, we rode down to the Canal Saint Martin, and then to the Place Charles de Gaulle, around the Arc de Triomphe, where the traffic seemed to pool and rotate in a dizzying nonsense.

Somewhere near where Edouard and Catherine had once lived in the tenth arrondissement, we stopped for him to show me the village market.

'We will have some coffee, and some pastries,' Edouard announced in his decisive manner.

As I stepped off the bike, he answered his phone. *Clémentine*. I could hear her speaking in French on the other side of the line.

'Why is she calling?'

'She wants to know why we've stopped.'

'How does she know we've stopped?'

'Because, the family is following our ride …'

He showed me an app on his phone — Liberty Rider — with which the French family were tracking us, like a GPS.

Another hour of beauty and slow riding later, we arrived back at Le Marais.

My last night in Paris, I met Coralie and Clém and their aunt Marie in a bistro near the Place de la Bastille.

I was slightly panicked about my luggage. I'd left dad's three-kilo memoir back in Saint Clair, but still I couldn't close my suitcase.

We talked about French-to-English translations, travelling, and Saint Clair, and Marie ordered a bottle of red wine.

Coralie gave me a French lesson.

'So, your first lesson, which comes at the end of the trip, is very important. The French translation of goodbye is *au revoir*,' she said in her dignified and decisive manner. 'It means *until I see you again*, because *voir* translates as *to see*.'

'Ah … It's not as final as *goodbye*?'

'*Non*,' she said. 'The only version of goodbye that is definite is *adieu*, which means we won't see each other until we're in front of God — God is *Dieu*.'

We ordered dinner, and the bread came with little pats of butter wrapped in gold. The portion sizes were thimble-thick, the same as dad's 1947 butter allotment for a week. I put a square in my handbag to take back to London, in case they were still 'out'.

Marie went to a choir practice, Laurence called to say farewell, and the sisters walked me to the Métro. We all caught the train together and said goodbye in the crowd when I got to Rambuteau station.

'*Au revoir,*' I said, trying not to cry. Clém was still holding my hands as the doors opened.

I lugged myself reluctantly out of the train, a new gift in my arms, balancing awkwardly. It was a painting, from Laurence. Wrapped in brown paper and bubble wrap, the canvas was wider than my large suitcase. It seemed Laurence had been painting furiously since the night at La Closerie des Lilas, leaving the phone unanswered even to Coralie in an effort to finish in time for my departure.

In the morning, I lugged the painting and my suitcases down to the street corner, but gave up the idea of catching one last Métro to Gare du Nord and instead decided to hail a taxi in the peak-hour Paris Monday. As taxi after taxi passed, and time ticked on, I started to panic. The Eurostar back to London left at ten, and it was now after nine.

'*Bonjour? Comment ça va?*'

A young man had arrived for work in one of the shops on Rue Rambuteau. Small, dark, French, he didn't speak a word of English.

'Ah, *je ne parle français. Pardon. Je suis australien.*'

'Ah, Hugh Jackman!' he smiled, then asked in French if I needed a taxi, called me one, and got a quote for the price, explaining it all to me with the help of his phone and my notepad. He added me on Instagram and I learned his name was Jon.

'*Un café?*' he offered, and I said no, to be polite, but he came back with one anyway, handing it to me and standing in peaceful silence with me as we sipped.

When the taxi finally arrived with just thirty minutes until the train left for London, I hugged him in thanks. He looked shocked, like it was just his duty.

When I got back to Australia, I found a message he'd sent me on Instagram: *Now you will have happy memories of Paris!*

I already did, lovely stranger, I already did.

Epilogue

The painting from Laurence arrived at my Melbourne doorstep the same day my plane delivered me back from London. Perhaps we were even on the same flight?

I unwrapped the brown packaging to see what she'd created from my photo of the lemon trees at Aucassin: an oil painting in a similar style to what she loved of van Rysselberghe's flecked landscapes of Saint Clair. When I first looked at it, I felt as though I was both back in Paris with the French family and in Saint Clair with dad at the same time. The colours combine soft beauty with hope, and the freshness of the present day. It's my most treasured souvenir.

I placed it in my bedroom, where I could see it every morning as I adjusted to the span of ocean between Australia and France, the worlds I'd covered, recovered, left and looped, the hearts that opened to mine and filled something I thought was destined to always contain loss. The turquoise and greens and citrus yellows in the painting are my perfect memory of Saint Clair, of a family who started as strangers across the sea, of their grandmother's letters, which led me to learn my own family story.

Something about the painting completes the cycle that started with searching for dad's portrait by Nolan. It never was a portrait by Nolan, as I learned by email when I was in Paris — instead it was possibly by another modernist student, and not actually of dad, but likely one of his brothers. But that doesn't matter. The painting led me on the search, its story carrying me through to an even more valuable treasure buried at the bottom of the hunt.

My painting from Laurence is more precious than a Nolan. A reminder to me that the dad I was born to cared more for life and love than holding and hoarding, and *that* is my inheritance. The stories he made of his life, the stories he left me, the stories that will never die.

Because stories, unlike paintings, can't rot or ruin, or burn in a house fire, or depreciate, or be fought over at auction. Because even when I hadn't known them, I'd lived them, because dad was in me and I couldn't help but follow his path. But like an inheritance I could only receive when I 'came of age', I'd finally dove into the 1.6 metres of diaries and papers kept safe by the oldest library in my home town, led by the promise of a mysterious email about a lost romance in London.

I know I had to be old enough — and understand enough — to fully embrace my inheritance. Until the pain of not knowing the answer to the question became more painful than the search for the answers:

Who was your dad?

Dad never mentioned anything about copyright to his material in his will, and because I didn't know what was published and what was not, I had to make up my own mind about how much time to invest in learning his stories. That was one of the hardest lessons of all — to honour dad's work without first needing permission. To take the time to value it, regardless of what others said and thought about my endless trips to the library and the time I spent unpicking and unravelling and transcribing things that might answer only a small scrap of a painful question.

I realised, through the course of the journey, I'd been asking the wrong questions about mum and dad's romance all along. I'd always wanted to know why mum had *left* dad, but I'd never asked why she had been drawn to him, once.

They shared a mutual passion for books, music, art, and poetry.

Epilogue

In the middle of a search for something else, a letter fell out of my sister's boxes of dad's papers. It was mum's handwriting, but it seemed unfamiliar. Mum had always written in clear capitals, as far as I could remember. But this was written in cursive script, gentle and curling. The letter was dated 1969 — the time she met dad.

It was a letter to a university friend who'd made it from Melbourne to London, talking of how she wished she could travel, how she wished she could write a book. As a twenty-one-year-old student at university, she was finding her feet and testing her dreams. The letter explained, finally, why she'd loved dad, even though she'd never said it out loud to me.

He wasn't afraid to fail; he wasn't afraid to try. He finished things and pitched them. He wrote and travelled and 'wasted' his 'fortunes' chasing his dreams. Some came off, some didn't.

To understand my inheritance from dad, I had to risk the same kind of failure. The possible waste of a year, of turning up to France and having no one to meet me, of no resolution to any of my questions. Of that same feeling I'd had that time in 2007, when I got to Gisèle's apartment just a little too late to find her forwarding address.

I only remember mum ever holding one art exhibition, and it is such a happy memory, of seeing her beautiful works appreciated and analysed and excitedly bid on, and knowing they were going on to hang in people's private rooms across Melbourne.

But before she died, we found she'd thrown her remaining works out on the street for hard rubbish.

We rescued some, but the rest were lost. None of them had her signature.

I've pored over the boxes long enough, assessed the facts, come to my own theories based on my own feelings and experiences — that someone who writes four complete books and thousands more manuscripts, even if many less are published or performed, is not a failure. Dad wrote hundreds of letters, radio scripts, and translations, but the memoir that led me through France is my most treasured of his manuscripts. And like me, despite rejection, he couldn't *not* write. It was an expression of his endless hope in life, a place where he always found peace. It was an expression of his belief in the spiritual regeneration of creativity; writing was his church and his peace.

Ivor contacted me a few months after I'd left the memoir in the Villa to say that he'd used it in an application to the French government to list Aucassin as a historic monument, so that the building — with all its precious history — won't ever be razed and ruined. The French respect for literature is such that dad's memoir can be used as 'evidence' of a building's importance.

The question 'Who was my dad?' used to stir others' grief, so I learned to swallow it. Until the French family gently insisted I ask again.

Someone once said to me that the antidote to shame is empathy, and perhaps that's why it was so important to know the times and the constraints dad was under, before I could understand that his story was not one of shame.

I used to feel shame about dad, but it's gone now.

Family stories are perhaps the hardest to unravel because there's so much at stake — namely, survival. If we ask the wrong questions, we might be thrown from the pack, having unwittingly jabbed a hot poker at the only people who can keep us safe.

I've repeated and questioned the *three fortunes* story long enough to know some answers. They aren't complete, but they're enough, for me.

The first 'wasted' fortune was probably the money he spent loaning Tucker and Kershaw the fares to get to England in 1947, and then buying a ticket himself. A few hundred pounds *was* a fortune, back then.

Another possible 'fortune' was from the sale of the original D.H.

Epilogue

Lawrence letter he'd acquired during the research for Aldington. He posted the original to an American institution in good faith, before he'd received a contract on the agreed fee — which was never paid.

The third, I think, came from selling the house his sister Kathleen left him when she died so that he could get back to France in the 1970s and finish his books on education.

Whether these really were the 'three fortunes', or whether the story even came from truth before expanding in the telling over time, it doesn't matter to me.

Like most stories, as you start to unpick them, the truth depends on who you ask. But his letters and papers told me what drove him and what he was always chasing: beauty and truth, something outside the mundane. The beauty and truth we both value so deeply, the stories he loved to write down.

It's as much a relief putting this down in a narrative form as it was heavy to carry it. The complicated slipknots around my heart took two years of unravelling, the lethal bonds of stories and myths and family beliefs undone at last.

Yes, dad suffered, like Mirka had warned me all those years ago, but he also made it to France. To people who felt like kin. To that sense of creative spirit and freedom and aesthetics he'd ached for in Melbourne.

I found that same France when I travelled there — a place that doesn't treat beauty as luxury, but instead as the way you simply must *live*.

Where dad found happiness and I lost grief.

And our mutual love of written words brought us together again.

So if you ask me now —
  Who was your dad?
  I would be able to tell you.
  And I would have to start with France.

References

Aldington, Richard
Lawrence of Arabia: a biographical enquiry. Collins; London; 1954.

Boyd, David
An Open House: recollections of my early life. Hardie Grant; Richmond, Victoria; 2012.

Bungey, Darleen
Arthur Boyd: a life. Allen and Unwin; Crows Nest, New South Wales; 2008.

Doyle, Charles
Richard Aldington: a biography. Macmillan; London; 1989.

Dutton, Geoffrey
Out in the Open: an autobiography. University of Queensland Press; St Lucia, Queensland; 1994.

Dutton, Ninette
Firing. HarperCollins; Sydney; 1995.

Fry, Gavin
Albert Tucker. The Beagle Press; Roseville, New South Wales; 2005.

Adrian Lawlor: a portrait. Heide Park and Art Gallery; Bulleen, Victoria; 1983.

Kershaw, Alister

Hey Days: memories and glimpses of Melbourne's Bohemia, 1937–1947. Angus and Robertson; North Ryde, New South Wales; 1991.

The Pleasure of Their Company. University of Queensland Press; St Lucia, Queensland; 1986.

Village to Village: misadventures in France. Angus and Robertson; Pymble, New South Wales; 1993.

A Word from Paris. Angus and Robertson; North Ryde, New South Wales; 1991.

The Denunciad; typescript; c. 1946.

Adrian Lawlor: a memoir. Typographeum; Francestown, New Hampshire; 1981.

McCaughey, Patrick

Bert and Ned: the correspondence of Albert Tucker and Sidney Nolan. Miegunyah Press; Carlton, Victoria; 2006.

Murray-Smith, Stephen

Dow, Hume (ed.); *Memories of Melbourne University: undergraduate life in the years since 1917.* Hutchinson of Australia; Richmond, Victoria; 1983.

Southey, Robert

'Denison Deasey' (obituary) in *The Corian: the Geelong Grammar School quarterly*, vol. 110, no. 1 (issue 356), July 1985. With contributions by Geoffrey Dutton and Stephen Murray-Smith.

Library Collections

Denison Deasey manuscripts, State Library Victoria.
Denison Deasey letters and diary, National Library of Australia.

References

Sunday Reed manuscripts, State Library Victoria.

Albert Tucker manuscripts, State Library Victoria and Heide Museum of Modern Art.

Stephen Murray-Smith manuscripts, State Library Victoria.

Geoffrey Dutton manuscripts, National Library of Australia.

Ninette Dutton papers, National Library of Australia.

Adrian Lawlor manuscripts, State Library Victoria.

Richard Aldington letters and papers, British Library.

Richard Aldington letters and papers, Southern Illinois University.

Guide to Notable Figures

Aldington, Richard (1892–1962)
English writer and Imagist poet. Rented the Villa Aucassin in Saint Clair from 1946 to 1951. Wrote numerous books, including the bestsellers *Death of a Hero* and *Lawrence of Arabia*. Commissioned DD to research and transcribe all the George Bernard Shaw letters, which formed part of the seminal research into T.E. Lawrence that informed the notorious story that Lawrence faked his war experiences.

Bailey, George (1920–2001)
American journalist who lived in France and visited Saint Clair in the 1940s. Wrote numerous books, including the bestseller *Germans*. DD planning to visit him in Berlin when arrested as a spy at the Hotel Floridor.

Boyd, Arthur AC OBE (1920–1999)
Australian impressionist painter, potter, and printmaker, considered one of Australia's most significant modern artists. Member of the Antipodeans movement. Painted DD in 1938.

Boyd, David OAM (1924–2011)
Australian painter and sculptor, member of the Antipodeans movement. Arthur Boyd's younger brother. DD paid his tuition at the Melba Conservatorium of Music in 1940, until he was conscripted. Introduced

DD and Gisèle in London circa 1950, was witness with his wife, Hermia, to DD and Gisèle's marriage in 1954.

Campbell, Roy (1901–1957)

South African poet and satirist, considered by T. S. Eliot, Dylan Thomas, and Edith Sitwell to have been one of the best poets of the interwar period. Lived in London and worked at the BBC when DD visited, secured radio plays for his 'friends', including Alister Kershaw, which got Kershaw the fare to France. Stayed with DD and Aldington in Saint Clair.

Deasey, Denison (1920–1984)

Australian writer, teacher, translator. Lived in London, Vienna, and France from 1948 to 1955, visited France in 1968, and lived in London, Germany, and France again from 1970 to 1976.

Delarue, Jacques (1919–2014)

French Resistant, Police Commissioner in Paris, historian. Wrote *The Gestapo*. Helped DD evade trouble during spy affair at the Hotel Floridor.

Dutton, Geoffrey OAM (1922–1998)

Australian author and historian. Met DD at Geelong Grammar. Lived in Saint Clair in the late 1940s after DD and Kershaw had met Aldington. Founded *Australian Letters* with Max Harris in 1957; also founded *Australian Book Review* in 1961.

Dutton, Ninette OAM (1923–2007)

Australian artist, broadcaster, author. Lived in Saint Clair in the late 1940s.

Foujita, Tsuguharu (1886–1968)

Japanese-French painter and printmaker. Known most famously for his drawings of cats in the 1930s. Met Albert Tucker in Japan during

World War II and gifted him two small doll paintings, which Tucker then gave to DD to sell in Paris in exchange for the fare to England. DD was accused of forgery instead, as Foujita was only known for drawing cats at the time.

Humphries, Barry AO, CBE (1934–)
Australian comedian, actor, artist, author, best known for his personas Dame Edna Everage and Sir Les Patterson. DD wrote the first article to explore his unique act.

Kershaw, Alister (1921–1995)
'Al'. Australian poet, writer, broadcaster. Travelled to England in 1947 and France in 1948 and never returned to Melbourne. Author of numerous memoirs about life in France in the 1940s and 1950s. Secretary of Aldington's estate until he died.

Lawlor, Adrian (1889–1969)
English painter and writer who relocated to Melbourne and became a member of the Heide circle. In 1949, DD published his book *Horned Capon*, about Melbourne bohemia in and around the town of Warrandyte.

MacNeice, Louis CBE (1907–1963)
Irish poet and playwright from the Auden Group, which included W.H. Auden, Stephen Spender, and Cecil Day-Lewis. Lived in London in the post-war period. DD described Roy Campbell shouting across at him in pubs and on London streets.

Mora, Mirka (1928–)
French-born Australian modern artist, member of the Heide circle. Emigrated to Melbourne in 1951 with husband George and ran Balzac cafe in Collins Street in the 1950s. Remembered a cheese-throwing incident with DD in Melbourne in the late 1950s.

Murray-Smith, Stephen AM (1922–1988)

Australian man of letters. Lived in London and Prague from 1948 to 1951. Founded *Overland* magazine in Melbourne in 1954. Both DD and SMS attended Geelong Grammar and joined the Commandoes in World War II. Wrote letter of recommendation for State Library Victoria to take DD manuscripts.

Nolan, Sidney OM, AC (1917–1992)

Australian modern artist, member of the Heide circle. Best known for his Ned Kelly paintings.

Peake, Mervyn (1911–1968)

English writer, artist, poet, illustrator. Best known for the *Gormenghast* books. Gisèle modelled for him in 1950 in London. She said that he wasn't proud of the *Gormenghast* books.

Southey, Robert AO, CMG (1922–1998)

Australian businessman who was president of the Liberal Party of Australia from 1970 to 1975. Went to Geelong Grammar with DD and served in the British Army during World War II. Wrote main DD obituary in *The Corian*.

Thomas, Dylan (1914–1953)

Welsh poet and writer who lived in London in the post-war period. Drank at The George, introduced to DD by Roy Campbell.

Tucker, Albert (1914–1999)

Australian modern artist, member of the Heide circle. Lived in Europe from 1948 to 1960 and famously built a caravan out the window of his hotel in 1949–1950 in Saint Germain, Paris. Gave DD some original paintings by Foujita.

Acknowledgements

First, I must thank Coralie Caron-Telders for doing what I didn't realise I wanted all my life: telling me a beautiful story of my dad, not wanting anything in return. Thank you for so generously sharing Michelle's letters when she'd only just passed away. And Michelle, thank you for keeping those letters all these years.

Clém, your emotional support, empathy, and understanding throughout the whole process — even when we had never met! — has propped me up so many times when I thought I was going mad. I don't think you realise how important your passion and encouragement has been to me. Thank you dearly, and for all your kindness with Gisèle and sorting out the paperwork with Sandrine.

To the rest of Michelle's family — Edouard, Laurence, Benjamin, Marie, Margaux, and Maxime — I'm so glad to know you all.

To my brother and sister: I could not have done any of this without your support, and wouldn't have wanted to. All I really cared about was getting something down that we three could have as our record. I'm glad we finally got to talk about how difficult it's been with all the scraps of differing information all these years.

Ayala, you're the best research 'partner' I could have hoped for: from sniffing out passenger ship records from 1947 and the cost of the fare to England, to recovering long-lost birthday cards from Gisèle, printing dozens of library things, double-checking other things, and, most importantly, holding on to all the (heavy) boxes of documents all these years. I love that we could combine forces for this project, even though looking through dad's papers was often painful for you, too. Thank you.

Dec, thank you for 'backing me up' in all of this, for helping with the army stuff, for the comrade-like chats about how bloody difficult and complicated it was to piece dad's story together, and for articulating the difficulties of the time in which dad lived, so that I better understood myself. Thanks also for making a start on the photos a few years ago and planting the idea in my head that I should continue the work.

My thanks to so many others:

To Mystic Medusa, for decades of encouragement, as well as that first short, sharp, swift message when I first heard from Coralie. To Margaret Ambrose, for similar immediate recognition and support — encouragement literally does 'give courage' ... particularly when I was so full of doubt!

To all my cousins who shared stories of dad, particularly Sarah and Mark, who helped me (finally) understand where the 'inheritance' came from.

To my friends and family and even strangers who became friends in the course of this research. A word, an ear, an unasked-for photocopy, a snippet of information, a translation, a connection, a kindness — it all meant more than you know.

To Russell Brooks, for contacting us with beautiful photos of dad (and us) from 1983, and, most importantly, stories of dad's love of Albert Camus and way of teaching.

To dear friends who loaned an ear or gave a hug or met me for lunch or coffee during my subterranean year visiting State Library Victoria. Claire Buckis, I loved our lunches at the Moat. Jason and Deanne, thanks for understanding the heaviness of all of this and just popping by with chicken soup, whisking me away for pho in Richmond, and, most importantly, believing in the story and encouraging me to pursue it.

Acknowledgements

To others who said things that helped me feel understood or encouraged in quite a strange and difficult process: Kingsley Baldwin (the line about DNA made it into the book!), Lia and Troy Simmonds, Cameron Watt, Kimberley Barter, Sacha Payne and Greg Muller, Karina Machado (thank you for the understanding chat and extraordinarily generous cover quote), Carla Coulson, Eleanor Jackson (for poetic texts of encouragement), Tim Haynes (for the translations and France info), Philippa Knack, Joanne Liberty and Eamon Dawson, Carmen Paff, Vanessa Hutchinson, Elisa Ventura, Carrie Hutchinson (for catching a train all the way to Sunbury after dinner to celebrate my first draft!), and Eliza Compton (I loved our birthday coffee in Paris!).

To Simon Clews. Thank you so much for the publishing advice, gracious fostering of connections, and speedy reply when I was in a real conundrum. You're incredibly generous. Thank you.

To my agent, Clare Forster — your calm, professional, and methodical approach was balm to an intensely emotional and complex project for me. Thank you.

To the entire team at Scribe, who saw the potential in this story from the beginning, particularly Henry Rosenbloom and Julia Carlomagno.

To my editor, David Golding. Thank you for such generous, intelligent, sensitive, meticulous, and thoughtful feedback (to such a complicated story!) on the second and third drafts. This story would be completely different without all your work, and I've learned so much from your approach. Editors really are the unsung heroes of books — and I feel so privileged to have worked with you!

To Laura Thomas (huge thanks for the wonderful cover), and to Cora Roberts and the entire publicity and marketing team for your enthusiasm.

To the Murray-Smiths — Joanna, Cleeve, and David. I loved that as soon as I contacted you about our dad's connection, messages pinged to my email inbox full of enthusiasm and understanding and memories of dad. Our mutual love of 'letters', written connection, and history gave me a taste of those fireside chats between dad and Stephen! Thank you. And Cleeve — your emotional support and inviting me over to see photos of dad was a miracle.

To all those I contacted in the course of this massive project who shared either information or anecdotes about my dad or the times in which he lived — every snippet, large or small, provided a clue to a huge life.

To Mirella and Peter Satoor de Rootas — thank you for helping us find Gisèle.

To the team at Heide Museum of Modern Art — particularly Lesley Harding and Kendrah Morgan, and to Darren at the Tucker Foundation, for letting me use 'Bert's' quote from the letter to dad. Also to the National Library Australia, for allowing me to print the portrait of dad by Arthur Boyd in this book.

To all the others I contacted who provided vital information or speedy replies or thoughtful conversation and help with photos over coffee: Sylvain Kershaw (thanks also for all those other letters!), Paul Cleary (it's hard to imagine I once thought those photos were taken in Timor), George and Philippe Mora, Jim Walker from the Australian Commando Association Victoria, Cheryl and Tony Hoban, Vivien Whelpton (your transcription work and camaraderie from afar was so appreciated!), Dr Andrew Frayn (for the Aldington help), Dr Karl James (thanks for confirming that dad's military record was hard even for the experts to decipher!), and the unknown manuscript librarian in Illinois who generously looked up my dad's material and photocopied parts of it to save me a trip to the USA!

To State Library Victoria, in particular, for keeping my dad's words safe and sound all these years. And to the National Library of Australia, for doing the same.

To my dear friend Jonathan Irwin for taking me on the '1947' tour of London and being so supportive, helpful with London research,

Acknowledgements

and encouraging throughout this whole process. To my cousins Chloe and Kirsty, with love, for understanding phone chats throughout the journey.

In loving memory, to my cousin Julian who told me fun stories about dad.

To Raphaël Dupouy, Josephine Marechal, and Ivor Braka for the miraculous trip to Saint Clair, and allowing me to see the Villa Aucassin and experience the warmth and beauty of the South just as dad would have felt it.

And to that nice man 'Jon' who bought me a coffee and ordered me a taxi on my last day in Paris —

It's the little miracles that make up the big ones …

Lastly, to my precious Sam — *Je t'aime, mon amour.*